HEAVY

HEAVY

HOW METAL CHANGES THE WAY WE SEE THE WORLD

DAN FRANKLIN

CONSTABLE

First published in Great Britain in 2020 by Constable

1 3 5 7 9 10 8 6 4 2

A CIP catalogue record for this book
is available from the British Library.

ISBN: 978-1-47213-105-8 (hardback)
ISBN: 978-1-47213-104-1 (trade paperback)

Typeset in Minion by Hewer Text UK Ltd, Edinburgh
Printed and bound in Great Britain by Clays Ltd, Elcograf S.p.A.

Papers used by Constable are from well-managed
forests and other responsible sources.

MIX
Paper from
responsible sources
FSC® C104740

Constable
An imprint of
Little, Brown Book Group
Carmelite House
50 Victoria Embankment
London EC4Y 0DZ

An Hachette UK Company
www.hachette.co.uk

www.littlebrown.co.uk

For Audrey, Axel and Bea

There are many heavy things for the spirit, for the strong, weight-bearing spirit in which dwell respect and awe: its strength longs for the heavy, for the heaviest[*]

Friedrich Nietzsche, *Thus Spoke Zarathustra*

[*] Friedrich Nietzsche, *Thus Spoke Zarathustra* (Translated by R. J. Hollingdale) (Penguin Classics, 1969), p.54.

CONTENTS

ACKNOWLEDGEMENTS

A massive thank you to Andreas Campomar for believing in this book, acquiring it for Constable, and encouraging me to have the courage of my convictions. Hails to Claire Chesser, Bernadette Marron and Lucian Randall for editorial steering and making *Heavy* as good as it could be. Horns up to Linda Silverman for overseeing the pictures included. Furious moshing is owed to Jess Gulliver and Aimee Kitson for connecting it to its rabid audience. A special thank you to my brother-in-arms, Luke Bird, for designing the jacket, and all the years of gig-going and sharing music together.

This book wouldn't exist without my agent Matthew Hamilton seeing the potential in the original proposal. Less interesting and astute people would struggle to see the attraction of metal music, yacht rock and Tottenham Hotspur – not Matthew!

The fact I have written a book at all about the unique power of heavy music is down to the platform given to me to consider the subject, and learn something of what it means to write about music, by John Doran and Luke Turner of *The Quietus*. Along with Anna Wood, they have commissioned and encouraged me, and invited me to interview some of my favourite artists. Running an independent culture and music website in the twenty-first century, not least one as good as *The Quietus*, is no easy feat. All power to them.

Lee Brackstone and Richard King gave me an opportunity to write about Napalm Death for the second volume of Faber and Domino's *Loops* journal a decade ago. Their advice at the time set me up to spend the subsequent years working out what I was doing.

I need to thank the individuals (and their representatives) who agreed to be interviewed for this project and on other occasions which contributed to it. To the bands and artists from other fields covered in this book, and the dozens of others I could have included, I hope that *Heavy* stands as testament to how you've impacted my life and wider culture.

Thanks to family, friends and colleagues who have participated in this journey, given feedback, or simply said, 'You've written *what*?!'

All my love to my children, Audrey and Axel. I wrote this book during the heightened state (and sleep deprivation) following Audrey's arrival in the world. How could I not be inspired by that? I'm grateful to Axel for tolerating me playing Judas Priest in the car on trips to the dump. Publishing this probably guarantees that they will both become minimal techno DJs later in life.

Lastly, I'd like to thank my wife, Bea. It's impossible to express my gratitude for her wisdom and the support she gives me in all aspects of our life together. I love you to death.

PROLOGUE:
SOME KIND OF MONSTER

On 12 July 2012 I went to see the band Baroness at the Barfly venue in Camden Town, London. The upstairs room of a pub with a capacity of about two hundred people, it was packed. Baroness were a few days away from releasing their third album, *Yellow & Green*. It moved further away from the sludgy metal of their early releases, into the cleaner, more panoramic territory that saw them begin to trouble the rock mainstream. They were undertaking a journey from a primordial swamp of heaviness to a loftier musical realm.

Baroness were turning into a very special band. They were led by singer/guitarist John Dyer Baizley – whose beautiful, highly detailed artwork, near pre-Raphaelite in style, adorned their records. On the Barfly's tiny stage he was flanked by Pete Adams, a lean, commanding presence, violently whipping his long hair – at points close enough for me to feel the swish of the air – while he picked out their intricate and thundering melodies on his Les Paul guitar.

In a room that small, hemmed into the top left corner hard against the stage, I experienced a pure, headlong rush of metal's heavy energy. The music hoisted the emotions of the gathered throng upwards. During 'Ogeechee Hymnal' a crowd-surfer appeared from nowhere, teetering on top of the tightly packed audience, before being swallowed up again. I had never seen a metal band sustain a sense of euphoria as they did, propelled by the rampant, wide-eyed, roll and tumble of 'The Gnashing'. They unsettled and moved with 'Eula'; berated and pounded with 'The Sweetest Curse'; the last song, 'Grad', which starts like nothing and swells to everything, ended the set with power that felt profound. After they put their instruments down, Adams and Baizley walked into the audience, laughing and exchanging well-wishes with fans. My girlfriend, unfamiliar with the band before then, had been so overwhelmed by the experience that she went up to Baizley and hugged him.

The next month, Baroness returned to the UK for another set of dates following the release of *Yellow & Green*. On 15 August 2012, having played the Bristol Fleece the night before, the band was on its way to Southampton in heavy rain when the brakes of their bus failed. The bus crashed through a barrier and fell thirty feet from a viaduct on Brassknocker Hill, near Bath. The impact was catastrophic for the band and its members – Baizley had been chatting to the driver at the front when it happened and his left arm was severely broken, and he also sustained a broken leg. Though Adams got away with minor injuries, drummer Allen Blickle and bassist Matt Maggioni both suffered fractured vertebrae.

Recovering in Bath's Royal United hospital, Baizley took a phone call from Metallica's James Hetfield. They shared the same management team. Hetfield had been through his own devastating bus crash on tour in Sweden on 27 September 1986, which resulted in the death of Metallica's mercurial bassist Cliff Burton. Hetfield rang the hospital to share some words of comfort and encouragement with Baizley. Baizley's left arm had been broken in seven places and it took surgeons eight hours to rebuild it with two titanium plates, twenty screws and 1.5 feet of wire. He spent months recovering. In spring 2013, Blickle and Maggioni left Baroness. A statement on their website said: 'Our bus accident left indelible marks, external and internal, physical and mental, you name it.' The bus driver was eventually fined just £365 for careless driving and using a vehicle with defective brakes.

I learned of the bus crash through browsing the BBC news website at work. I wondered how many people seeing this local Somerset news story had witnessed Baroness on these recent tours, or were even aware of the band's promise as a growing force – having to tour tiny British venues, an act for whom crossing viaducts in dangerous weather in a defective tour bus was an occupational hazard. Baizley and Adams eventually recovered and Baroness resurfaced again as a live band. They carried on – and theirs was the victory. But the crash was a stark reminder of the precious, vanishing power of heavy rock and metal music. Sound and fury can become nothing in the space of a moment. It also, strangely, began to cast that Barfly gig in a different, somehow historic light.

Baroness had used heaviness, in all its ineffable power, that evening. The crash seemed to be a warning that life and death can be a hair's breadth from one another: that they, that I, that anyone, could be snuffed out at any moment, and with it the memory of experiences like that concert. I began to feel a responsibility to understand heaviness in a way I had not attempted to before. I wanted to tell its story. I needed to share its mysteries.[1]

DESCENDING

I. Into darkness

I can't remember exactly when I stepped into the darkness. But I certainly knew when I was in it, enshrouded by heaviness. Metal and heavy culture form a massive part of who I am. Part-addiction, part-compulsion, when I hear a power chord tear through a venue I am like a shark that has smelled blood in the water. My pupils go wide and the animal side takes over. I am lost in the frenzy of the mosh-pit.

At a recent Deftones gig I managed to lose my wedding ring and my house keys while moshing. I should note that I am thirty-eight years old. I dived to recover the ring and only rescued my keys when a bemused bystander held them out inquiringly to the other members of the pit.

Where did this obsession with, this *possession by*, heaviness begin? I was born in 1982. When I was eight years old my dad brought home two cassettes: *Appetite for Destruction* for me and *The Simpsons Sing the Blues* for my younger brother. I was upset I hadn't received *The Simpsons* album. But that early introduction to Guns N' Roses clearly had an effect. Axl Rose reminded Dad of Robert Plant. Rose sounded phenomenal to me too. That *Simpsons* album was great as well, and being the blues, pretty heavy in its own way – particularly Homer's numbers.

I acquired an instinct for heaviness in other forms. My mum used to tape *Moviedrome*, the late-night BBC2 cult film show, for me. Judging from the date it was broadcast as part of *Moviedrome*, May 1992, I must have watched *Mad Max 2* on VHS when I was ten years old. The film's desertscape, carnival of dangerous weir-does and erratic energy blew my mind. By the time I watched *Apocalypse Now!* aged twelve or thirteen I brought my expecta-tions of heaviness to it, not the other way around. As napalm strafed the jungle in the film to the strains of The Doors I nodded: yes, this is so.

The Tarantino era began in the early nineties and following Oliver Stone's brazenly violent *Natural Born Killers* in 1994 (for which Tarantino wrote the script), the Royal Shakespeare Company promoted its new production of *Coriolanus* with a poster of a blood-drenched Toby Stephens in the title role with the tag-line: 'A Natural Born Killer Too'. I had the poster on my bedroom wall. It hung alongside KLF member Jimmy Cauty's famous Athena poster artwork for *The Lord of the Rings*. There was a wealth of publishing around the centenary in 1992 of J. R. R. Tolkien's birth that plunged me into an alter-native fantasy world where evil loomed seductively over the good.

What other conditions could have opened me up to the heavy ways? The same year, at an Edvard Munch exhibition at the National Gallery, I came face-to-face with *The Scream*. Maybe it was a particularly sweary performance by Meatloaf at Wembley Arena after *Bat Out of Hell 2* was released, in December 1993, that tipped the balance for ever in favour of loud theatrical magnificence?

Aged thirteen, already a grunge fan, I consulted a 1995 list that rounded up the best of the year in metal (from the now long-defunct *Raw* magazine) as a primer. Metal was spurned by the mainstream, which favoured UK garage, girl-power pop, big beat, trip-hop, drum'n'bass and Britpop. Metal was undergoing uncomfortable changes. At Reading Festival in 1997, aged fifteen, at a time when teenagers still used to queue at telephone boxes to ring home for their GCSE results on the eve of the festival, Marilyn Manson was the main support of Sunday headliners Metallica. The two camps of fans could barely conceal their disdain for one another. Metallica's *Load* and *Reload* albums became symbols for the supposed malaise that emerged in nineties' metal.

One Saturday, riding the tube, I caught the tinny but unmistakeable sound of Metallica's 'King Nothing' coming from the headphones of a Mr Normal reading a broadsheet while nodding his head along to the music. Perhaps metal was more popular than I thought? As a band that had sold 100 million albums, Metallica had long superseded the genre they epitomised. This bloke on the Piccadilly line represented vast swathes of regular people who had been touched by the power of the heavy at some point in their lives.

Aside from the cultural conditions, what psychological reasons could there be for me taking up the mantle of heaviness? My parents split up when I was eleven – but so what? It wasn't an uncommon occurrence. I was loved. I was not traumatised. I was certainly not disenfranchised. Quite the opposite – maybe that was why I needed the vicarious thrills metal and heavy culture promised. I didn't feel like an outsider, unless I wanted to be. I played by the rules, but I had developed a healthy scepticism towards authority.

The thing is, I'm not an exceptional person. And that's the point. Why are so many unexceptional people swept up by the power of heaviness? How has it enriched their lives? Has it been *good* for them?

II. The heaviest matter of the universe

This is a different kind of book about metal music. It will grab you, and turn your head – whether you want it to or not – to look at heavy culture in its eyes. It asks 'Why?' – *why* does metal music affect me and millions of other people so profoundly? The reason metal is so magical is its *heaviness* – the heavy. This journey is about uncovering what heaviness is, exploring it, and explaining how it shapes the world around us.

The mission of this book is to define what heaviness means to me, what it means to others, and how it binds other parts of culture to metal music. It will ask whether it has improved or impoverished society – but if you're reading this you're probably with me that it has accomplished the former. Heaviness is full-on, intimidating, exhilarating and addictive. Moreover, it feels very necessary, a kind of bloodletting for the excessive soul. It is for the person engaged with themselves and their emotions, who sometimes feels *too much* and wants to be consumed by sound and fury. It is a filter through which to hear, see and experience the world around you. Consuming this book, you will be staring right back at it.

Taking in my surroundings at a 2019 gig by Canadian cosmic death metal band Tomb Mold in a pub in north London, something struck me. Many in attendance were wearing 'battle jackets' – denim adorned with the patches of their favourite underground bands. They wore it like armour: in previous lives metalheads like this were Viking berserkers, the Roman Praetorian Guard or the soldiers first off the landing craft for D-Day. Heavy music emerged during a relatively peaceful period in the history of the West. This is the warrior class at play – let them be entertained.

I don't want to over-explain. There's an indefinable quality to heaviness which I have no desire to define. Rather than demystify metal music, I want to *re*-mystify it. Nonetheless, I also want to put it in its rightful place at the heart of the cultural landscape. Heaviness runs two ways: metal is an open, compelling and energetic type of music that absorbs musical and lyrical themes, aesthetics and atmosphere from other sources that share its weighty load – books, films and fine art – before pouring its heavy energy back into the wider culture. This is not the book that heaviness needs, but it is the book it deserves.

You are now putting on the sunglasses as 'Rowdy' Roddy Piper's character, Nada, does in John Carpenter's 1988 film *They Live*. When Nada wears the dark glasses, they act like a reality filter and allow him to see the dominion of the film's alien ruling class, particularly in the genuine messages beneath the advertising slogans all around: 'Obey', 'Consume', 'Stay Asleep'. After finishing *Heavy*, you will also have a similar ability to perceive heaviness, to be able to identify its defining qualities and see its influence everywhere. Prepare yourselves for what you are about to understand.

III. See the world the Heavy way

Samuel John 'Lightnin'' Hopkins once said, 'The blues is something that is hard to get acquainted with, just like death. The blues can come so many different ways, until it's kinda hard to explain.'[1] Heaviness has this elusive quality to it too. But it is an energy, an emotional intensity and a secret cause that runs through many things.

'Let freedom ring!' smiles the character Julie Ann, played by Hannah Murray, enjoying the liberty and hedonism promised by late sixties' America in the film *Detroit* (2017) just before events go south. Kathryn Bigelow's horrendous depiction of police brutality over one night in the city's Algiers Motel during the riots of 1967, which left three young black men shot dead, goes to the heart of continuing racial tensions across the USA today.

'Let freedom ring' is also a quote from the patriotic song 'My Country, 'Tis of Thee', written in 1831. It was co-opted for a roared refrain in Machine Head's 'Davidian', bastardised to 'Let freedom ring with a shotgun blast!' in a song about the law enforcement siege of the compound of the cult led by David Koresh – the Branch Davidians – in Waco, Texas, in 1993.

Machine Head's debut album, *Burn My Eyes* (1994), contained numerous songs that addressed the political, religious and social divisions that were pressurising America in the mid-nineties. 'Real Eyes, Realize, Real Lies' is an instrumental of mounting tension and turning-the-screw guitar, overlaid with field recordings of voices following the Los Angeles riots of 1992 that followed the acquittals of police in the Rodney King beating trial.

Across Bigelow's film and Machine Head's album, the phrase 'Let freedom ring' ties together the events depicted in Detroit in 1967, LA in 1992, and Waco in 1993. With their debut album, Machine Head traced a heavy seam through American culture. They blended hardcore aggression with their hard-headed Oakland attitude to make metal speak to a societal meltdown that is still ongoing.

Following the Las Vegas concert massacre of October 2017, singer Robb Flynn made a statement that he never wanted to play 'Davidian' again for those who took the line 'Let freedom ring with a shotgun blast!' as a clarion call to bear arms.[2] I felt it was a peculiar stance to take in the circumstances, as I always perceived the line as at least semi-ironic, considering the subject matter of 'Davidian'. America's tragedy of race and firearms is intertwined and ongoing, as it scars the conscience of modern metal. *Burn My Eyes* was at the time, and remains, one of the heaviest metal albums of all time. Musically it was uncompromising, and lyrically it dispensed with the genre's more fantastical subject matter and imagery, replacing them with the horrors of the world around us.

Violence, of course, has its place in heaviness. The band Vision of Disorder named their 1998 album *Imprint* after their singer Tim Williams was attacked in the street, leaving his face scarred by a knife wound. Love and pain have a prominent place too: Every Time I Die wrote a song called 'Petal' about singer Keith Buckley's wife's near-fatal experience while giving birth, invoking Macduff from Shakespeare's *Macbeth* with his screams that his daughter was 'untimely ripped' into the world. Life of Agony singer Mina Caputo wrote extraordinary threnodies like 'Lost At 22' before she had transitioned to a woman, opening up her life like the pages of a diary. Through heavy music, she has lived out a struggle with finding her place in the world, which continues. Metal is at home in the mode of tragedy: anger, fear and grief at the unavoidable loss of people and things we cherish in the physical world.

Heaviness is about emotional authenticity, what Justine Jones from Woking band Employed to Serve described to me as, 'Stark honesty about real-life experiences of ourselves and people around us'. She uses the writer John Steinbeck for lyrical inspiration: 'I feel emotionally connected to the characters and they're so believable that you can see parallels with his characters and people in your own life.' For Jones, the audience becomes a mirror and a means of catharsis. 'The lyrics that I write are a personal diary and are very therapeutic for me so, in order not to feel bare, I disguise them in metaphors so that people can take their own understanding of them.'

Speaking on the thirtieth anniversary of the release of . . . *And Justice for All* in 2018, Metallica's James Hetfield described his view of an apolitical anger that has seen his band attain rare status within and beyond the genre. 'We don't want to be a controversial band. We want to be solid, we want to be real, we want to tell the truth. Yes, we feel alienated: who doesn't? If you do, follow us.'[3]

Tell that to the detainees of US military interrogators during the second Iraq war in 2003, when they were subjected to a mix of the music of Metallica and children's character Barney the Dinosaur, in the hunt for information on the whereabouts of weapons of mass destruction. The US had previously blared Van Halen at Panamanian dictator Manuel Noriega when he took refuge in the Apostolic Nunciature of the Holy See, effectively the Vatican's embassy, in Panama City, in 1989. Metallica's music muscled up the barrage, as Sgt Mark Hadsell told *Newsweek* at the time: 'These people haven't heard heavy metal before. They can't take it. If you play it for twenty-four hours, your brain and body functions start to slide, your train of thought slows down and your will is broken. That's when we come in and talk to them.'[4]

Just as metal has been used as a weapon to weaken an opponent, it has been employed as a means of self-strengthening. In a paper entitled 'Suicide, Self-Harm and Survival Strategies in Contemporary Heavy Metal Music: A Cultural and Literary Analysis', co-authored by Charley Baker, associate professor in mental health at the University of Nottingham, self-harm is described as having a theme of 'a coping strategy, a relief of overwhelming or negative emotions, a catharsis, and as a way of feeling something other than numb'.[5] Catharsis, the process of releasing powerful emotions, has long been associated with heavy metal. I asked Baker about whether metal provides an equivalent kind of emotional outlet to self-harm: 'It's tricky to answer this one – given the increasing rates of self-harm and mental health difficulties young people in particular are facing. I think the lyric content and heaviness of the music in a range of metal subgenres is something that offers an identificatory mechanism, so self-harm or depression, for example, may be more widely acknowledged within the music itself (as opposed to pop or dance music, for example), potentially leading to people being able to identify with a particular song or band and then feeling more able to discuss their difficulties.'

Heaviness, for Baker – a fan as much as an academic with an interest in metal music – invites her to 'feel hard and think deep'. Metal music throws everything at you and, accordingly, it inspires people to throw everything into life itself, reciprocating that energy in a heavy lifestyle. This mirrors the energy exchange between band and audience at metal gigs, and – although Baker acknowledges that this exchange might not be unique to metal and heavy rock – that 'the heaviness – the depth, the bass, the screams, the emotions and the pulse of metal is something unique, something that in metalheads elicits powerful emotions'.

Metal neutralises dark subject matter and encourages listeners to recognise, acknowledge and own their desires, anger and pain, often in a loud and live environment. Baker encountered one fan at a Motionless in White gig who said that the band's music actively stopped them hurting themselves or getting low. Though one person does not make a dataset, Baker sees the conversation alive and well in the spaces where fans congregate on and offline. 'It is a commonly discussed issue throughout metal bands, metal forums, interviews, magazines, etc. Strength and survival are key messages in metal, and the neutralising-through-owning emotions expressed or identifying with lyrics can, I think, be one outlet that enables a different kind of acknowledging, openness and emotional and physical release for people.'

Dr Kate Quinn is a clinical psychologist working in NHS services in early intervention in psychosis. Her work with patients includes using 'voice dialogue', which is a psychoanalytically informed approach to understanding aspects of ourselves, including hearing voices. Sometimes this approach might be used for working with people who hear voices that command them to do harmful things. 'As a voice-hearing specialist,' she says, 'I often work with people who have voices who will say quite extreme things such as they should kill themselves or others. One of the most important ideas in voice dialogue is the symbolic nature of these experiences. They convey difficult feelings and important messages but not in a literal way – so there is a part that is legitimately angry, for example, but that doesn't mean you should literally kill anyone!'

Can we think about heavy music this way? That it is a means of acknowledging the parts of ourselves that we would rather disown? For Quinn, recognising and 'honouring' our disowned selves is a way of helping ourselves, whereas attempting to keep those selves at bay can often lead to distress: 'We might support people to find ways of "honouring" the energy that the voice conveys, so angry voices may like things – like the voice-hearer doing boxercise or listening to angry music – but that's not the same as acting on the voices in a literal way. I guess my thought is that we all have different aspects of self, which might not necessarily manifest as voices per se, but that the principle still applies.'

Quinn set up the website heavymetaltherapy.co.uk when she was working with young adults with emerging mental health problems and encountered a patient for whom traditional therapy techniques were not working: 'We came up together with the idea of using playlists and lyrics in the work, and that was the first time I managed to get him to do any homework! It also helped us to work out a few things that he couldn't tell me verbally, but could show through the music he brought to me. We used that approach to write his life experiences via lyrics and then also used this to describe coping strategies and ways to help.'

It was useful for Quinn that she had found herself returning to metal as a source of support for her own anxiety problems when they resurfaced as an adult, creating a common language with those of her clients who were receptive to it. The website is an extension of her voice-hearing work ('an amalgamation of peer support, recovery movement ideas and recovery stories'), with Quinn as the facilitator of a different kind of heavy metal online forum.

Listening to metal lets us identify those energies or voices within ourselves we might find difficult and helps us to contend with them through externalised heaviness. We are giving our disowned selves to the expression of heightened noise and emotions we receive from heavy bands. 'I think that for some people,' says Quinn, 'listening to metal, or performing, is tapping into those pushed-away parts of us and allows us to honour them in a safe way. I wonder if this may even help to reduce the risk of angry or violent behaviour as these feelings are channelled elsewhere and "processed" instead of building up.'

Heavy music is a tool to pick up and deploy in the exploration of our more difficult and complex emotions. It can be an outlet for, or means to absorb those sensations. Comedian and actor Rob Delaney now doesn't drink and uses it to replicate the intoxication of alcohol: 'I got into hardcore around age eleven when I started middle school and learned about Minor Threat, Black Flag and The Meatmen. Then, at age twelve, a friend gave me Slayer's *South of Heaven* and I'd listen to it on my Walkman delivering the *Boston Globe* every morning. All that music, of course, goes great with adolescence. Then my tastes expanded to all kinds of stuff, including classical, jazz, pop, whatever was interesting. But I never stopped listening to heavy music. I really dove back in hard when I got sober at age twenty-five. I think I liked, and still like, the "buzz" I got from loud, heavy guitars and drums and people screaming. So I definitely "use" heavy music to achieve a mood, whether or not that's healthy. I enjoy it in any case. I think also that the people who are good at metal, sludge, etc, are usually great musicians and it just makes me happy that someone could devote so much time and energy and skill to wanting to make nasty chug-a-lug riffs.'

Delaney is a well-known fan of Sleep and High On Fire, both bands involving guitarist Matt Pike, who Delaney describes as 'an amazing composer in any genre, and a truly virtuosic guitar player, but his music is always nasty, always dirty. It's like there's a war inside Pike between Bach and the Creature from the Black Lagoon.' When Matt Pike performs live in High On Fire, or even more so in Sleep, you get the startling feeling he is powering his wall of amplifiers with the molten energy diverted from the centre of the Earth – grounding them in its very crust. Pike's guitar playing, which channels sonic forces that operate on different, near-geological timescales, point to the finitude of our time on Earth. Things will come and go in your life. Your life itself will go. Heavy is for ever.

It can be surprising to see who draws on the power of heaviness while engaged in their own creative act. The novelist Elif Shafak, when asked in an interview what would surprise people about her, said: 'I am a huge fan of gothic metal, industrial metal, Viking-pagan-folk metal and metalcore. Especially dark, loud, aggressive, Scandinavian metal bands. I listen to this kind of music on repeat while I am writing my novels.'[6] That's all she had to say – I tried to coax more out of her on Twitter of all places, but she left it at that. We can understand that heavy fuels her, even if we are not allowed to know how.

Heavy metal has been described as having 'Wagnerian power'. As John Deathridge, Wagner scholar and Emeritus King Edward Professor of Music at King's College London, puts it, metal has its own visceral, internal logic: '"Wagnerian power", in relation to heavy metal, in my view refers to music with a deliberately physiological component. It's not music about beauty, form, "spirit", so-called programmes that conjure up extra-musical images, or even dance, but aimed deliberately at physical reactions: the body, the skin, nerve-endings, adrenaline-producing glands, not to mention the workings of conscious-changing mechanisms in the brain. Nietzsche got this right when he accused Wagner's music of being incapable of dance, yet capable of making him feel sick! That's a good, albeit negative, way of defining "Wagnerian power".'

Heaviness can be applied like a paintbrush to adjust the light and shade of a composition as necessary. Jock Norton, the singer/

guitarist of power trio Puppy, who blend poppy vocals with gritted instrumental crunch, sketches the melodic outline of their music with 'classic pop songwriting elements, but then the metal element is a way to colour that. Rather than that being the intrinsic thing. With a black metal band or a grindcore band that element is the focal point, whereas for us it's a way of colouring the songs.'

Heaviness is a way of understanding other things in unexpected ways. Football manager Jürgen Klopp is known for his 'heavy metal' style of football, in which control is seemingly forsaken for wild intensity and whirlwind surges of play. But that is merely appearance, because underlying this seemingly ferocious chaos is control, discipline and order – just as is the case in some of the most extreme forms of metal. The term 'heavy-metal football' came up when Klopp explained the contrast between his management style and that of Arsène Wenger of Arsenal: 'He likes having the ball, playing football, passes. It's like an orchestra. But it's a silent song. I like heavy metal more. I always want it loud.'[7] In Klopp's game, the players rally back and forth between attack and defence in overpowering waves: eleven men turned up to eleven.

Heaviness which, as we've seen, prefers the domain of tragedy, can be used to temper comedy. In the second season of 2010 HBO series *Eastbound & Down*, when buffoonish ex-major league baseball pitcher Kenny Powers adopts the persona of '*la flama blanca*', he puts on his Elvis-in-Las-Vegas-style outfit to a soundtrack of 'For Those About to Rock (We Salute You)' by AC/DC. AC/DC are not a metal band, but this is one of their heaviest songs: its opening smoulders steadily over almost funereal bass drum hits. It is deployed in the comedy to impart an atmosphere of faux solemnity to the character's transformation. It helps us to laugh with – and at – Kenny Powers, through our acknowledgement that the song is ridiculous but also mighty.

Listeners of heavy music might appreciate the value of Wenger's 'silent song', but they don't necessarily want it. They need the excessive energy of metal to spill over and overpower them and, in many cases, empower them. They want to share something with their fellow man and woman: to recognise our essential commonality through heavy sounds.

IV. Why heavy matters

Heaviness is an iron-rich bloodline running through the bedrock of culture. When you accept its power and identify it, the question becomes: how is it important and what does it teach us about the human condition?

Heaviness is about understanding that there are primal fears and concerns that underpin all human creativity. Death is the biggest one, the inevitable end of the journey. Tragedy is fuelled by the irreconcilable difference between our knowledge of life's finitude and our failure to live well within that: the crushing inevitability of an unhappy demise. *The Remains of the Day* is a heavy novel (originally published in 1989), film and, more recently, play, because its protagonist, head butler Stevens, cannot break from his sense of duty to express his feelings for housekeeper Miss Kenton. The intense, laden sorrow of the story has parallels with the cathectic outpourings of the doom metal genre. Tapping into the pure power source of heavy gives these emotions an expression and, in doing so, some kind of reconciliation and hope.

Heaviness is also about being honest about the evil that men do and looking at that unflinchingly. The sonic force and violence of metal is an assault on the senses and feels inherently confrontational. The same dynamic is at play when the viewer looks upon *Head VI* (1949) by Francis Bacon or watches the film *You Were Never Really Here* (directed by Lynne Ramsay, 2018): it is a heavy endeavour to look directly at representations of violence, suffering and fractured psyches, and to choose to absorb that energy. In doing so, we extract a kind of strength from the heaviness. Ultimately, it makes us feel better if we can weather the initial, visceral discomfort. Eventually, we can bathe in it, not because we have become inoculated against its effects, but because we relish its ability to sustain us.

So, read on and let me weave you a web of heavy matters. Whether you are a long-time follower of the heavy ways or a newcomer on the path, this book will leave you changed. Or at least, alter your perspective. This is an investigation into the reasons why metal is so powerful, what defines 'heavy' in music, and how heaviness transfuses culture and society: there is plenty of territory to explore.

This journey draws a line between heavy music and other works of art, and traces how deeply its roots penetrate the earth. I want to share a magnificent thing that is as misunderstood as it is adored. Both elusive and sometimes very sinister, I want to reveal heaviness in all its terrible beauty. It will drive you to discover music and other works of art that show the world in a different light.

1
ORIGIN MYTHS

'What in me is dark/Illumine' – John Milton, *Paradise Lost*

'This was me, this was my quest – a music
that wasn't there' – K. K. Downing

Heaviness has been with us since the dawn of time and the first exertion of gravity. In recorded history, it came to be welded into the framework of metal music during its development in England's industrial heartlands in the second half of the twentieth century. But heaviness also reaches further back and grasps some of the earliest tales that explore the human condition. The origins of its story are a fallen angel, an iron giant teetering on the precipice, a young man on a quest in a land of metalworking and a wizard attempting to reach the stars. In the music of Led Zeppelin, Black Sabbath, Judas Priest and Ronnie James Dio, we find the myths which heavy music was built upon: a fallen world of human overreach and an intuition that there is something beyond the realm of the day to day.

I. Lucifer falling

Like water bursting through a broken levee, Led Zeppelin flooded into my life in 2003, when I was twenty-one years old. I had just been through a break-up, and something about that torrid period meant that I started listening to Led Zeppelin properly – to my vulnerable ego, their music was also responding to me – and I couldn't stop. In the midst of guitarist Jimmy Page's remastering drive of their back catalogue, I was mainlining their music. I often sat, heavily stoned with friends in my student flat in Edinburgh, watching the 1970 Royal Albert Hall gig they had just released on DVD. The spontaneity, energy and absolute fearlessness of the gig was a revelation. It was a performance later described by vocalist Robert Plant as an 'absolute shock' when he watched it on the same DVD thirty years-plus after the performance: 'I was just hanging on for dear life, really.'[1]

Following that childhood obsession with *The Lord of the Rings,* references to Mordor and Gollum in the lyrics to 'Ramble On' weren't cheesy to me – they connected. By the end of that record-breaking hot summer of 2003, I had the artwork that inspired Zeppelin's Swan Song record label logo (Lucifer in freefall, two arms extended to the sun) tattooed on my right shoulder. It was derived from William Rimmer's beautiful 1869–70 line drawing, *Evening (The Fall of Day).* I was pleased with the original drawing's small differences to the Swan Song version of Lucifer: the one arm extended up, another hooked behind his long hair, and a sunburst at the apex of his left wing.

It is said heavy metal fell from the sky. Rimmer's glamorous Lucifer, with his flowing long hair, muscular physique and almost lovelorn posture, is a visualisation of the Lucifer of John Milton's epic poem *Paradise Lost* (1674). The chief rebel angel is a symbol of the republican revolt of the seventeenth-century English Civil War. In contrast to the prosaic, bland platitudes spoken by God and Jesus in the epic poem, Satan charms with convoluted proclamations; he is seductive but specious. He is hard to resist, and heavy metal music, even in its prototypical stages, made sure its audiences heard him out.

The summer of 2003 was emotionally raw for me, but revitalising with the pain and thrill of new beginnings. Zeppelin reached deep into me and plucked at a chord that seemed to run through my entire being. There was one song in particular that resonated – 'Dazed and Confused'. It has an atmosphere of an encroaching storm, a bass-led melodic descent from heaven (and into hell), with Plant singing of getting what he hadn't bargained for, and of the soul of a woman being created 'below', which for years I misheard as 'for love'. The song is massive in length and breadth, a wide-open vista in which the band paints abstract images, especially when Page takes a violin bow to his electric guitar strings. Page's guitar-playing on the record becomes a low droning imitation of distant whale song and, when he played the song live, he transitioned into the ominous lead refrain of Holst's 'Mars: the Bringer of War', sounding very much as if massive, dreaded planets were coming into view.

Led Zeppelin set a historic standard for how to approach live performance. Even a comedy performer like Rob Delaney speaks of their influence in their command of a stage: 'I will sometimes remind myself when I walk onstage to do stand-up, "This is a stage. Led Zeppelin performed on stage. You are lucky to be on a stage and you must give your performance the energy and care that Led Zeppelin would give an audience. This audience could be anywhere else and they've chosen to spend their entertainment dollar with you. Don't betray them."'

On 10 December 2007, I saw Zeppelin live: something I thought I would never witness. That night at the O2 arena in London's Docklands (a venue I love for its garish faux-American sports arena atmosphere), with Page framed in a pyramid of green lasers during the guitar bowing, 'Dazed and Confused' thundered out with more force than before, because he had down-tuned his guitar to accommodate Plant's lower vocal range. It dragged the original recorded incarnation of the song to hell with even greater heaviness. As Plant said at the time: 'The trouble is now, with rock'n'roll and stuff, it gets so big that it loses what was once a magnificent thing, where it was special and quite elusive and occasionally a little sinister and had its own world nobody could get in.'[2] But it's easy to focus on Page and Plant whereas, in the case of 'Dazed and Confused', the band's power is hammered home by the rhythm section of bassist John Paul Jones and drummer John Bonham, whose son Jason played the 2007 gig.

John Paul Jones's role was highlighted by drummer Mac Poole in the oral history of the band, *Trampled Under Foot*: 'Musically, out of all four of them, I would put John Paul Jones as being the fucking man. He may play a very simple line on "Dazed and Confused", but the guy's thinking for the mood is so musical, and that makes it work. Jimmy's a great guitarist, but without Jones in the band – without that fundamental – it would be nothing.'[3] When I interviewed Dave Grohl about collaborating with John Paul Jones in their then new band, Them Crooked Vultures (two years after Zeppelin performed at the O2 arena), Grohl defined the chemistry at the heart of the Zeppelin rhythm section: 'The only way it works is when it's entirely real and everyone's playing off each other, and you sort of lose the pattern and the choreography, or the plan and you just go. And in order to do that you have to be in a band of people that trust each other, and you all have to feel safe with each other to do it. I'm sure that's what Zeppelin did. All the bootlegs I have there are moments that are completely insane like, "What the fuck are they doing?! They're all going in four different directions!"'

Earlier in the same interview, Jones had explained the alchemy of the right rhythm section, this time working with Grohl: 'As a bass player you work with so many drummers in your life, you can spot the ones that are going to work real quick and they are very few. Well, there are various levels of how they work. Some, it will be all right, others, it's going to be magic, and Dave was one of those magic ones.'

John Paul Jones tied heaviness to a plunging, lead weight melodic centre and roamed with it. No Zeppelin performance was the same – the setlist and running order of the songs might not change but the course of the musical channel would meander through them. There was freedom, and a sense of discovery, but also a sense of momentous *will* (as consecrated in occultist Aleister Crowley's directive, 'Do what thou wilt', which fascinated Page[4]): go where you want in music and the world, and decide your own fate. Confuse yourself and let life confuse you. Fall from the sky and explore the fiery depths. For me, that electric connection with Zeppelin in 2003 was the end of the beginning of living a life of heavy music.

II. Iron Man has his revenge

There is a story so well-known about the creation of Black Sabbath's sound, it is as if it was etched in stone and brought down from the mountain. Like the best stories, it bears retelling.

Among the dark, satanic mills of Aston's industrial heartland, an eighteen-year-old Tony Iommi arrived to work at the sheet metal factory where he made a living as a welder. It was the mid-sixties and he was about to embark on a tour with his band The Rockin' Chevrolets, but as fate would have it, the plant was short-staffed and Iommi had to help work the metal presses. Unused to the labour, he trapped his hand in the machinery, slicing the tips off two of the fingers on his right hand.

As he stood staring at his ravaged hand could Iommi have realised, somewhere deep down inside him, the significance of this moment? Because this ending – the end of his time at the factory and what he thought was the brutal end of his musical ambition – was actually a beginning, and the inception of one of the biggest musical genres in the world.

Instead of giving in to despair, Iommi drew on his courage and ingenuity to forge a new way forward. Encouraged by the example of Django Reinhardt, the legendary guitar player whose playing continued despite having two fingers of his left hand badly burned in a fire, Iommi began experimenting with ways to continue his music. He fashioned homemade thimbles for the tips of his fingers, initially made from melted-down washing-up bottles. The lack of feeling in the fingers of his fretting hand meant he had to slacken the strings on the guitar to ensure he had the purchase he needed. The result was a downtuned sound, and a slower style, sculpting heavy riffs from a morass of distortion.

Iommi soon formed a band called the Polka Tulk Blues Band – after a while it was known as simply Polka Tulk – then Earth, which in turn was renamed Black Sabbath. The original line-up – John 'Ozzy' Osbourne on vocals, Terence 'Geezer' Butler on bass, Bill Ward on drums and Iommi – played an atomic blues that was the beginning of the metal sound.

The tolling bells and thunderstorm that introduce the track 'Black Sabbath' give way to a dissonant tri-tone riff (known

musically as 'the devil's interval') and lyrics depicting a visitation from Satan himself. It came out of a jam on the encroaching, planet-sized menace of the main figure of Holst's *Mars*,
which we've already seen that Jimmy Page also enjoyed playing
live. Unaware of the significance of the musical interval – a
taboo in religious music through the centuries dubbed *diabolus
in musica* – Iommi simply felt 'something was moving me to
play like that'.[5]

'Black Sabbath' introduced the tropes for which heavy music
has become famous and massively popular. That figure in black at
the foot of the bed of its lyrics is the devil, but also a shadow self
– externalised, recognised though disowned, and planted into
the song. Musically, the song took the hippy notion of saying
'heavy' to describe something in benign harmony with the
universe, cast it in iron and tossed it into the North Sea to sink to
the bottom.

I got into Black Sabbath as a teenager, years before I listened to
Zeppelin. Getting into metal in the mid-nineties coincided with
the reformation of that original line-up of Black Sabbath, and the
launch of Ozzfest – a touring festival designed for them and/or
Ozzy to headline. Long an influence on a generation of heavy
musicians, during the last decade of the twentieth century
Sabbath stepped out of the shadows in a massive way. My first
Sabbath album was a fifteen-track compilation called *Between
Heaven and Hell* (1995). Although far from comprehensive, it
was well-sequenced and, despite running to just a single disc,
didn't fear to include a number of songs from the band's sketch-
ier, post-Ozzy line-ups. It ended with 'Black Sabbath' itself, but
began with 'Hole in the Sky' – a thrashing piece of bedsit psychedelia. The song had strange lyrics that were both cryptic and
introspective ('The synonyms of all the things that I've said/Are

just the riddles that are built in my head'), and which also described some kind of visionary astral projection ('Hole in the sky, take me to heaven/Window in time, through it I fly').

The second track on the compilation was 'Into the Void', the closing song from 1971's *Master of Reality*. It sounded incredible to me: the portentous opening slide down the guitar fretboard, which then reversed into a slovenly blues climb, followed by the throttling of the engine-room main riff to within an inch of its life. It is an urtext in heavy music, with its lyric about escaping a burning Earth in a spacecraft. It is lumbering, it is slack, but it moves together with an awesome intensity and momentum. In 2015, after Jamaican author Marlon James won the Booker Prize for *A Brief History of Seven Killings* (a novel inspired by the attempted murder of Bob Marley in 1976), James hosted an episode of BBC 6 Music's *Paperback Writers* programme (on which authors choose their favourite music) and selected 'Into The Void'.[6]

What was the appeal of this song – forged in the furnace of industrial Birmingham by a poor, white, working-class band – to a young black kid from Jamaica? Forced to watch a documentary at high school called *Highway to Hell*, that painted rock music of black origin as the work of the devil, and in doing so introducing James to a host of illicit heavy rock acts, it was probably the very fact it *was* forbidden.[7] How could James not be drawn to Sabbath's propensity for groove and swing? Bill Ward's jazzlike chaos on the drum kit is undeniably their secret weapon. Theirs was never a straightforward form of plodding rock. But more than that, Sabbath embodied a raw heaviness that smashed any cultural boundaries. The prose of *A Brief History of Seven Killings* has a grand, almost occult darkness in its multi-stranded story about the fallout following the attempted assassination of Marley – a difficult, impenetrable gloom and seething intensity, drawn from the same power source as Sabbath. Looking at it another way, the same ominousness that runs through the music of Sabbath *is* that source.

One of Black Sabbath's most audacious compositions – a series of titanic riffs welded together – is 'Iron Man'. It sits as a partner to the other epic from 1970's *Paranoid* album, 'War Pigs'. Not so much a comment on the horrors of conflict as a performance of those horrors themselves, I've always felt 'War Pigs' left other anti-war songs like Bob Dylan's 'Masters of War' as burnt-out husks along the sonic highway. It was more recently used to devastating effect as it played out for the best part of two minutes at the beginning of the final episode of the second series of *Fargo* (2015). The song soundtracked an on-foot police pursuit of two fugitives, also being hunted by a rifle-toting psychopathic family gang member.

As former Black Flag frontman Henry Rollins pointed out in BBC Four's *Classic Albums* episode on *Paranoid*, it is a marvel the way that the band plays a full-tilt section in 'Iron Man', over which Iommi can play a solo with the fluidity and speed afforded by those manufactured fingertips, before shifting two gears down into the drilling-rig steadiness and immensity of the pre-chorus riff.[8] Iommi wrote solos with as much melodic character as his riffs; they burrowed into my brain, never to leave. 'Iron Man' features one of his most well-conceived musical figures – his guitar invokes hulking machinery coming to life. The song is a story of a man transformed into steel by a magnetic field when time-travelling to save humanity, after which perceived betrayal he pledges to destroy the human race. The song begins with a sequence of questions: whether he is alive, what's going through his head and what's the risk that he will fall.

It has stark parallels with *The Iron Man* by Ted Hughes, published in 1968, two years before the Sabbath song was released. Hughes's story begins with one of the great opening lines: 'The Iron Man came to the top of the cliff.' Like the song, it then poses a set of questions (How far had it walked? Where did it come from? How was it made?) before the enormous iron man steps into nothingness, plunging from the cliff, smashing into pieces. Hughes's iron man then slowly pieces himself together in a beguilingly logical sequence, starting with his right hand recovering his eye with a little help from a seagull. After reassembling himself, he feeds on farm equipment, and is met with the same hostility and confusion that greet the subject of Sabbath's song. He is lured to a covered-over pit by a boy, falls into it and is trapped. He emerges in the latter part of the story to become mankind's saviour as he battles a 'space-bat-angel-dragon' on our behalf, which he out-matches. He then encourages the creature to sing its music of the spheres to humanity, bringing about lasting peace on earth. The iron man that Hughes imagines has the opposite impact to the one depicted in the lyric of Sabbath bassist Geezer Butler.[9]

However, it is hard not to conflate the two. In a friend's caravan at the most easterly point of the British Isles on the Ardnamurchan peninsula in Scotland, I remember putting the song on one evening and looking out towards the nearby lighthouse as the song's opening steady bass drum thud, tortured guitar pitch-bends and grating spoken word introduction reverberated in the confined space. I half-hoped, half-expected in the spectacular highland dusk, to see the iron giant appear at the land's end and plunge into the sea: heavy metal personified.

III. Forged between the hammer and the anvil

Born in 1951, in the post-World War II baby boom, Judas Priest guitarist Kenneth 'K. K.' Downing dragged himself out of poverty on a quest to realise his own vision of heavy metal. The 'very dark world' he came from that he described to me, and the working-class community of the Black Country he grew up in, fuelled his need to escape. In his book *Heavy Duty* (2018) he describes a suburb of West Bromwich called Hilltop, 'where the horizon, assuming you could see it at all, was dominated by steel-rolling mills and foundries set against a dense, grey backdrop', providing 'a noisy, gritty, industrial soundtrack' which ground down the residents.[10] Judas Priest's heavy metal has often been equated to the sound of the industrial Midlands, but it is the working-class nature of the band, and the abuses they withstood, which imbued their music with its crucial power.

Character might be developed while working in factories, but earlier in life people are moulded by their experiences in their front rooms, their close-quarter family lives. Or, in Downing's case, when he was crammed into a bed with his sister and cousin, forced to spend his childhood days in a glorified shed in the bottom of his cousin's garden that had been constructed by a parent deeply paranoid about his children coming into contact with the outside world. Downing described to me the 'virtually sinister' circumstances of his upbringing, ruled over by a father who was an inveterate gambler down at the dog-racing track, but was himself haunted by the death of his younger brother – who fell from a cooling tower on the day Downing's father took a day off from the same workplace to go betting on horses.[11] Accordingly, his dad felt the horses saved him, when really they were the start of his condemnation.

Even more than feeling the indignity of being hungry and not having shoes on his feet, Downing was embarrassed about the family's lack of proper furniture and carpets, about his parents, and his home. Some release came in the form of his older sister's crystal radio set, tuned to Radio Luxembourg. That was when his quest for a new form of music began. 'I was always looking for something I suppose,' he said. 'What I consider now to be working class, workman's blues or white kid's blues.' Two songs gave him a sound that contained an embryonic form of heavy metal, as defined by the use of fuzzbox distortion: 'You Really Got Me' by The Kinks and 'Eve of Destruction' by Barry McGuire.

Downing began a search for something 'darker and more meaningful' in music; something with a heightened emotional impact. Going to see Jimi Hendrix live in 1967 as a sixteen-year-old confirmed in his mind what he was after. For Downing, Hendrix was emphatically heavy metal: 'Because musically the riffs and the sound of the guitar were detached from everything else in existence. Everything else was blues and progressive blues, and I could reel off the bands left, right and centre, and I liked a lot of the bands. But it was kind of play safe, stand still, and we'll play our style of blues type of thing. Hendrix came over and all hell was let loose really.' Downing saw the impact immediately – how an ostensible pop band like The Who morphed into an instrument-smashing monster in response to Hendrix trashing his own guitar. The beast had been awakened, but still it was in its inchoate form. And it still lacked something, according to Downing: 'It didn't seem to have the emotional content that was geared up for people like me – who went through what I did when I was growing up.'

Even Black Sabbath was not there yet, in Downing's eyes. Happy as he was to hear a band write songs based around riffs, their 'Stonehenge metal' (his coinage) was too primal. He craved something more polished, that had not only the flamboyance and technique of Hendrix and Cream, but also an outstanding singer with an extraordinary vocal range.

When Rob Halford joined the early incarnation of Judas Priest in 1972, he was that virtuoso. In response to the 'soft harmonies' of the multiple guitar bands from the West Coast of America such as James Gang, Allman Brothers and Grateful Dead, Downing had wondered what a band with 'really heavy harmonies' would sound like. When guitarist Glenn Tipton, a more blues-orientated and commercially minded player, joined Judas Priest in 1974, Downing's vision of playing 'a music that wasn't there', which 'came from inside of me' was ready to be executed. Judas Priest's heavy metal pitted the Downing–Tipton axis, fired by a crackling tension and creative sense of one-upmanship, against Halford's histrionics. They crafted a new, ornate, sometimes overly shiny steel blade that they wielded with increasing efficiency as they hurtled towards the 1980s.

On 'Victim of Changes', the opening song from Judas Priest's second album, *Sad Wings of Destiny*, released in 1976, the transition from progressive heavy blues into heavy metal plays out in the song itself. It begins with Downing and Tipton in unison but slightly apart, executing those heavy harmonies Downing dreamed of, etching out patterns of melody and counter-melody, before a two-tiered bluesy descent into the song's fist-pumping main riff: a turbo-charged blues, coruscating like burning chrome. The song, at nearly eight minutes long, is actually two blended together: Downing's 'Whiskey Woman' and Halford's 'Red Light Lady'. The former describes the ravages of a woman drinking herself to death – the despair of seeing someone destroyed by the working-class lifestyle and the emotional pain when 'another woman's got her man'. Whereas the latter reposi-tions the subject as the singer's lost love ('once she was beautiful/once she was mine'). Putting the songs together created a subtle but affecting perspective change: we are no longer onlookers but also implicated in this woman's downfall. The song showcases Halford's piercing voice in acapella breaks between the riffs, and the more delicate timbre of his mid-range after the subdued break in the action, before his sky-ripping falsetto shriek sees the song out. Downing takes the extended first solo and in performances, ranging from an enormous gig in San Bernardino, California, at the height of the band's powers in 1983, to one 2008 performance of the song at the Seminole Hard Rock Arena, Florida, he sounds like he is blasting away his childhood demons for good. His play-ing makes an emphatic statement: victim no more.

'Victim of Changes' is remarkable and became a longstanding piece of music, played consistently through the years in the band's live sets. This was not only because heavy metal was being forged in its piledriving passages and in its scope of ambition, but because it packed the emotional punch that Downing wanted to deliver.

The following song on *Sad Wings of Destiny* shows one of the parallel paths Judas Priest would take. 'The Ripper' is under three minutes and is leaner, with a simplified, chugging main riff, a menacing half-time groove and sporadic, sharp jazzlike guitar flourishes. It picks up pace and slows down again like its focal point, Jack the Ripper, stalking one of his prey on the streets of the East End of Victorian London.

The third song of the album, 'Dreamer Deceiver', is in another mode again. With a trippy set of guitar chords, softly delineated like Sabbath's *Paranoid* album cut 'Planet Caravan', and Halford's jaw-dropping vocal shifts in register, this was a sound they soon moved away from in large part – but what a waymarker it was. Just compare it to the in-for-the-kill fury of 'Dissident Aggressor' from the following year's *Sin After Sin*. This is a song gritty enough to get covered by Slayer (in 1988), and even they failed to out-do the original. Judas Priest's early performance of 'Dreamer Deceiver' on *The Old Grey Whistle Test* in 1975, with Downing in an out-sized white fedora and a long-haired, open-shirted Halford, is another moment in time which crystallises something that came to bother Downing as the seventies progressed: how the band looked.

Back when he was at school, Downing had acquired a second-hand leather satchel to replace a tatty canvas bag. On it, he carved some of his favourite bands' names, filling the scoured letters with pen ink: the Small Faces, The Rolling Stones, The Troggs. Though he didn't want his own band to have the kind of uniformity that defined the look of the pop stars of his childhood, in the mid-sixties, he told me that a decade later he felt that a uniform look with individual differences (something like the characters of 1960 film *The Magnificent Seven*) would make the band look as powerful as they sounded. 'It's something to bond us together. So that when we hit that stage we have more strength, more meaning. We can send out more of a message and more of a performance. I was convinced it was the right thing to do. Of course, the denominator was denim, leather – leather particularly. We could all wear the same fabric but have different designs or whatever that would make us look more like a shit-hot, polished platoon in the game: a force to kill.'

In his book, Downing talks about taking Halford to his favourite shop in London to fit him out with the leathers that would become Judas Priest's definitive style.[12] Downing recalls the band members looking at each other behind the curtain before performances and drawing a feeling of power from their respective gleaming spikes and studs. This look was established by 1978's *Killing Machine* album, with the band on the sleeve sporting the necessary armaments in clothing and inside showing the songwriting skills necessary to mount an assault on the mainstream. Only bassist Ian Hill was holding out, with his billowing, white satin shirt. The song 'Hell Bent for Leather' said it all, and was preferred as a less violent album title for the American release of the record. Their reimagining of 'The Green Manalishi (with the Two-Pronged Crown)' from the Peter Green-led, progressive blues-rock period of Fleetwood Mac, acknowledged their origins and also left them behind in the afterburners. Rosław Szaybo's cover artwork, of a mannequin face with laser bursts reflected in its sunglasses, topped with a studded leather crown, reinforced the future-facing aesthetic. The only thing left over from the illustration of a mournful Lucifer from the cover art of *Sad Wings of Destiny*, was his satanic trident, which has served as the band's symbol from the mid-seventies to this day.

Through the late seventies, Judas Priest created a visual language for heavy metal, by taking their audiences into a leather-clad world. It was a subversive thing to do – and in retrospect looks like a *Queer Eye* makeover of tired seventies' rock clothing trends. It was countercultural, it was silly, and it was *strong*. Think of the uber-buff, cartoonish subjects of the art of Tom of Finland: leather transformed Judas Priest into superheroes. The transition was so bullish that it made the look and feel of heavy metal ripe for satire as much as celebration. But they summoned an army, drawing their fans into an illicit, alternate world in the same way that director William Friedkin did in his film *Cruising*. In the story, police officer Steve Burns, played by Al Pacino, ventures undercover into New York's S&M clubs, and the 'heavy leather' (as Burns's commanding officer puts it) gay scene, on the hunt for a serial killer. Released in 1980, *Cruising* coincided with the release of the band's ultimate expression of this new worldview: *British Steel*.

British Steel's cover depicts artist Szaybo's hand cradling a razor. The band chose a version in which it didn't draw blood – *British Steel* contained the possibility of violence, but left it tantalisingly close, rather than realised.[13] Rather than repel the mainstream, the band's imagery drew it in. Judas Priest appeared on *Top of the Pops* not once, but twice, around the album's release: to play 'United' and 'Living After Midnight'. Two of the simplest songs on the album, they were also two of the most feel-good on a record fuelled by direct, short and sharp, positive energy. As Downing told me, 'By the time *British Steel* came around, we had the music, we had the look, we had the album cover – we had everything that we needed to go forward from that point and – what the hell? – we still ended up on fucking *Top of the Pops*!' Downing had executed the reverse feat of bands like The Who, who he had seen go from pop to rock when he was growing up: Judas Priest had transitioned from being a heavy metal band to a (partial) pop band.

British Steel's finest moment is 'Grinder'. Disappointed though I am that it wasn't the inspiration for the name of gay hook-up app Grindr, with its lyrics about avoiding the 'straight and narrow' path in life, it is a joyful and defiant anthem to non-conformity. In the late nineties, Halford would join inheritors of his crown, Pantera, onstage to deliver its piston-pumping celebration of 'self-reliance'. Halford's vow to fly the 'open skies' like a 'mighty eagle' and cast off the mind-forged manacles of the system – the grinder 'looking for meat' – represents the fulfilment of Downing's goal to leave the quotidian prison and traps of working life in his past.

Although in *Heavy Duty* Downing nominates 'darkness, religious doubt, betrayal'[14] as the three core themes of heavy metal music, Judas Priest are actually a testament to hope, loyalty and belief. Downing was driven by his conviction in a previously non-existent heavier form of rock music, and Judas Priest successfully mobilised their fanbase to believe in them. As he told me, 'Finding music gave me everything, really. And at that point it did become my religion because it was what I believed in, what I wanted to do. It was my interest, it was my escapism. It was everything to me.'

As a side note here, it's important to recognise that though Judas Priest, like Black Sabbath and Led Zeppelin, are one of the cornerstone bands in the origins of the heavy rock legend, there was also a constant bubbling up of bands from the heavy underground as the sixties turned into the seventies. Judas Priest drummer Dave Holland cut his teeth in the band Trapeze, alongside future Deep Purple frontman Glenn Hughes (their 1970 album *Medusa* and its title track in particular, is stunning). Another drummer, Marc Bell, was part of the hard-rock power trio Dust, long before he morphed into Marky Ramone of the Ramones. Where would stoner rock be without Grand Funk Railroad's incendiary 1969 song 'Inside Looking Out'? Much less stoned, for a start. There were a host of others: Leafhound, Buffalo, Sir Lord Baltimore, Captain Beyond, etc. They constituted an underground which fed the iconic bands of the day and contributed in their own way to the erection of the heavy monolith.

K. K. Downing has not been an active participant in Judas Priest since 2011, when he retired. But he still considers himself a member of the band. His relationship with Tipton (both lead players, both songwriters) has not been without acrimony down the years, and he was upset not to brought back into the fold in

2018 when Parkinson's disease had taken too much of a toll on Tipton for him to perform live any longer. Downing's often dim view of this critical partnership is sad, because it suggests theirs was a relationship of compromise more than cooperation for much of the time. The heavy metal sound they refined in the four years from *Sad Wings of Destiny* in 1976 to *British Steel* in 1980, remains the gleaming backbone of the genre to this day. What started as a means of escape became a way to unite: Defenders of the Faith gathered around their Metal Gods.

IV. Dio in excelsis

Rainbow's song 'Stargazer', from their 1976 album *Rising*, imagines a people enslaved to a hubristic wizard. The song tells of how they have broken their backs to build an immense tower of stone for the arch mage, from which he might launch himself and fly. All the while the sun is obscured by his immense shadow. He jumps from the apex of the tower, falls rather than flies, and a rainbow rises, guiding the people back home.

This is the masterpiece of guitarist-sorcerer Ritchie Blackmore, built on a riff that dives and sweeps upwards, its path cleared by the magewind provided by drummer Cozy Powell and bassist Jimmy Bain. The grand, ascending chords of the pre-chorus section move upwards as our mind's eye follows the wizard's climb, accented and off-set by Tony Carey's keyboards. It is an extraordinary performance by the band, but vocalist Ronnie James Dio's singing and the craft of the storytelling in the lyric – the warning at the centre of this ego-driven act – soars even further. The way he poses the question asked by this enslaved people – 'Where do we go?' – at the end of the first chorus, in a long drawn-out note echoing as if from the precipice itself, contains all the emotional intensity that made his songwriting the first and last word in high-fantasy heaviness.

The symbol of the tower is particularly potent in the fantasy fiction of the twentieth century. It represents a phallic need for dominion over its surroundings. The subject of 'Stargazer' might have been Saruman the White, the wizard from *The Lord of the Rings*, whose black tower Orthanc is the central feature of his stronghold, Isengard. The wizard's subjugation of the natural world around him is said to represent Tolkien's disapproval of the industrialisation of his native west Midlands in the early twentieth century, as much as it refers to the mechanised horrors of World War I.

The tower has other significance as a symbol. In Ursula K. Le Guin's *A Wizard of Earthsea* (1968), on the northern-most cape of the island of Roke, where there is a school for wizards, stands the Isolate Tower. Here, the Master Namer presides over pupils memorising countless names: in the archipelago of Earthsea, to know something's true name is to have mastery over it. The process of naming also helps maintain the equilibrium of the world. The tower, a place of learning and silence and words, represents stability.[15]

Ronnie James Dio was something like an itinerant wizard. His journey ended in May 2010 when he died of stomach cancer while he was fronting Heaven and Hell – the reformed version of Black Sabbath he first led in the early 1980s when he replaced Ozzy Osbourne as vocalist (initially, Tony Iommi, who had become sick of Sabbath towards the end of the seventies, had suggested to Dio they form an entirely new band).[16] On 1980's *Heaven and Hell*, Dio effected a change in Sabbath worthy of a master magician. The album's final song, 'Lonely is the Word' – Dio's lofty, melancholy ode to fading achievement after a lifetime of being 'higher than stardust' – leads him to conclude, 'Maybe life's a losing game'. The sheer drama of Dio's delivery brings out a stunning solo from Iommi which, like the narrator of the song, just keeps going and going, moving from introspective subtlety to glorious moments in the sun.

In *A Wizard of Earthsea*, the wizard Sparrowhawk is led by a moment of antagonistic competition with a peer to rip open a hole in the fabric of the world and summon a shadow from the other side of life. He pursues the shadow to the ends of the known world of Earthsea and the open sea of its most eastern reaches, filled with regret at the critical mistake he made as a student: 'I was too much in haste, and now have no time left. I traded all the sunlight and the cities and the distant lands for a handful of power, for a shadow, for the dark.'[17] In the third book of the Earthsea cycle, *The Farthest Shore*, Sparrowhawk lies injured and drifting in a chapter titled 'Children of the Open Sea', with a name echoed in another *Heaven and Hell* masterpiece, 'Children of the Sea'.

On Dio's next album with Black Sabbath, *Mob Rules*, 'Falling Off the Edge of the World' sees him assume a similarly resigned view of life. The song opens in a mournful mode – 'I think about closing the door/And lately I think of it more' – as Dio wails over the kind of grandly subdued guitar passage Iommi wouldn't have considered playing before working with the elvish balladeer.

Dio and the song rouse themselves on an upsurge of swelling strings as Dio laments he should be at the 'Table round', serving 'the crown', presumably King Arthur. Arthurian legend was a rich wellspring for Dio lyrically, going back to 'Lady of the Lake' from Rainbow's *Long Live Rock'n'Roll* (1978). Sir Thomas Malory's *Le Morte d'Arthur* (1485) had immortalised the characters of Merlin, Arthur, Guinevere and Lancelot, and the knights of the round table – England's great origin myth sits prominently in northern European ideas of faith, authority and the trials of leadership. This was irresistible to an imaginative New Englander lyricist like Dio, who had been born in Portsmouth, New Hampshire, in 1942.

Released in 1981, like Sabbath's *Mob Rules*, was John Boorman's film *Excalibur*. This was a project Boorman conceived after unsuccessfully attempting to get an adaptation of *The Lord of the Rings* off the ground. A film I also saw when I was very young, Boorman's adaptation burned into my consciousness with its eighties' medievalism, or as the Dio-era Black Sabbath puts it: 'Neon Knights'. What struck me was the effulgent armour, alternately wry and doom-laden Merlin and soft-focus male gaze of its insouciant sexism. Unlike the wizard of Dio's 'Stargazer', Merlin is successfully able to summon enough dragon's breath so that Uther Pendragon can walk across the clouds from the clifftops in order to enter castle Tintagel and have sex with the object of his lust, Igrayne (Pendragon is disguised as her husband). Pendragon is wearing a full suit of armour as the couple conceive Arthur, but presumably has his penis unsheathed, whereas Igrayne is fully naked. My guess remains that it takes a bloody long time to take armour off and put it on again, and Pendragon needs to be ready to beat a hasty retreat.

Excalibur places itself beyond the reach of parody. Since Monty Python had already sent up the Arthurian legend six years earlier, in 1975's *Monty Python and the Holy Grail*, any silliness in *Excalibur* is overwhelmed by its dreamlike, operatic tenor. Like heavy metal itself, there is nothing you can accuse it of, or lampoon, that it hasn't already knowingly made part of its fabric.

In the film, Arthur's aggression and insistence on a battle to the death with Lancelot, though clearly out-matched, could have been the scene parodied by John Cleese as the Black Knight in *Holy*

Grail ("Tis but a scratch!' the Knight famously remonstrates, when his left arm is lopped off by Arthur) – except that *Excalibur* came afterwards. Instead, it develops into one of the film's more moving moments, as Arthur breaks the sword Excalibur in a fight he should never have pursued. 'My pride broke it. My rage broke it.'

What also imbues *Excalibur* with its ineffable register and atmosphere of being something far greater than it really ought to be, is its use of the music of Richard Wagner. Themes of intense foreboding from 'Siegfried's Funeral March' in Act III of *Götterdämmerung* ('*The Twilight of the Gods*') are used at the film's opening, when Arthur pulls the sword from the stone and, most effectively, in the film's final scenes, as a dying Arthur instructs his knight Sir Perceval to return Excalibur to the Lady in the Lake. An exaggerated, huge, blood-red sun setting beyond Cornish cliffs makes the scene look like an opera on stage itself. The use of Wagner's music invests the film with an unyielding sense of significance: an emotional intensity and high drama that are the hallmarks of heaviness.

John Deathridge, Emeritus King Edward Professor of Music at King's College London, thinks the use of the piece is well-placed: 'It's not a coincidence that the scene at the end has water at its centre. The obsessive repetitive rhythm of the march, the re-assertion of E flat going back to the *ängstlich* water-bound opening of the whole cycle, the sword returning to the water, as if to the mother's womb, yet with uncertainty, leaving the listener begging for more.'

Deathridge himself grew up in the industrial heartland of Birmingham in the forties, fifties and sixties. His father was in the metal business – he patented a blacking process for car and lorry chassis and owned a small factory in Corporation Street. His father's best friend, Arthur Street, also had a business dealing with metals and was a metallurgist who co-authored a Penguin book, *Metals in the Service of Man*, that went to eleven editions. Both men were opera fanatics: Street conducted rare operas in a society he founded, with Deathridge's father singing tenor. There are distinct correspondences between the working men who immersed themselves in opera as a means to blow off steam in what Deathridge acknowledges was a 'dreadful' and 'philistine' environment and, in the same industrial region, youths like Tony Iommi and K. K. Downing, leading their own parallel lives and forging their own musical paths into similarly heavy – if amplified – music.

By using Wagner in *Excalibur*, John Boorman makes a distinct connection between the northern European perspectives of Malory and Wagner as interpreters of the mythic figures of Arthur and Siegfried. The latter also appears in Norse myth as Sigurd, a character who vanquishes a dragon, takes possession of its hoard and dies at the hand of a conspiracy. Joining the two figures harks back to what Deathridge calls the 'syncretic thinking' of Wagner: 'Wagner even conflated Friedrich Barbarossa [a medieval Holy Roman Emperor] with Baldur [a Norse god], with Siegfried, and so on. So why not Arthur and Siegfried? Wagner didn't do that; but Boorman is following a similar non-objective logic which, in a dream narrative – which is what *Excalibur* essentially is – makes sense.'

Wagner had read *German Mythology* by Jacob Grimm, a treatise of the relatedness and archaic origins of languages from the mid-nineteenth century that established 'Grimm's Law'. In Deathridge's introduction to his 2018 translation of Wagner's *The Ring*, he describes Grimm's Law as 'proof that Germanic and proto-Indo-European languages have common ancestors in ancient languages like Greek and Latin' and that 'he also did more than most to collect massive amounts of data about German mythology to propose, albeit on less secure grounds than in his work on language, that one can logically trace its disparate strands back to pure archaic origins.'[18]

There is a shared wellspring of myth from which these heavy works of art are drawing inspiration. The overriding message – whether in Dio's lyrics, Le Guin's Earthsea novels or Boorman's film – is that wizards and kings must pay the highest price for hubris. It's a long way to climb the tower, and further to fall.

Following *Mob Rules*, Dio and Iommi's relationship began to turn sour. Dio was fired from Black Sabbath and began to put together a solo project, born out of frustration, under his own name. His intention was to recruit a young guitar hero, preferably a British one. In Dio's eyes, British players had more desire in their hearts, on the grounds of not being American and from the birthplace of rock'n'roll. He wanted someone with 'romance in his soul, beauty in his playing'. It was via former Rainbow bassist Jimmy Bain that twenty-year-old northern Irishman Vivian Campbell was recommended to him. The first rehearsal with Bain, drummer Vinny Appice and Campbell was enough to convince Dio. He described the band's playing as 'magic'.[19]

Campbell's ascent as a young guitar player capable of the hyper-expressive, fiery style that would mark out eighties' metal, coincided cruelly with the death of Randy Rhoads. Ever since Ozzy Osbourne had gone solo at the beginning of the decade, Rhoads had played guitar with him. One night a tour bus driver took Rhoads up in a light aircraft that clipped the bus on its third attempt to playfully rattle the sleeping inhabitants: in the ensuing crash, the driver, Rhoads and makeup artist Rachel Youngblood, also on board, were instantly killed. Rhoads was an astonishing talent who still casts a long shadow today, particularly in his pouring of classical influences into the mould of metal guitar playing. But on 19 March 1982, he came crashing to earth.

Dio released their debut album *Holy Diver* in May 1983. The title track adjured listeners to 'ride the tiger' of life's challenges and uncertainties. But a few years into the 1980s, heavy metal began to split into vicious new forms, and was compelled to respond to a threatening new geopolitical reality that ripped through the fantastical visions of Dio. By then, his position as a founding father of the genre was assured. He was celebrated with renewed vigour in the years leading up to his death, when he reunited with Sabbath bandmates Tony Iommi, Geezer Butler and Vinny Appice in Heaven and Hell. When he died, he managed something the subject of 'Stargazer' could only dream of: he ascended into that firmament for ever. More strangely, since his death he has continued to posthumously perform on stages around the world as a hologram, spreading metal lore in a resurrected form.

2
NUCLEAR WINTER
AND ITS MALCONTENTS

'Blow the universe into nothingness/Nuclear warfare
shall lay us to rest' – Metallica, 'Fight Fire With Fire'

'We were a button push away from
oblivion' – Ronald Reagan[1]

———————

Visions of the end of the world fuel heavy depictions of humanity's demise. In the eighties, the prospect of nuclear apocalypse was very real and intruded on the day to day lives of millions of people paralysed between two superpowers squaring up to each other. Metal responded, or rather, it was *forced* to mutate itself as a result. As more extreme forms of the music emerged it became a coping mechanism and a way of facing down the threat and its attendant feeling of powerlessness. The nuclear winds of fury that were unleashed in metal music exploded into popular consciousness like never before.

I. Push the button

On 20 November 1983, the US station ABC Television broadcast *The Day After*, a made-for-TV movie that imagined the devastation and fallout of a Russian nuclear attack on US soil. It drew a hundred million viewers and, for years afterwards, retained the record for being the most-watched television film in history.

Set mainly in Kansas City, Missouri, it depicts the escalation of tension between NATO and Warsaw Pact countries through glimpsed news broadcasts, incidental radio transmissions and overheard conversations. We learn that NATO has exploded three nuclear bombs over Russian troops who have invaded West Germany. When the USSR fires retaliatory missiles and the nuclear bomb hits Kansas City, Jason Robards's character – who witnesses it from the freeway thirty miles away – describes it as 'like the sun exploding'.

The film follows the lives of several groups of people – college students, farming families, hospital workers – most of whom live in rural communities: the middle of nowhere. The stinger here is that this is the cold war and there's no such thing as the middle of nowhere when the country's nuclear arsenal of intercontinental ballistic missiles is stored in silos in just such quiet, sparsely populated regions of the country. When the massive attack of three hundred Russian intercontinental missiles is launched, the agricultural areas of Missouri are a key target.

In 1983, things had changed since the Kennedy era with its doctrine of 'mutual assured destruction' (MAD). No longer assuaged by theoretical deterrence, the US had adopted a policy of 'launch under attack'. Both the Americans and the Russians had concluded that, with Soviet submarines in the Atlantic and American bases in Europe, the gap from launching to impact on either side could now be six minutes. This meant that it might be necessary for one or the other to launch their own missiles in *anticipation* of an attack or at the first warning that missiles were in the air.

All of this globe-destroying military posturing was wide open to human error. As Taylor Downing notes in his book *1983: The World at the Brink*: 'No matter how sophisticated the systems were, how thoroughly the structures governing the use of nuclear weapons had been prepared and the protocols rehearsed, it was always an individual who had his finger on the button.'[2]

Metallica wrote the song 'Fight Fire With Fire' while they were touring their first album, *Kill 'Em All*, through the latter half of 1983. It remains to this day a startling, raze-it-to-the-ground depiction of a world in which two superpowers are poised to wipe each other out, depending on who blinks first. Starting with an unusually nuanced, major key acoustic guitar introduction written by their most accomplished musician, bassist Cliff Burton, it is soon consumed by the firestorm of the tremolo-picked guitar work that took the relatively new form of thrash metal to another level of aggression. James Hetfield spits out the opening lines that question the biblical axiom of eye-for-an-eye: 'Do unto others as they've done to you/But what the hell is this world coming to?' At the same time the song revels in its nuclear wind of speed and fury. It's not so much with fear, but with relish, that he concludes each chorus: 'We all shall die.'

This was extreme music for extreme times. Fuelled by the fears of nuclear annihilation and hardened by America's neoliberal view of the world, metal music underwent a fusion process of its own: it collided hardcore punk with speed metal, with catastrophically heavy results.

Sonically and lyrically, the nuclear bomb was perfect fodder for the thrash bands of the time. Already snarling and out to shock, the prospect of total death fuelled their sardonic nihilism. When Dave Mustaine, a raging alcoholic and brattish guitar *wunderkind*, was fired from Metallica, he formed a band that was named after the new unit to measure a million deaths from a nuclear explosion: the 'megadeath'. This had been coined by American scientists as their bombs' measurements in megatons increased and increased. In Megadeth, Mustaine went on to reference the submarine missile launch technology in Megadeth's classic song 'Rust In Peace . . . Polaris'.

One of the other 'big four' thrash acts, Anthrax – though named themselves after a biological weapon – spawned the most overt nuclear war-inspired band of the mid-eighties. Again, it was kicking out a member, bassist Danny Lilker, that led to the formation of the new act, Nuclear Assault. Their 1986 debut, *Game Over*, traded heavily in nuclear Armageddon, as did the artwork by Ed Repka, which depicted the fleeing populace of an American city silhouetted against an enormous burnt-orange mushroom cloud amidst downtown skyscrapers. There was an unnerving parallel with the Chernobyl nuclear reactor explosion that lit up the night skies over the Ukrainian city of Pripyat in April of that year, six months before the album was released.

Nuclear Assault were a less technically assured thrash-metal band, instead combining frantic tempos and melodic flurries with more sculpted breakdowns. This muscular, politically acute speedwork became known as 'crossover'. Thrash was born of the fusion of punk and metal, but like a further fissile process, cross-over metal drew the components out and refined them further.

The mushroom cloud was again the centrepiece of the cover of Cro-Mags' *Age of Quarrel*, also released in 1986. Firmly rooted in the hardcore punk scene, Cro-Mags's songs were bare-bone attacks of one to two minutes' length, often using a handful of brutal riffs. As violent and boiled-down as the songwriting was, Maxwell 'Mackie' Jayson's supple drumming explored the spaces between the onslaught and made him one of the outstanding drummers of the scene. The band's primitive name and sound belied the spirituality at its lyrical centre. Lead singer John Joseph McGowan, once a typical New York street thug and drug dealer, was now a Hare Krishna after 'the veil of illusion was lifted' through his encounter with the religion in the early eighties. He remains an avowed 'straight-edge', free of drink and drugs, and a vegan: his book on the subject is the punchy *Meat is for Pussies*.

Joseph is adamant that seventies' punk was merely moaning and crying about the state of things, whereas eighties' hardcore was much more solution-oriented: 'It's not corny to try and dig into your mind and your soul and find out what the fuck we're doing in this material world.'[3]

As such, the quarrel at the heart of Cro-Mags's beatdowns is that of social justice ('We Gotta Know') and the toughness needed to get by in Manhattan's Alphabet City ('Survival of the Streets'), as much as goading the forces of anarchy and waving goodbye to 'World Peace'. Cro-Mags were reporting on the impact that global tensions were having on communities at ground level. The mushroom cloud represented a potential global cataclysm, but the cracks in society they saw forming around them reflected the thousands of smaller stresses being exerted by Ronald Reagan's neoliberal agenda.

II. You're on his list

What framed the nuclear threat in the 1980s – casting Russia as the 'evil empire' and the Middle East as a crucible for global terrorism and instability – was Reagan's doctrine of actively seeking to roll back Communism and the USSR's influence throughout the world. This was underpinned by unfettered economic globalisation, building up the military–industrial complex and pouring money into related technological innovation (such as the much-vaunted American 'Star Wars' defensive shield initiative). Reagan was attempting to Make America Great Again by facing down any nation that stood alongside the opposition – with all the homegrown jingoistic sentiment that encouraged.

Stormtroopers of Death (aka S.O.D.) was an inevitable reaction. In 1985, Danny Lilker made peace with his Anthrax ex-bandmates Scott Ian (guitar) and Charlie Benante (drums) to form a band revolving around a fascistic character Ian had created called 'Sargent D'. Sargent D is part-Judge Dredd, part-Drill Instructor Hartman from Stanley Kubrick's 1987 film *Full Metal Jacket*. He is illustrated on the cover of the S.O.D. album *Speak English Or Die* as a soldier's withered skull, chomping a cigar – an anarchy symbol is carved into his green helmet: he was Iron Maiden's 'Eddie' mascot on steroids.

Like thrash and crossover's depictions of nuclear holocaust, *Speak English Or Die* recoils from its own blunt chauvinism by also revelling in it. Their lyrics and message were determinedly politically incorrect. By today's standards and, considering the twenty-first century refugee crisis in the Mediterranean and elsewhere from wars being prosecuted in the Middle East, the title track's 'Boats and boats and boats of you/Go home you fuckin' slobs' leaves a very bad taste in the mouth. That's before we come to song titles as direct as 'Fuck the Middle East'. The band were adamant this was all purely satirical ('a fucking joke'),[4] and their crunchy, rampant, straight-to-the-jugular music suited the take-it-or-leave-it tenor of their lyrics. They were deadly serious about the send-up – and out to piss people off.

Elsewhere on the album they were simply in it for the dark laughs. 'The Ballad of Jimi Hendrix', a five-second crank-out of the opening melody to 'Purple Haze', ends with singer Billy Milano flatly declaring: 'You're dead'. It was the first of a whole series of S.O.D. live 'tributes' to popular music's fallen soldiers: from Kurt Cobain to Jim Morrison to Michael Hutchence to Tupac Shakur.

S.O.D.'s musical influence has been huge. Opening track 'March of the S.O.D.' has one of the greatest riffs anywhere in metal and is still played live by Anthrax. Love them or hate them (and it would be hard to see a band like them starting out in today's climate without getting dismembered on social media), they held a mirror up to a pig-headed, stars-and-stripes way of seeing global politics that sought to rearrange the world in the image of the United States. As they warned: 'Sargent D is coming, and you're on his list'.

S.O.D. introduced at least one innovation into their music: the song 'Milk' had a new type of drum beat that soon became known as the 'blast beat'. Like the product of encroaching radiation sickness, the blast beat was a mutation in thrash metal: the sheer noise terror of machine-gun percussion. The drummer rattled off alternate kick drum and snare sixteenth notes, cymbals smashed however they pleased. The blast beat became the foundation of grindcore (an even more extreme variant of metal which was as close to simulating nuclear meltdown as was sonically possible). The genre was best represented in the UK by Napalm Death and in the US by the band Terrorizer on their album *World Downfall*.

Like S.O.D., Terrorizer was a supergroup side-band, comprising members of death metallers Morbid Angel (bassist/singer David Vincent and drummer Pete Sandoval), who dispensed with their exploration of ancient and satanic evil for a more socially engaged condemnation of The Evil That Men Do. The psychic and societal damage done by the threat of nuclear war was as catastrophic as the event itself and the band posited a post-human landscape free of people. The listener is buffeted by the album's globalist angst and bleak social commentary. The chorus of its lead-off track, 'After World Obliteration', reads like post-apocalyptic haiku: 'Suffering/Deep in our minds/After World/ Obliteration'.

Ironically, the album's release on 13 November 1989 was pre-empted – by four days – by the fall of the Berlin Wall, heralding the beginning of a period of relative stability between the world's superpowers. It also opened the door for western bands to play in the Eastern Bloc and Russia; an opportunity seized by Time Warner when it staged the Monsters of Rock Russia on 28 September 1991. It was a free concert at Tushino airfield in Moscow attended by a staggering 1.6 million heavy music fans. It saw Metallica, then at their commercial and creative peak, play the country for the first time – the footage of the event is truly jaw-dropping. Despite the surreal setting of an airfield still littered with old war planes,[5] helicopters circling perilously close to the crowd, the inevitable crushes and the over-zealous phalanxes of Russian military acting as de facto security guards, Metallica's performance was imperious. East and West were reconciled with each other in a celebration of thrash metal. Of their back catalogue, most of the songs Metallica played that day were from their second album, 1984's *Ride The Lightning* – with the notable exception of its opening track: 'Fight Fire With Fire'.

This would be a great place for the story to end, but history does not work like that. The representation of the mushroom cloud, signifying that heaviest of deaths, was absorbed and neutralised for almost a quarter of a century after the Berlin Wall came down. But the nuclear threat never went away. Instead, it went underground and bided its time, waiting for humanity to make its final mistake; US policy to this day remains 'Launch under attack'. In 2013, as tensions about North Korea's atomic programme started to mount, and before the fragile nuclear deal between the US and Iran was struck, another debut album was released with that familiar, explosive motif present (amid other lurid and grotesque imagery of hardship, pain and suffering): Power Trip's *Manifest Decimation*.

Manifest Decimation – with its cavernous, reverb-drenched drums, razor-wire guitars, dive-bombing solos and from-the-abyss vocal agonies – could have sounded like a pastiche of 1980s' crossover. But it didn't – it was for real – and Power Trip's meteoric rise in the underground and mainstream metal scene reflects a new world order with the same simmering tensions. The even more incendiary follow-up from 2017, *Nightmare Logic*, is thrash for the Trump era. As their singer Riley Gale told me: 'In the last couple of years or so, it seems I am in a waking nightmare . . . it's very different from what I remember the world being like eight years ago when the band started. So it's having to cope with this reality that the world really has gotten as bad as it seems and feels to me.'

A new generation are channelling the thrash and crossover they loved as kids to confront the reality of the second decade of the twenty-first century as young adults. The cold war nuclear stand-off was reflected in an arms race for heaviness that culminated in the ultimate extreme music attack: grindcore.

Heavy music in the eighties was perfectly suited to interpret a world teetering on the abyss of self-annihilation, laughing hysterically as it rode its own sonic bombs to their target. In doing so, its bands were at the vanguard of interpreting a new reality of internecine destruction. They enacted the devastation in music, defused the threat, and made it processable as entertainment. The bomb is yet to drop. In contrast, this weaponised form of metal continues to be deployed, unleashing its own massive energy – the audience joyfully moshing in the debris of the fallout.

III. Fire on the mountain . . .

Where better to test nuclear weapons than a landscape that appears dead? The desert of Nye County, Nevada, was the test site for the atomic bomb from 1945. The programme ended in 1992 and was soon superseded by an elemental, desert rock that exploded out in waves of atomic, blissed-out power.

The fusion of punk and metal that created thrash continued to be refined, to the point that the increasing virtuosity of its musicians would often over-balance the feel for frenzy and attack that originally defined it. The near-athletic fretwork of guitarists like Marty Friedman was pushing arena-sized acts like Megadeth to new heights, but the music became forensic in how carefully it was constructed. Not so out in the Palm Desert, near Joshua Tree, southern California. There, a young musician called Mario Lalli, aka 'Boomer', owned a generator that he took out into the desert. He hosted parties at which his band, Yawning Man, played. Circulating these generator parties was a group of high school kids who formed a band named Katzenjammer, then Sons of Kyuss and then, simply, Kyuss.

With his roots in the hardcore punk scene, Kyuss guitarist Joshua Homme played with a direct, no-frills style, wrapped it in swathes of distortion, and created landscapes with riffs that evoked the ancient, wind-blown sands of the desert. Drummer Brant Bjork and bassist Nick Oliveri were Black Sabbath fans who created the kind of loose, play-around-the-beat rhythm section that had made Sabbath's vision of heaviness so impactful. Singer John Garcia's honeyed voice contained enough grit to sail over the tar-thick melange, with abstract, intoxicated dream-scapes of songs like '50 Million Year Trip', appearing on 1992 album *Blues for the Red Sun*. That song moves through chiming psychedelic passages, fades out entirely, then drives back in. On 'Green Machine' there are vague pledges to shut down the capitalist system. And probably best of all, there are threats of being burned by Garcia's lighter on 'Thumb' – a song that might depict some kind of abduction scenario, but ultimately just makes it clear that by listening to Kyuss 'you're on desert ground'.

Blues for the Red Sun blazed through the metal scene like a wildfire whipped up by the Santa Ana winds. Producer Chris Goss has since described it as a rejoinder to the glossy thrash of the period concocted in LA and the Bay Area: '1990 was an era of perfect metal. It was very staccato. Typing . . . it was heavy metal typing.'[6]

Kyuss had guitars tuned down to the centre of the Earth, chan-nelled through bass cabinets, and oversized drums – all enlarged to provide a soundscape that could attempt to fill the wide-open spaces of the Mojave Desert. The result was what Goss describes as 'a lava bubble of frequency'. On 'Freedom Run', the pivotal track on *Blues for the Red Sun*, John Garcia tells a tale about some kind of fuck-the-world Bonnie and Clyde-esque relationship. But like all of Kyuss's songs, the desert itself is the subject, the 'million miles of desert sun', stretching mirage-like in front of anyone wandering out there. Accordingly, the song makes a journey, from a tight main riff through gravelly vocal-led breakdowns, and Homme surging up the fretboard, adding playful grace notes to Bjork and Oliveri's semi-false endings (something Kyuss perfected on the following album's 'Supa Scoopa and Mighty Scoop').

The desert wind of Kyuss reached all the way up to Seattle where it impacted on Dave Grohl, who was in the middle of Nirvana's *Nevermind* blowing up. It caused him to stop and ponder whether Goss was the right producer to get to work on Nirvana's follow-up album. As he said to me, 'You know what's so funny – I remember when I got *Blues for the Red Sun*, I played it for Kurt and said, "Dude, we should have this guy record our next album," and he listened to it and he came back and he said, "Are you serious?!"' Nevertheless, in the media Grohl proselytised that the future of grunge lay in Palm Springs, not Seattle.

Something about this band from the desert resonated very deeply with Grohl, who had himself grown up feeding off the passion and aggression of punk-rock drummers in bands like Bad Brains, Black Flag, Void, Faith and Nomeansno, before being knocked off his axis by Led Zeppelin's *Houses of the Holy* (1973) and the feeling and groove of John Bonham.

Grohl evangelised about *Blues for the Red Sun* in Nirvana interviews, grasping the secret, underground nature of Kyuss, as his own band attained unprecedented popularity. He told me he felt particularly connected to Homme, who he first met when Kyuss were playing with friends of Grohl's, The Obsessed: 'The two of us come from similar backgrounds, y'know? He grew up out in the desert – I grew up in a suburb. We both come from tight families. We both love rock'n'roll but, when we discovered punk rock, I think we were attracted to the criminal element of it. The fact that it was underground and it was our secret and it was our little world. And I think that we were attracted to the same things musically and then, when we started bands and started touring, we both did van tours. We both slept on a lot of floors. We both were on labels that nobody knew about. We just sorta had the same paths, and Nirvana blew up. But when something like that happens it doesn't necessarily change you as a person, it just changes everything around you. So it didn't change my love for all of those things I loved before. It just made this band a lot bigger, or whatever.'

The desert sound – fuzzed-out guitars, reverberant drums, soulful vocals – incubated in a small, community music scene in this part of southern California, spilled out inexorably, like encroaching sand drifts. The sound is one in awe of the monumentality of its natural surroundings. Its alien, escapist nature accounts for its persistence today, and why desert rock-themed gigs and festivals take place as far afield as dreary Europe.

Kyuss built a bridge between classic rock and metal. When I first met my friend Hallam in my early twenties he was a huge Free fan. He introduced me to their debut album *Tons of Sobs* (1969). I reciprocated by playing him Kyuss, which he had never heard. He was instantly hooked. Hal was, and remains, a superb guitar player. We formed a power trio, with me on bass, called Orchis – named after an exotic kind of orchid. And the Latin word for testicle, as it turned out. Oh well. Our career was short-lived, but it was a blast playing those simple, Kyuss-style songs to handfuls of adoring fans.

The desert is as uncompromising a landscape as it gets, but it also offers the sheer space for psychedelic exploration, as depicted in Michael Antonioni's *Zabriskie Point* (1970) when the two protagonists make love at the titular location. The landscape itself can be foreboding, such as in artist Georgia O'Keeffe's painting *Black Place II* (1944) – darkness vying with metallic greys and a central fissure signifying division in the rock-hard landscape – or her more faithful representations of the rolling reds of New Mexico.

New Mexico was the site of the Trinity nuclear tests presided over by J. Robert Oppenheimer in July 1945. Famously, he thought of the Hindu holy book the *Bhagavad Gita*. Recalling the event in 1965 he said, 'We knew the world would not be the same. A few people laughed, a few people cried. Most people were silent. I remembered the line from the Hindu scripture, the *Bhagavad Gita*; Vishnu is trying to persuade the Prince that he should do his duty and, to impress him, takes on his multi-armed form and says, "Now I am become Death, the destroyer of worlds." I suppose we all thought that, one way or another.'[7]

The desert is also an inherently violent landscape, as another Seattle traveller to the region later depicted. On the 2005 album by the band Earth, *Hex; or Printing in the Infernal Method*, Dylan Carlsen (a former friend and roommate of Kurt Cobain) traded massive distortion for a cleaner, ringing guitar sound, as if it rebounded off the timeless edifices of the desertscape. An instrumental album, it was inspired by Cormac McCarthy's novel *Blood Meridian, or The Evening Redness in the West* (1985), which concerns the scalp-hunting Glanton gang who massacred Native Americans for bounty in the mid-nineteenth century. In the novel they undertake this murder with increasing ferocity and blood-crazed senselessness.

Heaviness can be small and insidious, like a creeping doubt or fear, but more often it is defined by massiveness, and rendered in gigantic and mythic scale that speaks to broad and often uncomfortable human truths. This passage from near the end of *Blood Meridian*, spoken by the huge and unnerving character known as 'the judge', shows the desert as a theatre in which humanity is incapable of the scale of passion and vivacity required to answer the demands of life itself. Life's scale and hardness resists its own living:

> A man seeks his own destiny and no other, said the judge. Will or nill. Any man who could discover his own fate and elect therefore some opposite course could only come at last to that selfsame reckoning at the same appointed time, for each man's destiny is as large as the world he inhabits and contains within it all opposites as well. This desert upon which so many have been broken is vast and calls for largeness of heart but it is also empty. It is hard, it is barren. Its very nature is stone.[8]

IV . . . and it rages out of control

After Kyuss dissolved in the mid-nineties, Homme started another project with Oliveri and Kyuss drummer, Alfredo Hernández. With Queens of the Stone Age, Homme seemed set on dispensing with the earth, wind and fire that fuelled Kyuss, leaning into a synthetic sound that was more catchy and danceable. But Homme carries that sense of what he calls 'desert threat' with him wherever he goes. QOTSA is a collective which has recruited many musicians over the years. Homme is its leader and makes the rules, but as he told me, he is part of a crew: 'Well, I see Queens of the Stone Age as a pirate ship, and there's a false assumption that the captain is the most important role to play. If the rigger fails – you die, if the cook fails – you die, if the captain fails – you die.'

Under Homme, there can be no secrets in bands, and no role envy: if you're going to take drugs, take them, but don't hide it. If you are playing drums, don't whine about the bass player. Having admired each other for a decade, Grohl joined QOTSA for 2002's *Songs for the Deaf*. He destroyed the drum kit again after having had a long furlough, adding insane fills to 'No One Knows' and battering-ram intensity to 'A Song For the Dead'. Grohl even recorded the drum-heads and the cymbals of his kit separately in order to avoid bleed over and to keep the album's sound as dry as possible.[9]

With Mark Lanegan also aboard as a second-string vocalist, QOTSA's strongest line-up was complete. They played Glastonbury in 2002 before the album had even been released. The BBC footage of the event showed the new songs being greeted with hushed adulation. QOTSA were growing as a band, but Grohl's inclusion shook the mainstream awake, injecting a menacing swagger into what amounted to one of the most accessible formations of heavy rock. The band would roll into the backstage areas of festivals like the Glanton gang, as Grohl recalls: 'That was fun, man. Walking backstage at a festival, the bus would pull up and you'd have a backstage and everyone sitting around, and catering, and all the other bands. And it was total *The Good, The Bad and The Ugly*.'

For Homme, QOTSA was always a gang, and going backstage he was carrying their flag, which in this incarnation was particularly intimidating. Out of his peripheral vision he often saw a path being cleared for the band, as they stumbled and grunted their way past everyone else. There was what he calls a 'respectful fear' that the band carries around itself still, but was particularly special in that era: 'We were like a steamroller with thirty-two clowns on it. It's really funny, until you get fucking rolled over.'

Homme's greatest successes are sometimes dogged by controversy or incident. He can read a bedtime story for the under-sixes on BBC channel CBeebies, but also have to apologise after kicking a female photographer in the face during a performance.[10] Falling down seems to be part of the process. 'I don't mind falling down because I find the coolest shit on the floor. I've won a few things in my time but I've never learned anything whenever I've won something.'

Like the desert that threatens to consume all around it, or the atomic energy radiating out from a nuclear test, popular culture has mutated under the heavy influence of Homme: from conducting numerous Desert Sessions recordings with PJ Harvey and others, taking up the drum stool himself with Eagles of Death Metal alongside long-time friend Jesse Hughes, to producing the Arctic Monkeys, to forming Them Crooked Vultures with Grohl and John Paul Jones: 'There's no rest around here. I won't play in a band where rest is one of the key functions. Not with anybody, because it's not that important. Rest is not that important.'

The Kyuss song 'Whitewater' states that 'you move your own mountain', and Homme continues to work from the sanctity of the desert expanses, often the Rancho De La Luna studio in Joshua Tree which is part-sanctuary, part-chemistry laboratory. It is a place of psychedelic ceremony in the stillness of the desert that trims away the fat of existence and perpetuates a uniquely contagious heavy attitude.

Joshua Homme is the most high-profile proponent of heavy messages from the desert: 'That's all I've ever wanted, though. To play for respect, y'know? I don't care about money. I'm married. I don't care about girls – except my girls at home. I don't want any stuff. I want to make something that will last for ever and I want to do what is least done to my notion of the least done thing, which is to be consistent for an entire lifetime. And to always try and merge art and commerce together. I like to do all right but I like it to be respected for its art. And I like to keep changing all the time without losing a sense of self, and that's not easy. And quite often you lose many people but that's what a career is. I feel like I wouldn't be able to do this unless I'd done Kyuss and Queens and Eagles of Death Metal that way. How would I be able to do this, y'know? I don't think too much about what was. The past and future take care of themselves.'

3
ROMAN WILDERNESS OF PAIN

'Nazarene/I've come to bestow you this crown of
scorn' – Bloodbath, 'Blasting the Virginborn'

'I devour the pediculous corpse/Whetting my palate as
I exhume/The festering stench of rotting flesh/Makes me
drool as I consume' – Carcass, 'Exhume to Consume'

If metal did not have religion to rebel against, it would have had
to invent it. As a symbol of staid, patriarchal authority,
Christianity has long been the avowed enemy. As hosts of the
crucifixion, the Romans created a framework for cruelty handed
down the ages, which is now gleefully picked apart by extreme
metal. The representation of the destruction of Christ lends itself
to blasphemy and is ripe for anyone wanting to convey a simple,
shocking 'fuck you' to authority, even if Christianity has become
a soft target compared to other forms of religious radicalism.
Beyond the targeting of the figure of Christ, the heaviest questions
lie in death itself and how we reconcile ourselves to our
inevitable demise.

I. Once upon the cross

The Passion of the Christ is Mel Gibson's love letter to the destruction of the body of Jesus, and more broadly, the destruction of the male body itself. The 2004 film came out amidst the emergence of 'torture porn' – the *Saw* franchise and its ilk. *The Passion's* harrowing gore is a cinematic ordeal masquerading as religious devotion. At the time it drew criticism for alleged antisemitism – the onscreen Jewish Sanhedrin priesthood, led by Caiaphas, are fanatically keen to condemn Jesus. But the film makes it clear that the gubernatorial framework that enabled the crucifixion was that of the Romans. In the film (as in the Bible), Pontius Pilate, the prefect of the Roman province of Judaea, washes his hands of the matter; but it is his men that perform the whipping, scourging and crucifixion of Jesus. The film's most excruciating scene bears witness to Jim Caviezel's Jesus having lumps of flesh torn from his back by a scouring whip fixed with metal claws and shards of bone – at one point exposing his ribcage. The overseeing Roman soldier finally says, '*Satis*' ('Enough'), before instructing his men, through a simple hand gesture, to turn Jesus on to his back, exposing his chest and stomach. Gibson leaves enough time for the blood to drain from the audience's faces in horror – then his torturers 'do' the other side.

Flaying religious icons is not unique to Christianity. Aztec priests paid tribute to Xipe Totec, their 'flayed lord', by wearing the skins of human sacrifices.[1] Nevertheless, the Passion of Jesus Christ is an event that set a historical standard for two millennia of depictions of suffering. Christianity was born during a tumultuous succession of cruel and Epicurean Roman emperors, who tolerated it as a curious *religio licita* ('permitted religion') in the city of Rome. Emperor Nero took a more hardline view and made Christians the subject of garish murder in the Colosseum.

When metal's extremity was fast evolving in the eighties, Christianity's stifling moralism was an easy target for its anti-authoritarian intent: blasphemy was one of metal's sharpest weapons. As death metal evolved, its blood-soaked visions were wrapped into zombie apocalypse fictions as well as serial killer lore, and it was always seeking out new portraits of pain. Representations of the destruction of Christ himself fed the genre's nightmare machine, as did the demise and inevitable putrefaction of all bodies as earthly vessels. At the same time, it was a darkly humorous genre. Like Charles Baudelaire's poem 'Une Charogne' ('A Carcass' – from 1857's *Fleurs Du Mal* [*Flowers of Evil*] collection), about a pair of lovers who stumble across a rotting body in the street, death metal revels in the fact that, hey-ho, we are all 'To moulder among the bones of the dead'.[2]

The result is often very cruel comedy and the genre's cartoon-ish extremity still has the power to shock and offend. At an event to launch his contentious novel *The Good Man Jesus and the Scoundrel Christ* in 2010, when he was challenged from the audience that calling the son of God a scoundrel was 'an awful thing to say', author Philip Pullman replied: 'Yes, it was a shocking thing to say and I knew it was a shocking thing to say, but no one has the right to live without being shocked. No one has the right to spend their life without being offended.'[3]

Slayer adopted the Roman eagle as a symbol under which to rally their fans. On 1986's *Reign In Blood* they fell over themselves to invoke evil in all its forms, as singer Tom Araya filled his songs full to the brim with lyrical poison. 'Altar of Sacrifice' and 'Jesus Saves' – though not live classics like 'Angel of Death' and 'Raining

Blood' – are still two of the album's pivotal songs: the first segues beautifully into the second with an intercession worthy of the Antichrist, a passage where the drums are afforded lots of open space for steady snare hits and sixteenth-note ride cymbal decoration. 'Altar of Sacrifice' depicts a Satanic ritual in which the subject transforms into the demon Baphomet ('Transforming of five toes to two/Learn the sacred words of praise, hail Satan'). After the connecting passage, on 'Jesus Saves' Slayer slides into a viciously fast mockery of anyone who would follow Jesus ('In an invisible man you place your trust'). What maddened Slayer, as it did many metal bands of the period, was the hypocrisy of Christianity. Though metal was wrapped up in notions of the end of times, in their eyes the eschatological nonsense of evangelical Christians was unforgivable. This is one of the interesting ironies of the evolution of blasphemous extreme metal: that it arguably applied a keener moral rectitude to the struggles of life than did monied, Bible-belt preachers.

Chuck Schuldiner's band Death expressed similar qualms on the 1990 album *Spiritual Healing*. Throughout the album, Schuldiner plays out an electrifying, duelling-guitarists' battle with James Murphy. Murphy's style was very distinctive – favouring weird chromatic patterns and sudden, often very graceful leaps across the fretboard that drove Schuldiner's squalling soloing style to adopt its own internal logic and character. The title track is a death-metal symphony of multiple movements that encompasses grandstanding theatrics, burning-angel speed and its repeated 'Practise what you preach' grooving refrain. In the song, Schuldiner speaks to the neglect of someone who has died at the hands of evangelism, a form of 'holy death' and martyrdom through religious belief: 'Preach the good word/Speak no more, prepare to burn/A justified torture?/From this may others learn'.

The cover art by Ed Repka (mentioned above for his Nuclear Assault artwork) depicts a bald, almost ghoulish patient in a wheelchair wearing a hospital gown. It is more disturbing now considering that Schuldiner himself would himself contract a terminal illness (he died of brain cancer in 2001). The patient stares out with vacant, red-rimmed eyes as a cowboy preacher puts his hand on his head, with the other extended in a kind of blessing. The crowd, as Repka's sketch notes state, are 'forcing sick guy to submit to preacher's healing'.[4] In the final version, the middle-aged woman to the preacher's left, and the man to his right, bear a resemblance to Margaret Thatcher and Ronald Reagan.

On Morbid Angel's debut album, *Altars of Madness* (1989), the Floridian band constructed more of death metal's harrowing architecture. They created a place for particularly acute religious suffrage on 'Maze of Torment': 'Stricken from the holy book deliverance to pain/Effigy of Jesus Christ burning in your mind'. On second album *Blessed Are the Sick* (1991) the devilish perspective of 'Day of Suffering' took direct aim at Jesus himself:

Lord of light
I will swarm against you now
Gods perverse
Wickeds at my side
Misery
Thorns to lance your every word
Nazarene
Now I crown you king in pain
Suffer

Morbid Angel were joined in the Christ-baiting canon by New York's Immolation, particularly on the tremendous 'Higher

Coward' from 2000's *Close To A World Below*, and Incantation, who started as they meant to go on with the profanity of 1992's *Onward to Golgotha* and 1994's *Mortal Throne of Nazarene*. Around 2000, I wore Morbid Angel's *Gateways To Annihilation* T-shirt in a remote Scottish pub with friends. It went totally silent while I ordered the drinks. The drinkers eventually relaxed and let the devil in amongst them.

These unflinching, demonic reports of Christ's suffering correspond to the near-ecstatic levels of physical pain depicted by painters such as Caravaggio in the seventeenth century. Then, the city of Naples was under Spanish rule and subject to the religious policing and cruelties of the Spanish Inquisition. The Spanish-born Jusepe de Ribera was a painter in the city during this period, when the horrors of the Inquisition were a common sight in much the same way that atrocities were on public display during the Roman rule over Jerusalem. *The Martyrdom of St Bartholomew* (1644) shows the near-naked apostle of Jesus looking directly and piteously at the viewer as he is being flayed alive, a decapitated statue of the Roman god Apollo lying underneath him – Jesus seems suspended in air, just as he is between life and death, with the drunken executioner beginning to strip the flesh from his arm. In Ribera's *Christ Mocked and Crowned with Thorns* (1638), Jesus similarly looks out at us with dark, bloodshot eyes, as he is crowded by executionary thugs, the blood weeping from the cruelly crowned rim of his head. Ribera and Morbid Angel and their death metal ilk made art of Jesus's suffering hundreds of years apart.[5]

Artists like Ribera and death metal bands induce both a revulsion and fascination with the Christian fetishism of cruelty. This instils a suspicion of religious authority, and with it all authority, that is hard to shake. Death metal's torture of Christ is a way of subverting the messiah and generally pissing off the hypocrites in the church who want to mediate our relationship with God. The extent to which its progenitors identify, and even sympathise, with the abuse of his son by perpetuating the images of his suffering is a tantalising grey area. Which rock musician doesn't have something of a messiah complex? But having these apostate lessons taught to us by death metal, it is difficult to hear anyone thank 'God' for a success or achievement and not smile darkly at the blank devotion that means they won't, or can't, credit themselves for what they've done in their lives. The fact that countries still imprison, and even execute people, for the crime of blasphemy, seems preposterous – the Irish referendum that removed the crime of blasphemy from its constitution in 2018 was an obvious step against such regressive legislation.

The collision of nascent Christianity and the excesses of the Roman empire was brilliantly fictionalised in the mid-eighties in *The Kingdom of the Wicked* by Anthony Burgess. The novel follows two narrative strands, juxtaposing the work of the apostles after Christ's ascension with the reigns of the Roman emperors Tiberius, Caligula, Claudius and Nero. One of the novel's best scenes is when Nero (in disguise) visits the home of the apostle Paul. Nero's obsession with the pleasures of the body draws him into an exchange that speaks to the heart of the Christian preoccupation with the body's demise and what it promises:

'So you people see death as a gateway to a better life. If you have been good.'

'Caesar puts it simply and well.'

'The destruction of the body is nothing?'

'Painful perhaps, but acceptable – more than acceptable to the just.'[6]

None of this is much of a laughing matter. But one of death metal's finest modern bands started as a 'drunken side project' which then evolved into 'a death metal elite'. That is how Mikael Åkerfeldt put it onstage at the Wacken Festival in Germany in 2005 while performing with Sweden's Bloodbath. The cover of their superb live album, *The Wacken Carnage*, features Christ's dismembered foot with a nail driven through the ankle, photographed in the pallid, forensic style of the severed hand on the poster of the first *Saw* film. Åkerfeldt's day job is lead singer and guitarist of Opeth, a progressive metal band that incorporated a huge amount of light and shade into their long, complex compositions which – as the years progressed – became lighter and lighter. In promoting the 2019 Opeth album *In Cauda Venenum*, Åkerfeldt confessed, 'It's an impossible mission, to be the heaviest.'

In Bloodbath, he was later joined by Opeth's drummer Martin Axenrot and members of fellow progressive act Katatonia, who had similarly taken a softer path in their later years. Bloodbath lanced the boil of extreme brutality that increasingly festered underneath the surface of those bands. Founded in the late nineties as a tribute to the classic death metal bands of ten years previously (and named after a song by the band Cancer), Bloodbath's sound was drawn from the mid-frequency, buzzsaw characteristics of a now-discontinued guitar pedal, the Boss HM-2, made famous by fellow Swedes Entombed. Bloodbath was a gore-soaked laugh, evident in the tattered clothing and fake blood they donned for that first-ever show at Wacken. As later singer Nick Holmes put it to me, 'When you take it too seriously, you've failed.'

The members of Bloodbath sought to keep the music fun and anti-professional. They recorded their first EP the day after a party, Åkerfeldt threw up on the studio wall[7] and they used a cut-up technique for the title track 'Bleeding Death'. Each of them wrote a line, folded the piece of paper the lyrics were written on, showing only the last word for the next person to rhyme. The quality of the band was hard to keep down, though. By the time they wrote the EP *Unblessing the Purity* in 2008 they were nailing their Christ-baiting lyrics and blast-beat enthusiasm firmly to the cross.

Opening up with the firestorm of 'Blasting the Virginborn', the four-song EP is as good a piece of death metal as was ever released, rounded off with a pounding mid-paced classic in the vein of Morbid Angel called 'Mouth of Empty Praise'. A gleeful massacre of Christian innocents ('Trapped inside a burning field/Sheep of god'), it becomes a litany of the names of demons after its avalanche-like breakdown: 'Azazel/Belial/Abaddon/Leviathan'. On this EP, and the follow-up album *The Fathomless Mastery* (2008), it is like Åkerfeldt has sacrificed his voice to Satan himself, such is its astounding depth and ferocity. On a counterpart track to 'Mouth of Empty Praise' from that album, 'Iesous', he uses several of the names that Jesus was known by in the Middle East, underpinned by a hammering, fractured, torn-from-the-depths melodic bedrock: 'Eeso/Yeshua/Iesous', then reaching lower than almost ever before in his guttural vocal range for the final condemnation: 'Die by our rage'.

When Åkerfeldt could no longer make the time for Bloodbath, and was concerned about the business demands its growing success entailed, Nick Holmes took up the reins as singer. Already well known and loved for his work in British gothic-doomers Paradise Lost, he brought a plague-pit, quasi-monastic malevolence to his character in the band on *Grand Morbid Funeral* (2014) and *The Arrow of Satan is Drawn* (2018). The latter release suggested that the God of Emptiness is the saviour we need during the crisis of late capitalism.

A straightforward, Bradford-born northerner, Holmes is unmoved either way, as he told me. 'I am one hundred per cent an atheist so I can play with the divisions between Satan and God and I don't care who gets offended either way.' Heavily inspired by the gloriously overwrought visions of evil espoused by proto-black metal bands like Venom and Bathory, and German thrashers Sodom, Holmes cares less that the songs have coherence than that their overall impact of cascading pestilence overwhelms the listener. Well into middle age, youthful at heart, and tainted by his early immersion in the blood-spattered origins of death metal, it is now hard to shock him: 'When Glen Benton [lead singer of Deicide] burned the inverted crucifix into his forehead, that was a classic one.[8] Like "Oh my God, this guy's fucking terrifying".' For Holmes, knee-deep in lyrical blood and guts and destruction, self-harm like that in service to the cause might be permitted, but cruelty to others is not: 'If you started killing a cat, you've taken it too far.'

Holmes watches hundreds of horror films a year to feed a subconscious hungry for rotten lyrical fodder. As well as that, the edifices of the church and religious imagery are a necessary source of fascination: the 'dark cathedrals claiming souls' of his Bloodbath song 'Bloodicide'. On 'Morbid Antichrist' he wanted to write about an Antichrist-type figure who found religion later in life, influenced by the formerly alleged religious awakening of Charles Darwin, but thought it was sounding too sensible and re-committed the subject of the song to the dark side: 'So I spurn the predatory heavens above/So I serve only the beast inside and all the suffering.'

The Antichrist is accounted for in *The Kingdom of the Wicked*, although there are historic disputes where the number 666 originated. In Burgess's novel it originates with the emperor Domitian and the amount of money he owes in a bet with a one-eyed man named Scrupulous, chalking the sum DCLXVI on the wall: 'The number has ever since been the mark of the beast, expanded in the secret writings of the Christians to an abbreviation of Domitianus Caesar Legatos Xsti Violenter Interfacit, meaning that the Emperor Domitian is violently killing the legates or representatives of Christ.'[9] Death metal's obsession with both Christ and the Antichrist has its bloody origins in the Roman empire.

The Arrow of Satan Is Drawn suggests that the Antichrist's work is not done. The artwork for the album by artist Eliran Kantor is a painting of a bedroom with a white crib in the foreground buzzing with flies, as the mother and father sleep in a bed in the background. The thick black strip down its side evokes grief and ceremonial mourning, or something more austere, like an armband worn by totalitarian and fascist regimes. The artwork is unusual since it is subtle and disturbing in what it alludes to: a child who has died in the night, yet to be discovered by its parents.

As he told me, Kantor was only given the album's title and left to come up with a concept to fit it: 'I like it when the artwork serves as another metaphoric layer for the title, as opposed to fleshing it out directly. In this case, that would be painting Satan with a bow and arrow. The title to me sounded like an act of initiating an unholy war on the righteous. So my mind went into thinking about a symbolic act in which the couple on the cover are asleep while their baby is long gone by the time they would wake up.'

In Kantor's mind it is a satanic equivalence to the scene in *The Godfather* (1972) where the severed head of a prized thoroughbred horse, owned by film producer Jack Woltz, is placed next to him in his bed while he sleeps; it is an act of mafioso retribution for refusing to cast boss Don Corleone's godson in one of his films. Woltz awakes screaming at the discovery in blood-soaked silk sheets.

The album cover shocked Holmes. 'It's a weird one. When I first saw it, it made me feel quite uneasy. I didn't know what to think. But it's provocative and I guess that's what you want, in a way. At first I wasn't sure whether I liked it or not because I thought, Maybe this is too much.' Nevertheless, it was Kantor's artistic response to the 'creepy' vibe Holmes brought to Bloodbath – a sense of inchoate evil – that made Kantor veer away from physical violence or gore. The image puts story above time and place, and there are no historical markers in the image (most obviously no modern technology) to distract from the horror of the scene. It retains a quality which Kantor finds 'in a lot of children's books, fairy-tales and lullabies, which are timeless'.

The damage inflicted with the image is emotional and that is almost worse than the genre's depictions of physical violence. As for Holmes's sense of shock, Kantor is happy to elicit such reactions from hardened death metal musicians: 'A long time ago I found a way to both please myself without compromising while also pleasing others – I'm fortunate enough to pick which projects I take in, so I'm already excited about the direction, have things in common with the bands and even their fan base, and share the need of coming up with something new and original. And that's why you get these reactions, because what I go with is usually not the obvious and familiar choice, but I trust the bands and audience would still "get it" because we share similar goals and taste, and they also know I really dive in to the subject matter and don't just touch its surface.'

Kantor's experience of creating art for metal albums has reinforced his belief that similarities can be found between different artistic expressions in culture that share attributes that are 'unsettling, intense, weird, scary, distorted and hard to watch' or, indeed, hard to listen to. It reflects his experience growing up. 'I was collecting bugs as a kid, and was into *Nightmare on Elm Street* in elementary school, and even after I got into metal, I still got into [artist] H. R. Giger way before I got into darker metal like death and black metal. So it wasn't that the music influenced my taste in visual art, it's that it all comes from the same place of being drawn to certain attributes, aesthetics and atmosphere.' It amounts to a commonality of heaviness: 'When I think of "heavy" I think of something that's intense and carries an impact. Maybe something that's not easy to digest because it brings out emotions that are not very calming. Heavy demands your attention and can't just be in the background.'

Like all great cover art, Kantor's artwork is a prism through which to see an album, and sets an emotional tone that frames the listening experience. For Kantor, it is 'the same as what a soundtrack can do to a movie scene – when you couple sonic art with visual art, you add another dimension that directs the listener's imagination, and get it closer to how you want your music to be perceived and experienced. To this day, [Metallica's 1984 album] *Ride The Lighting* sounds "blue" to me while [Metallica's 1986 album] *Master of Puppets* sounds "red and brown".' Metal music's sonic strength and vividness has long been accompanied by, and reinforced with, the hallmarks of the genre's visual aesthetics, from Judas Priest's leather onwards. Playing with these tropes, and subverting them where necessary, can create visual art that impresses and shocks with renewed force. And, ultimately, it makes the experience of the music heavier still.

II. The snake bites back

For the cover of Venom Prison's 2016 debut album *Animus*, Eliran Kantor painted a truly horrifying scene. A shaft of light illuminates a muscular, long-haired man stripped of his clothes, held in position on one side by a sepulchral-looking figure with a bloodied knife, while another woman clasps his mouth shut. It's by looking at the image a little longer that you notice the blood dripping from his groin, and the lizard-like tail emerging from the woman who is evidently feeding him his own genitalia.

The artwork was a direct response to a song called 'Perpetrator Emasculation' – a stinging rebuttal of what its lyric skewers as 'misogynistic culture'. Venom Prison blazes through the song in ninety furious seconds. It contains a succinct recommendation for the punishment that should be exacted on rapists: 'Your kind deserves decimation/Castration/Genital mutilation'. For Kantor, the imagery that came to him from the song 'stood out to me because I have never seen a piece of artwork, let alone an album cover, in which a rapist is being castrated by a gang of women who then feed him his own genitals'.

It is a piece that strongly recalls the historical cruelty of Caravaggio and Ribera: 'I was never the most versed person in art history and could talk to you about music ten times more, but I've observed and absorbed a lot of classical art through the years and it stuck with me. For instance, you can show me a crop of just a knee from a Ribera painting or an eye from a Caravaggio piece, and I would probably know which piece it is from, while I can't really tell you much about the stories behind these pieces, the artists' biographies or the art movements and schools of that period.'

Venom Prison singer Larissa Stupar was, like Nick Holmes, taken aback when she first saw the piece in its early stages. She told me, 'When he sent us the first sketches and the concept, I have to admit that at first people weren't sure: "Can we do that? Is it going to be too offensive? What are people going to say?" And then we just thought to ourselves: this is exactly what this album is about. This is exactly what the music feels like. This should be it.' The lizard-like appearance of the women in the piece came under instruction from Stupar to Kantor: 'After I came up with the composition, Larissa commented that she likes to think of the women she writes about as demons and mythical creatures, strong and angry, inhumane in their appearance but human in their emotions.'

Larissa Stupar was born in Russia and grew up in Germany, before moving to Wales and joining Venom Prison. Stupar knew she wanted to bring a 'feminine perspective' to death metal, a genre that plays around with savage violence, often targeted at women, reflecting the terrible reality of murder, rape and domestic abuse statistics worldwide.[10] Nonetheless, it can be grossly misogynistic. Exhibit A for the prosecution is Cannibal Corpse's infamous 'Fucked With A Knife'. 'Even though I love Cannibal Corpse,' said Stupar, 'and I love loads of bands that have misogynistic content – because they are amazing bands and because they started all of this – I do feel like women haven't always been really welcome, active participants in metal. Metal has changed over the years but the lyrical content has mostly stayed the same. And I think we do need to go with the times and do need to progress. We need to show that women are a part of this. And we can do just like men can do. I was sick of having to read all of these misogynistic lyrics that target women and specifically speak about rape.' The lyric of 'Perpetrator Emasculation' is unpleasant, but is justified vengeance for the decades of violence the genre has doled out towards women.

A period of being made to go to bible school from ages twelve to fourteen convinced Stupar it was 'good to know the enemy'. As such, she likes to turn the tropes of evil, manipulative women on their heads. She based the final song on the album, 'Womb Forced Animus', on the character of Lilith, who in Jewish mythology is Adam's first wife, supposedly demonic and wanton, but in Stupar's hands a necessary opponent of the male religious order: 'Indomitable to the patriarchal force of the lord/Feeding the devil by means of the umbilical cord'.

Set deep within the yawning chasm of the opening chords of the song is a sample from the 2003 film *Monster*, in which Charlize Theron played serial killer Aileen Wuornos: 'I'm good with the Lord. I'm fine with him. And I know how you were raised, all right? And I know how people fuckin' think out there and, fuck, it's gotta be that way. They've gotta tell you that "thou shall not kill" shit and all of that. But that's not the way the world works, Selby. Cuz I'm out there every fuckin' day living it. Who the fuck knows what God wants?'

For Stupar, Venom Prison's poisonous name symbolises a means to finally subject patriarchy to the serpentine power of women: 'I know the serpent in the Bible is not necessarily a positive thing and for me it's connected to femininity, and gives the image of women particularly being snake-y and not trustworthy, and having ruined the paradise for humans. Knowing there is this image that is vested in Christianity I thought to play around with it and turn it around. So, for me, the snake is something powerful. It's not necessarily a bad thing being smart and being able to trick people. It can be a good thing as well. I just really like playing with these kinds of traditional uses of that thing, and give them a new spin.'

Stupar continued this exploration through the prism of Buddhist concepts on 2019's *Samsara*, naming the song 'Dukkha' for the Buddhist concept of suffering and 'Narakha' after the Dharmic name for hell. Second track 'Megillus & Leana' is about the seduction of the female Leaena by the transgender Megillus, as recounted by the Syrian rhetorician Lucian in his *Dialogues of the Courtesans* from the second century AD. Stupar believes the pressure Venom Prison were under to produce their follow-up album manifested itself in even more savage performances.

Stupar acknowledges that raw and emotionally honest emotional content is as important as rhythm, distortion and sheer volume. She cites Nicole Dollanganger's ambient dream-pop: Dollanganger created a lot of her music while being treated for anorexia, before collaborating with grindcore act Full of Hell and touring with the hardcore metal band Code Orange: 'It's beautiful, it's angelic and her voice is really nice, but she sings about self-destruction and destroying her own body and bulimia and throwing up and just wanting to die, and bleeding and stuff like that. And that's so heavy. So for me, you don't really need to be really loud and be really fast and have beatdowns. Sometimes it's just enough to be emotional and self-destructive, for example.'

Stupar discovered the extraordinary power of her voice on antifa marches in Germany when she was sixteen years old. As she roared slogans, people around her remarked she should be a singer in a band. A period in a crust punk band and then in hardcore act Wolf Down concretised how she wanted to make music with a message: 'Ever since I've been in a band I always wanted to write content that was political to some extent because I feel if you have the opportunity to say something then you should.' On 'Corrode the Black Sun' she returns to the fascism that comes from the distortion of the Nietzschean concept of the 'übermensch'/'Superman', which towered over twentieth-century Germany, the country she grew up in, and the 'passing chauvinism as collectivism' that dogged Russia, the country of her birth, when it was part of the Soviet Union.

With Stupar leading from the front, Venom Prison refilter death metal through a feminist lens. She returns to familiar themes on 'Celestial Patricide' – about a hypocritical god crucifying his 'coward son' and positing Satan as a 'saviour' when God's lineage of patriarchal dominance is passed down through a world order of kings and priests. Musically, Stupar describes the band as 'extreme metal with death metal influences': their dense, layered sound is thick with breakdowns, frenetic black metal guitar runs, and often pulls back and out to grand instrumental passages. It is all delivered with the lacerating precision of Lilith gelding the Christ-like subject of Kantor's nightmarish cover of *Animus*.

III. Rotten to the gore

Bloodbath's *Nightmares Made Flesh* (2004) saw another vocalist, Peter Tägtgren, take the helm during one of Mikael Åkerfeldt's breaks from the group. He presided over some of the band's most notorious material. Deviating from their usual blasphemous intent, 'Eaten' is Bloodbath's signature song – a slow, flesh-stripping grind of massive power. It was inspired by Armin Meiwes, aka '*der Metzgermeister*' ('the master butcher'), a cannibal who advertised on a now-defunct internet forum called the Cannibal Cafe for a willing subject to eat. An engineer from Berlin, Bernd Jürgen Armando Brandes, answered the advertisement, culminating in his death at the hands of Meiwes, but not before they attempted to eat Brandes's penis together. Meiwes kept the body for ten months and used it for food – he described the taste of human flesh as 'like pork but stronger'.[11]

In Bloodbath's 'Eaten', the song unfolds from the perspective of the victim who, like Brandes, is desperate to be eaten: 'I've had one desire since I was born/To see my body ripped and torn'. This pulverising mock-celebration of cannibalism demonstrates death metal's capacity for ludicrous extremity. It makes something hilarious out of the emetic recesses of the human imagination: the wish to find that special someone 'to suck my heart and lick my guts'. The designer of the cover of this book is Luke Bird – he is also a good friend of mine and a Bloodbath fan. I supplied the lyrics of 'Eaten' to Luke's brother and best man, Tom, in advance of Luke's wedding. It was a proud moment for us all to hear them recited during Tom's best man speech in a beautiful venue in Northumberland.

'Eaten' was the subject of an academic study into whether metal fans are more violent, or fucked up in the head, than the average person on the street. Researchers at Macquarie University, Sydney, played 'Eaten' to a few dozen death metal fans and non-fans whilst showing them violent imagery to see if death metallers were more desensitised. The results showed they weren't. However, the control track used for comparison was Pharrell Williams's 'Happy', a heinous song that would provoke sensitive listeners to acts of sickening auto-cannibalism, surely? A report of the study on the BBC's site had a typically dry Nick Holmes response to the non-revelation that death metal listeners had normal responses to violence: 'I didn't personally write them [the words], but I would be frankly astounded if anyone listened to that song and then felt a desire to be eaten by a cannibal.'[12]

'Eaten' has its antecedent in a song released fifteen years earlier, 'Exhume to Consume', by Carcass. Guitarist Bill Steer uses a throaty groan that is an excellent approximation of the sounds of the undead in the zombie films of George A. Romero. He sings of the desire to feast on the flesh of the dead by disinterring their corpses: 'Ulcerated flesh I munch/Rotting corpses are my lunch'.

The lyrics are emitted in short, crammed bursts, over an atrocity of double-bass drum and serrated guitar lines. The song encapsulates the band's transfiguration from grindcore (or, more pointedly, 'goregrind') propagators to death metal masters.

Carcass was the project of three close friends: Jeff Walker (bass, vocals), Ken Owen (drums) and Bill Steer (guitar, vocals). They were (loosely speaking) a Liverpool-based band, but to be more exact they were located in the Wirral: the prosperous, middle-class, largely rural area outside of the city. Steer had known Owen since they were eight or nine years old – Steer moved to the Wirral from North Shields and Owen from Wigan. They both had Scottish mothers, who were also school teachers. When they found they had that in common, they became firm friends. Walker did not come into the picture until Steer was sixteen, but Steer was immediately impressed with Walker's self-deprecating attitude and energy. Walker wanted to get things done, and one of the first things he suggested was getting Owen on drums in their new band, despite his total lack of experience.

Steer's family home had two attic rooms. He lived in one, and the other – afflicted by a fair amount of dry rot – was where Carcass tried to work out what they were doing. Steer's parents were absolutely neutral about his music, which in his eyes was perfect. Carcass knew which bands they liked and who they wanted to emulate from the underground: from the fuzzing grindcore of Repulsion, who came from Flint, Michigan, to the early death metal of Florida's Death – sounds all put through what Steer calls the 'Carcass mincer'. Perhaps more importantly, they knew what they did not like, which was the proliferation of British bands who were trying to be the next Metallica and the hair-metal bands who were filling the pages of metal magazines *Raw* and *Kerrang!*.

Carcass quickly tired of the juvenile gore of the early death metal scene and, between them, Walker and Owen began to create a vision that was at once more sophisticated and more visceral. They took the forensic view of the pathologist. They examined death itself – the post-mortem decay and degradation of the human body. Their songs laid these remains out on a mortuary table and described the processes of disease, death and autopsy in an impenetrable medical-ese, which they felt was somehow more adult – more fresh – in all its purulence. Similarly, their music was assembled from ragged emittances of murky, blasting fury. The songs on their twenty-two-track debut album, *Reek of Putrefaction* (1988), were vulgar ('Genital Grinder', 'Vomited Anal Tract'), punning and darkly humorous ('Festerday'), and told tasteless stories in collections of tracks, sequenced in bursts (see the electrocution of a foetus and the after-effects in 'Foeticide'/'Microwaved Uterogestation').

The early output of Carcass was crude, but even then was saying something pointed about how society treated death. *Reek of Putrefaction*'s cover artwork deviates from the illustrated imagery and conventions of metal up to that point, instead confronting us with a collage of photographs of dead and rotten corpses and body parts which, arresting as it was in the late eighties, was covered up on reissues to avoid giving offence. As Walker put it to me: 'In our western society at least, all the horrors of the abattoir or the funeral parlour are sanitised and behind closed doors.' Carcass placed the imagery of death on the shelves of high-street record shops.

Musically, they created a lot of confusion, or at the least a challenge, and were happy to leave it to others to interpret what they were doing. Steer recalls the 'total bemusement' of the audience at the Swinging Sporran venue in Manchester at one of their early

John Dyer Baizley *(foreground)* and Pete Adams of Baroness perform at The Fleece venue in Bristol on 14 August 2012, the night before their catastrophic bus crash. *(© Prog Magazine/ Getty Images)*

Baroness's tour bus lies across a road having fallen from a viaduct on Brassknocker Hill, Bath, after its brakes failed in heavy rain. Baizley was sitting up front, which bore the brunt of the impact. *© SWNS)*

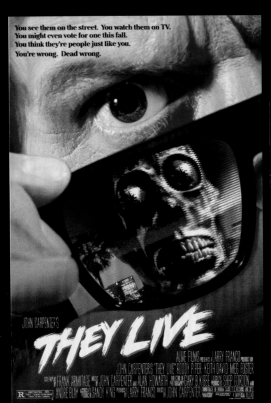

You see them on the street. You watch them on TV. You might even vote for one this fall. You think they're people just like you. You're wrong. Dead wrong.

'Rowdy' Roddy Piper's character Nada dons a special pair of sunglasses in John Carpenter's *They Live* which act as a reality filter, revealing the film's alien ruling class. Time to put on your *Heavy* sunglasses. (© *Universal/Courtesy Everett Collection/Mary Evans*)

The Branch Davidians' Mount Carmel compound outside Waco, Texas, burns during the ATF raid in 1993. The religious group were the subject of the first song, 'Davidian', on Machine Head's album *Burn My Eyes*. (© *Gregory Smith /Getty Images*)

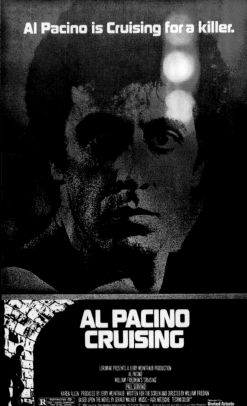

Al Pacino is Cruising for a killer.

AL PACINO CRUISING

William Rimmer's 'Evening (The Fall of Day)' was the inspiration for Led Zeppelin's Swan Song Records logo and the tattoo on my right shoulder. (© *Everett and William Sturgis Bigelow Collection/Bridgeman Images*)

Cruising, directed by William Friedkin, sees Al Pacino's undercover cop enter a world of 'heavy leather'. Likewise, Judas Priest donned leather to lead their audience into another world in the early eighties. (© *United Artists/Courtesy Everett Collection/Mary Evans*)

Hell Bent for Leather: K. K. Downing *(left)* and Rob Halford of Judas Priest performing in 1980.
(© Paul Natkin/Getty Images)

Looking less like a wizard and more like Witchfinder General, Rainbow guitarist Ritchie Blackmore poses alongside his elven vocalist Ronnie James Dio in 1975. *(© Fin Costello/Getty Images)*

Cro-Mags taking it to the neoliberal world order onstage in Chicago, 1987.
(© Stacia Timonere/Getty Images)

The Wild Bunch:
Queens of the
Stone Age in
2002. *(left to right)*
Mark Lanegan,
Nick Oliveri, Josh
Homme, Dave
Grohl and Troy
Van Leeuwen.
*(© Hayley Madden/
Getty Images)*

Darkness vying with metallic greys
in Georgia O' Keefe's *Dark Place
II*, a foreboding representation of
the landscape of New Mexico.
*(© 2020. Image Copyright The Metropolitan
Museum of Art/Art Resource/Scala,
Florence)*

'Nazarene/Now I crown you king in pain': Jim Caviezel as Jesus in Mel Gibson's horrifying *The Passion of the Christ.* (© *Newmarket Releasing/ Courtesy Everett Collection/Mary Evans)*

Jusepe de Ribera's *The Martyrdom of St Bartholomew* – a depiction of bodily suffering that expresses a fascination with pain and cruelty, as does the lyrical imagery of death metal. (© *Mary Evans/Iberfoto)*

'The title to me sounded like an act of initiating an unholy war on the righteous': Eliran Kantor's cover for Boodbath's *The Arrow of Satan Is Drawn.* (© *Eliran Kantor)*

Perpetrator Emasculation: a rapist is given a taste of his own medicine in Eliran Kantor's artwork for *Animus*, the debut album by Venom Prison. *(© Eliran Kantor)*

Larissa Stupar and Ash Gray of Venom Prison upending the conventions of death metal onstage in 2018. *(© Roberto Ricciuti/ Getty Images)*

At home with Cradle of Filth. *(left to right)* Dani Filth, Robin Graves and Nick Barker. *(© Mick Hutson/Getty Images*

'Bequeath to me thy fiery kiss/ To sever thin mortality': Edvard Munch's *Love and Pain*, aka *Vampire*. *(© De Agostini Picture Library/ Bridgeman Images)*

Nice church – it would be a shame if something happened to it. An illustration of Fantoft Stave Church, Bergen, Norway, in happier times before the church burnings that accompanied the second wave of black metal. *(© Nastasic/Getty Images)*

Careful with that knife. Isabelle Adjani in Andrzej Żuławski's *Possession*, in a rare moment of (relative) calm. *(© Courtesy Everett Collection/Mary Evans)*

Arik Roper's far-out artwork for Sleep's *Dopesmoker*, with its 'stoner caravan' of Weedians. (© Arik Roper)

The greatest sci-fi film that never was? The documentary *Jodorowsky's Dune* is an ode to anyone who strived and failed to execute a bold artistic vision. (© Collection Christophel/Alamy Stock Photo)

Sleep's Matt Pike onstage at Alexandra Palace in 2012. 'It's like there's a war inside Pike between Bach and the Creature from the Black Lagoon,' says Rob Delaney. (© Gary Wolstenholme/Getty Images)

gigs. But that's not to say it didn't leave a positive impression. Alongside Napalm Death (for whom Steer played guitar on their first two albums), Carcass managed to capture the underground zeitgeist in an unexpected way and reach a far wider consciousness than their peers. Napalm Death's ultra-short songs and indecipherable vocals, and mass media exposure, made them something of a curiosity. Steer remembers that, 'in those years, 87–89, when Lee [Dorrian, vocalist] and I were in the band, it was always on the verge of being a joke to a lot of people. We did have some very straight characters coming to gigs just for pure novelty value.' It is probably because of the extremity of what Carcass were doing that radio DJ John Peel picked up on their music. He invited them to record two sessions at Radio 1 (one in December 1988 and one in December 1990) and even declared *Reek of Putrefaction* his album of the year for 1988 in the *Observer*, saying, 'I like the idea of defining for yourself an area of operation as apparently limited as hardcore and then finding room for innovation within that area.'[13]

Carcass also felt they were playing within set parameters. In Walker's eyes they simply 'bastardised the blues' and Steer was emphatic about retaining those self-imposed limits when he spoke to me. 'I'm not interested in music that's confrontational and challenges people in that way. I just like, if possible, good singing, good playing, good songs.' Familiar with the alternative musical scene and harsh industrial noise acts like Whitehouse, Steer had an aversion to breaking the rituals and conventions of a live performance: 'I actually regard myself as quite conservative musically. Because I'm really not interested in blowing anybody's minds. And the very word *experiment* just worries me, in the context of music. To me, a gig is a musical performance: it's not a research laboratory.'

Their second album, *Symphonies of Sickness* (1989), had more characterful, memorable songwriting. After that, the musical development of the band was rapid, even extraordinary. They began to stretch the skin of death metal and sew it into new shapes. On third album *Necroticism: Descanting the Insalubrious* (1991), Carcass saw their music as nearing (a sickly form of) progressive rock in scope and execution: bringing in samples, keyboards, and then state-of-the-art recording techniques. The songs were lengthening: no longer the nasty, short and brutish rip-and-run approach of *Reek of Putrefaction*, they reached up to ten minutes in length and experimented with rhythm and melodic shapes, akin to movements in a piece of classical music. *Necroticism* feels like an elaborate Frankenstein's monster in construction, mirroring the process related in one of its singles, 'Corporal Jigsore Quandary': 'Such a perplexing task/To fit the remains in the casket/Uliginous mess so quiescent'. Today, the band's live performances are masterclasses in adding and subtracting song excerpts from their back catalogue and reconfiguring them into collages of songs past and present. Despite its bloating in ambition, perhaps *Necroticism*'s best song, 'Incarnated Solvent Abuse', is also one of its shortest – it concerns someone getting high off the 'mucilage vapours' of a corpse.

The cutting humour of the north is ever-present in the work of Carcass, like a *risus sardonicus* on the face of one of their imagined cadavers. As they continued to strip their music back, Walker drew harder on his crust-punk upbringing, got more serious, and pulled his lyrical focus back to a broader view of man's inhumanity to man. *Necroticism* was released just a few weeks after Metallica's *Black* album and Nirvana's *Nevermind* in 1991. For the next Carcass record, in Walker's frank formulation, it was 'a case of cutting the crap'. They did that on their own terms.

Steer could not get into the rigidity of the opening track of the *Black* album: ' "Enter Sandman" is so completely unfunky and on the one. It's like marching music. It's got no swing to it whatsoever.' He wanted to infuse the music of Carcass with even more touch, expression and groove – the result was an undeniable masterpiece of the death metal genre: *Heartwork*.

The new intention of Carcass was clear from glancing at the sleeve of the 1993 album: the chaotic assemblage of garish images was gone and replaced by an abstracted spinal column with blood IV line in a Christ-like pose attached to the peace symbol, in an image by artist H. R. Giger. An original version of the piece, named 'Life Support 1993', had been pilfered for a Deicide bootleg called *Deny The Cross*, but Giger agreed to reproduce it in burnished metal for *Heartwork*.[14] The album's opening song, 'Buried Dreams', had an unprecedented density, the result of 'stacking' the guitars, layering no fewer than four rhythm guitar tracks on top of one another. Steer traded solos with second guitarist Michael Amott – who had joined Carcass in 1990 and had played a more minor role on *Necroticism* – in an extraordinary interplay of guitar leads that out-did Death's *Spiritual Healing* from three years earlier. Walker's opening snarl makes the scope of the album plain: 'Welcome, it's a world of hate'.

Heartwork simply *flows* – the cadaver's stitches have dissolved, and Steer and Amott's guitar playing could change the mood of a song like 'Carnal Forge' almost at whim with a beautifully executed legato guitar solo. The album has the cold, clean sharpness of a surgeon's tools, which is why it is keenly recalled on their 2013 comeback album, *Surgical Steel*. You can draw a clear line from the cattle-like subjugation of the workforce of 'Arbeit Macht Fleisch' from *Heartwork* to the 'The Granulating Dark Satanic Mills' of *Surgical Steel*. Walker described both songs to me as 'a romantic tribute to my youth. I grew up in an industrial town. I literally grew up on a road with factories where there were chimney stacks.' But Walker cannot say the band forged its music in that environment. 'That's what bands like Black Sabbath and Judas Priest will say, and quite rightly. Carcass was not rehearsing in an industrial town in the north. We were rehearsing on the Wirral.'

Walker addressed religion on the *Heartwork* song 'Embodiment': 'This effigy of flesh/Corporeal christi, nailed'. The main verse riff sees the band slow things down to a self-abasing drudge – then the guitars leap and vault; the pendulous rhythm picks up pace before slowing again. As guitar solos burst fitfully through the drudgery, the torturing mechanisms of humanity turn slowly.

Christ returns as a subject of 2014's 'Zochrot' from the *Surgical Remission/Surplus Steel* EP (leftovers from the *Surgical Steel* sessions), which draws a direct line from the crucifixion to the ultimate act of human destruction, the Holocaust: 'Nazarenes avenged the vaticide/Sculpturing the ashes of the six million who died'. Walker explained its message of cruelty down the ages to me: 'The whole song is about the cycle of violence. The Jews, allegedly, and the Romans, crucified Christ, and then in World War II we had the Holocaust. The Jews have been persecuted for the past two thousand years to a certain extent because of that.'

The band had dissolved after 1995's *Swansong*, an album that Steer moulded with a classic heavy rock sound that a lot of the fanbase objected to: 'I stretched the whole concept of Carcass to breaking point.' The interim period before their live reformation in 2008 saw drummer Ken Owen suffer a cerebral haemorrhage in 1999 that left him unable to play drums to the giddying extremes he could before. I saw the reformed band at Leeds

University for the Damnation Festival in November 2008, with Michael Amott temporarily returning on guitar. At that point Amott was arguably the most famous member of Carcass thanks to the band he had formed after he had left – Arch Enemy. His Arch Enemy bandmate Daniel Erlandsson filled in on drums. Owen was in attendance, though, and played a spontaneous drum solo. They even played 'Edge of Darkness', a *Swansong*-era song that opened the 1996 posthumous compilation *Wake Up and Smell the . . . Carcass* (its cover consisting of a photo of the dead President Kennedy with his head blown open and brain exposed). 'Edge of Darkness' (sharing its name with a paranoid, nuclear-age, eighties' TV series that starred Bob Peck) seethes with a cool, pitch-black intensity, aligning heavy blues with death metal's inherent ferocity to herald 'a new dark age'.

One of the surprising effects the pathologically obsessed music of Carcass has had, and one Walker is tickled by, is to send fans towards medical careers: 'I'm not deliberately trying to influence people or to put a positive or negative effect on people. But I can take comfort in the fact that I've met people who became doctors or nurses or pathologists or veterinarians, or who work in funeral parlours – and it's based on their interests from listening to Carcass, which is kinda cool. I think most people would look at a Carcass record, read the lyrics, and think of it as a very negative piece of art. It is, but it's had a very positive effect on people. I don't think everything has to be so friggin' positive to make people become positive. I grew up watching lots of thrillers and horror from the 1970s, but I have zero interest in wanting to kill people. Well I do, but not because of that . . .'

In their killing of Christ, the Romans created a potent framework for death metal to express its blasphemies. They created an icon of physical pain and a symbol of bodily destruction that cried out down the centuries, and which was deeply alluring for the songwriters depicting the gross agonies defining death metal. Bloodbath are one of many bands playfully killing Christ again and again as an expression of disobedience, and also a recognition that death comes for us all. Venom Prison are turning those religious myths on their head in savage new ways.

Carcass took a pathologist's interest in the minutiae of corporeal decay and then zoomed out to paint a picture of humanity's capacity to kill on an industrial scale. The Romans also built the first roads – it's just that we happen to drive cars down them now. The resulting grind of modern life takes its own toll, as Jeff Walker concludes: 'I was watching a programme about the motorways on BBC Four, about the highways agency, and a couple of times they had jumpers who were on the bridges and they had to close the motorway. I think one of these queues went on for twenty-four hours, and basically the motorists were so frustrated they were just telling the guy to jump. That sums up humanity, really.' Day to day, death can be dull, inconvenient and downright banal. Death metal elevates it again to be lurid and fascinating – telling bloody stories for the ages and keeping our inevitable demise front of mind.

4
CROSSING THE THRESHOLD

'The wind was high that night, and as the creaking
door swung on its hinges, every noise seemed
like the sound of a hand struggling with the
lock, or of a foot pausing on the threshold'[1] –
Charles Maturin, *Melmoth the Wanderer*

Transgression is important to metal: no doorway is forbidden and boundaries are to be crossed. Taboos are to be exploited and orthodoxies usurped. Black metal brought to the genre what gothic fiction did to popular culture in the eighteenth and nineteenth centuries: the supernatural and the subversive. As radical and challenging to the order of things as black metal was when it emerged, it remains a remarkable exemplar of breaking down barriers.

I. A gothic romance

'Jesus is a cunt'. It's (still) a shocking thing to say. Cradle of Filth came up with the phrase sitting on the lawn of the house of their record label owner's mother. They thought it sounded anarchic.[2] They asked printers in Hadleigh, Suffolk to print a new T-shirt design – in which 'Jesus is a cunt' was emblazoned on the back in huge, block-capital letters. The printers flatly refused. It was bad enough without the full-length photographic image of a naked, masturbating nun that covered the front. The *Vestal Masturbation* T-shirt created offence all over the globe, sold in tens of thousands, and caused the kind of upset that results in small fines and a day in the magistrates' court, as was the case for fan Paul Kenyon.

Kenyon was arrested in 1996 for wearing the shirt in London and found guilty of committing 'profane representation' under the 1839 Metropolitan Police Act by Bow Street magistrates court. He was promptly fined £150. Even the band was hoisted by its own petard, when drummer Nick Barker was arrested for wearing the garment in the port of Dover the following year waiting to catch a ferry. He was released two hours later and still made the band's slot at the Dynamo Festival in Holland. The T-shirt would go on to cause controversy for years afterwards in a number of incidents.[3] Rapper Iggy Azalea wore the shirt in an Instagram post from New Year's Eve 2018/19.[4] She subsequently removed it. It is still not wise to call the Son of God a cunt.

The T-shirt coincided with Cradle of Filth's second full-length album, *Dusk . . . and Her Embrace* (1996). It was a new formulation of the deadly serious black metal forged in eighties' Sweden by Bathory and propelled to infamy by the inner circle of its second wave in the early nineties. Cradle of Filth instilled black metal with a new gothic sensuousness. In doing so, frontman Dani Filth had an uncanny knack of capturing the public imagination. His vocal range varied from growls to high-pitched shrieks to somewhere of his own hysterical level: a unique falsetto scream unmistakeable and impossible to imitate. But it was easy to make fun of it. During Bloodbath's *Wacken Carnage* set in

2005, Mikael Åkerfeldt exhorted the audience to respond to him in a death metal growl, then higher pitched screams, and then finally a 'Dani Filth voice'.

At university, an appreciation of black metal was one of the more unusual ways to bond with fellow freshers. I met 'French' Ed (he was French and called Ed) one night when he latched on to the fact I was wearing an Emperor T-shirt. Ed really loved Cradle of Filth. The theatricality of Dani Filth was a massive part of it. Ed was quite flamboyant himself. He had written an ultra-violent horror novel as a pre-teen and appeared on a French talk show to discuss it alongside Jean-Michel Jarre. He still had his telephone number.

On *Dusk . . . and her Embrace*, Dani Filth is accompanied by spoken-word passages and backing vocals by a classically trained singer, Sarah Jezebel Deva. The songs are full of ornate melodicism as much as they are savage speed and Barker's relentless battery. The lyrics of songs like 'Funeral in Carpathia' and 'A Gothic Romance (Red Roses for the Devil's Whore)' concern seduction, 'supreme vampiric evil' and, most crucially, 'vulvic revelry'. Cradle of Filth's music objectifies women in every sense: they are treated as idols of reverence and respect, but also of a leering male fascination. The near-softcore artwork of previous album *The Principle of Evil Made Flesh* (1994) and EP *V Empire or Dark Faerytales in Phallustein* (1996) constituted naked glamour models daubed in blood and depicted in fantasy scenarios of lesbian lust. They used the photographic archive of the S&M-leaning Redemption Films in homage to a kinky and rather cheap Hammer horror aesthetic.

On *Dusk*'s title track and Cradle of Filth's subsequent concept album, *Cruelty and the Beast* (1998), Countess Elizabeth Bathory takes centre stage: 'Elizabeth/My heart belongs to thee'. She was a legendary figure from European history who was supposedly a vampire of genocidal proportions in the vein of Vlad the Impaler. But accompanying her are other powerful female figures, such as Sumerian goddess Ereshkigal (who governs the nether world, a 'land of return', death and darkness into which her sister and enemy Inanna descends);[5] Lucrecia, a Roman noblewoman whose rape triggered the rebellion which converted Rome from monarchy to a republic; as well as Edgar Allen Poe's raven-haired beauty, Ligeia, from his short story of the same name published in 1838. Dani Filth's storytelling is a whirling collision of the gothic, fetish-club eroticism and as many mythic tropes as he can cram in.

The overall effect is intoxicating and at once transports us to a wooded Transylvanian landscape. Dani Filth superimposes it onto the flatlands of his native Suffolk, itself populated by the ghosts of the witch-hunts that took place there during the seventeenth-century English Civil War. Cradle of Filth's songs, as verbose, convoluted and deeply atmospheric as they are, are part of a gothic tradition of transgressive lust that stretches back to Samuel Taylor Coleridge's 'Christabel', a poem written in the late eighteenth century. In the poem, the titular character becomes bewitched by a woman called Geraldine, who bears a strange mark on her body. Their encounter takes place amongst a host of supernatural ephemera, such as Geraldine's inability to cross water. The poem was supposedly a template for Sheridan Le Fanu's influential short story 'Carmilla', published in his collection *In a Glass Darkly* in 1872. Like Geraldine, Carmilla is a mysterious and beautiful young woman who is entrusted to the care of a family and their daughter, Laura. Also, like Geraldine, Carmilla cannot cross a boundary without invitation. This time, she is revealed to be a vampire as well as the subject of Laura's

overt desire, entwining the sickness of Carmilla's vampiric afflic-
tion and the pair's attraction to each other.

The push–pull tension of their obsession plays out like the
dialogue of one of Cradle of Filth's black metal paeans. As narrated
by Laura:

> She used to place her pretty arms about my neck, draw me near
> to her, and laying her cheek to mine, murmur with lips near
> my ear, 'Dearest, your little heart is wounded; think me not
> cruel because I obey the irresistible law of my strength and
> weakness; if your dear heart is wounded, my wild heart bleeds
> with yours. In the rapture of my enormous humiliation I live in
> your warm life, and you shall die – into mine. I cannot help it;
> as I draw near to you, you, in your turn, will draw near to
> others, and learn the rapture of your cruelty, which yet is love;
> so, for a while, seek to know no more of me and mine, but trust
> me with all your loving spirit.'[6]

Cruelty and love bleed into each other. Perhaps it is the fact
that its story is told so well in 'Carmilla' that Cradle of Filth's most
overt reference to the character is in the instrumental that was
originally recorded as part of *Dusk . . . and Her Embrace* and then
resurrected as a bonus track, 'Carmilla's Masque'. A keyboard-led
piece of music, icy notes akin to rain tinkle over dramatic percussive rumbles and tolling bells; a woman weeps and another
disdainfully laughs among the synth-strings.

Carmilla and Laura's relationship is illicit and titillating, and
also ambiguous. Cradle of Filth's portrayal of love is savage and
also beautiful. It echoes Norwegian artist Edvard Munch's 1895
painting *Love and Pain*, in which a flame-haired woman leans
into the exposed neck of a male lover, commonly interpreted as a

vampire sinking her teeth into her victim. The painting is also known as *Vampire*. As Cradle of Filth describe the act on the song 'Dusk and Her Embrace' itself: 'Bequeath to me thy fiery kiss/To sever thin mortality'.

Cradle of Filth took black metal over the boundary into a sensuous, near-pornographic place. Though they toured with Norwegian black metal bands such as Emperor, their rose-tinted, lush productions differed greatly from the austere, folklore-driven extremity of the second wave of Scandinavian black metal. The inner, satanic black circle of the Oslo scene was infamous for church burnings and murder and its central figure was Øystein Aarseth, a.k.a. Euronymous, the guitarist of Mayhem. He was immortalised in the 2019 film adaptation of the 1997 book *Lords of Chaos: The Bloody Rise of the Satanic Metal Underground*, directed by ex-Bathory member and pop video director Jonas Åkerlund. Euronymous had shot into worldwide consciousness two decades before, when he was brutally murdered by band-mate Varg Vikernes on 10 August 1993.

Euronymous had run a label called Deathlike Silence and was determined to realise black metal's ornate gothic potential, want-ing to leave sex to the side. As Ivar Bjørnson, the guitarist of his friends in the band Enslaved told me, 'That's where he saw black metal or extreme metal, as a continuation of these [artistic traits], not as a new punk thing where we were wading in blood and pissing on people's heads, but more of an impressionist black-and-white. A gothic cathedral is the picture that he wanted to paint with music – like the *Nosferatu* movie before vampires became sexy. Where things are cold and derived from human emotion but contain the larger energies.'

Euronymous was akin to a travelling apostle, spreading the bad news of the black metal genre. He taught more sophisticated guitar-playing techniques – the chilling diminished chords and chromatic scales which gave black metal so much of its grand, intimidating atmosphere. He also recommended the forefathers of sequencer music such as Klaus Schulze and Brian Eno.

He walked where he wanted to walk, musically speaking, producing at least one masterpiece in Mayhem's *De Mysteriis Dom Sathanas* (1994). It bears a monochromatic image of Trondheim's Nidaros Cathedral cast in blue on the cover. It is the only Mayhem album to feature both Euronymous and his eventual murderer, Vikernes. Bjørnson told me: 'He was really important and, as a guitarist he was very, very interested to the point of obsessed in new ways of using the guitar to create a larger sound. Now it's commonplace but in those days when we heard the demo tapes of *De Mysteriis Dom Sathanas* it was crazy. No one had thought of using more than maybe two or three strings at most – that's what they were doing beforehand, and now there were several guitars with several harmonies on top of each other. There were glissandos and all these kinds of things that his friends had picked up from classical music and so on, and prog rock. And he would bring his guitar, go round on trips visiting his bands on his label: we'd sit around for three or four hours and he'd teach techniques and riffs and so on, bring along some new vinyl recommendations. And that's the relationship we had with the guy.'

If Cradle of Filth are associated with the gothic figure of Carmilla, then Euronymous is more like Melmoth from *Melmoth the Wanderer*, another classic of gothic literature, written by Charles Maturin and published in 1820. Melmoth is an immortal man, condemned to walk the Earth for ever due to a pact with the devil. As the character himself puts it, he is ' "a being who was commissioned on an unutterable errand – even to tempt spirits in woe, at their last mortal extremity, to barter their hopes of future happiness for a short remission of their temporary suffer-ings" ".[7] Within its structure of numerous narratives-within-narratives, Melmoth seems to visit one incarcerated subject of his infernal interest at will. The person reports their encounter:

> 'I felt I had never beheld such eyes blazing in a mortal face – in the darkness of my prison, I held up my hand to shield myself from their preternatural glare . . . he came and retired appar-ently without help or hindrance – that he came, like one who had a key to the door of my dungeon, at all hours, without leave or forbiddance – that he traversed the prisons of the Inquisition, like one who had a master-key to its deepest recesses.'[8]

Euronymous held black metal's master key. Though he is not remembered with the fear that Melmoth rouses in those he encounters, he was accused of involvement in the church burn-ings that defined Norwegian black metal in 1993. As with Cradle of Filth's *Vestal Masturbation* T-shirt outrage, it made the Oslo music scene the subject of British tabloid fascination.

Just as the beautiful wooden Fantoft stave church in Bergen, Norway, burned on 6 June 1992, in *Melmoth the Wanderer* the Spanish Inquisition's headquarters in Madrid is set ablaze: 'The night was intensely dark, but so strong was the light of the confla-gration, that I could see the spire blazing, from the reflected lustre, like a meteor.'[9] An impassive witness of the scene – though, like Euronymous, never directly implicated in causing the blaze – is the silhouette of Melmoth, 'a human figure placed on a pinna-cle of the spire, and surveying the scene in perfect tranquility.'[10]

II. Of Wolf and Man

Kristoffer Rygg was just fifteen years old when he first entered the gloomy, 'tomblike' atmosphere of Oslo's Helvete ('Hell') record shop, run by the twenty-two-year-old Euronymous.[11] The shop formed the dark nucleus of the second wave of Norwegian black metal. The older denizens of the store would press demos, purportedly 'pure evil', into his hands. Typical of the initiation rites of the shop, it took Rygg a year to work his way into its inner circle. He also understood he needed something a little different musically to push his band Ulver – Norwegian for 'wolves' – through some of the mundanity that already marked the scene. On nights out in Oslo he repeatedly approached Jon 'Metalion' Kristiansen, who ran the Head Not Found label, and told him that he should sign Ulver. When Rygg sent him a five-track demo the band had recorded called *Vargnatt* ('*Wolf Night*'), Kristiansen soon agreed.[12]

The press release Kristiansen sent out in spring 1995 outlined the first three Ulver albums that Head Not Found were planning to release. It described Ulver's music as '*trolsk*' ('lugubrious') metal that emitted a melancholy inspired by, and emanating from, the Norwegian landscape. The first album, *Bergtatt* (or *Spellbound: A Folktale in Five Parts*) (1995), was not far from the flowery and, at times, somewhat ridiculous poetic mannerisms of Cradle of Filth. It drew on Norwegian folk tales and wolf mythology in lyrics written in an old Norwegian linguistic style. This was pleasingly translated into an 'olde English' equivalent for the liner notes of the *Trolsk Sortmetall* (*Trollish Black Metal*) box set, released in 2014. For example, the first album is set in a medieval world where 'Norwegian Nighte turns colde/When howling wolves do sing' ('Capitel III: Graablick Blev Hun Vaer'/'Part Three: She senses Eyne of Grey').

Rygg obligingly wrote brief mission statements for their album sleeves: 'Through Ulver, we have tried to draw a musickall Picture of a different Realitie: A Mythickall Worlde of Phantasie that will not fade, change or sink into Oblivion.' This was the start of a creative approach to 'potent imagery' and artistic sources that fuelled their career from that point onwards, as Rygg put it to me, 'almost paraphrasing certain national poets or folklorists – things we were obsessing about back then'. *Bergtatt* hones in on traditions of abduction in Norse mythology and the figure of Huldra, a creature masquerading as a fair maiden who lures men into the realms of the 'Netherworlde'. As the album title is literally translated, 'spirited away by the mountain'. Such representations of wild, free women – the goddesses and temptresses of nature – have a dangerous and fascinating allure, often leading to men's downfall. The male subjects of Cradle of Filth's songs run into the arms of these women, whereas Ulver's are kidnapped by them. There is something fearful and chaste about this period of Norwegian black metal.

Ulver's second album, *Kveldssanger* (*Twilight Songs*) (1996), explored the acoustic and incantatory heritage of ancient Norse music. Their lupine storytelling found its ultimate realisation on their third album, *Nattens Madrigal* (*Night of the Madrigal*) (1997). The album was deliberately made to sound as scratchy and primitive as possible and rumours swirled around its release, the best being that it was recorded in the forest as the band blew their recording budget elsewhere.[13] Structured into eight 'hymns' which each focus on some aspect of the relationship between wolf and man, the songs take the form of chapters telling a tale of a tragic figure – a 'Wanderer in this infernal night' ('Hymne III: Of Wolf and Hatred') – who is damned to avenge lost love by destroying his former lover, his victim ensnared by the cursed magic within him.

In his notes for the album, Rygg stated, 'We see the Werewolf as an Image of the Beast in Man . . . in the presentation of this concept it hath been natural for us to choose a violent musickall Expression, seeing that the lycanthropicall Idea embodieth much untamed force.' But the music, though certainly forceful and definitely primitive (you can hear them plugging their guitars into the cranked-up Marshall JCM 800 amps), is carefully wrought and, despite its buzzing harshness, moments of melodic sophistication, rare in the genre, are frequently uncovered. This is particularly clear in the sparse acoustic break a minute into 'Hymne I: Of Wolf and Fear' followed by the interplay between the guitars singing through their two channels and delineating a textured, moving passage from the 2 minute 22 second mark that speaks to the beauty lurking beneath the ferocity of black metal. Werewolves make explicit the lonely outcast figure in history. They were woven into the folklore of Europe much like vampires, and with *Nattens Madrigal* Ulver were soaking up the gothic werewolves of writers Sabine Baring-Gould and Montague Summers. But Ulver were about to shape-shift themselves.

Nattens Madrigal was their definitive black metal statement. It was recorded in 1995 and by the time it was released, two years later, Rygg had come to think that the mythological well they were drawing on was running a little dry. For many listeners it enthroned them as the ultimate black metal band. Not one, but both, of Tony Soprano's children had Ulver's *Nattens Madrigal* cover art as a poster on their walls in HBO's *The Sopranos* (presumably the same poster used twice to decorate the respective bedrooms).

Much of what fascinated Rygg was drawn from a wider, Christianised canon of work, including gnostics like William Blake. Ulver soon departed on a new sonic journey that began with *Themes from William Blake's The Marriage of Heaven and Hell* (1998). They then really opened up new, cinematic vistas on *Perdition City*, subtitled *Music to an Interior Film*, in 2000 – an album awash with pulsating electronica and a more avant-garde expressionism.

Ulver's 2017 album *The Assassination of Julius Caesar* started with a title representing an event which Rygg told me was 'a pivotal moment in history', one that changed society. Classical Rome is a natural destination for Ulver – a place where, like its founders Romulus and Remus, the band can be, as Rygg puts it, 'sucking on the tit of the wolf mother'. The album signalled a shift that even for Ulver was extreme: a move into pop music. But rather than the pop of Ariana Grande or Katy Perry, this was a solemn pop more akin to Depeche Mode and Tears For Fears, and the longest distance it seemed possible to be from their roots. That said, the album is a collision of imagery across history, marrying the classical and ancient to the contemporary – those things that were analogous or conspicuous to the band, common denominators that amount to what Rygg describes as 'an associative journey in time and space'.

Opening track 'Nemoralia' is named after a festival of light in honour of the Roman goddess Diana, but is also about the great fire of Rome that occurred on 18 and 19 July AD 64 under the emperor Nero's watch. It refers to his burning of Christians at the stake as a consequence, the bodies of whom 'Illuminate the garden/human candles'. Most arresting is a reference to another Diana, Princess of Wales, hunted to her death by the paparazzi in August 1997 when she was killed in a car crash with her lover Dodi Fayed in a tunnel in Paris – 'Her sexual drive/Stop dead under the river'. Rygg describes the band as having a thing for the 'blue-blood' traditions of England. They are fascinated by the

British royal family, as much as they are with papal ceremony: 'We've had our eye turned towards Rome and the Vatican business for a long time.'

This fascination started with 2005's *Blood Inside* and was consecrated with a follow-up EP of *Caesar* off-cuts in 2017 titled *Sic Transit Gloria Mundi* (Latin for *Thus Passes Earthly Glory*). On 'Echo Chamber (Room of Tears)', the titular room is where a newly elected pope puts aside his cardinal's red robes and dons the papal white, often overwhelmed by private emotion. In the song, Rygg makes a connection between the seventy-seven participants in the papal election, the seventy-seven slain by Anders Breivik in Oslo and on the island of Utøya on 22 July 2009, and the 7/7 terrorist attacks in London in 2005. Ulver sought to write a lyric with the emotional distance and dispassionate perspective of a news feed. As Rygg sings on another song, 'So Falls The World': 'Tragedies repeat themselves/In perfect circles'. Ulver aim to get at the heavy truth of tragedies repeated down the years. As Rygg put it to me, the song was 'a realisation of the nature of man and things, and just how exposed and vulnerable we are as human beings. Thus passes the glory of the world, quite simply.' Ulver's concern is one of being pursued by the past, as it catches up with the present: 'History haunts us, it's been haunting us for years and years and years. At some point you just have to acknowledge the fucking Armageddon.'

By framing these things in a grand pop style, Ulver position themselves as documenting the decline of the post-World War II liberal consensus much as the Roman empire did, two thousand years earlier. In doing so they pose a question, as Rygg formulates it for me: 'How long will the ghosts of our time haunt us? What will they call us? The World War Era? The Genocidal Age?'. The teenager who made the *Trolsk Sortmetall* trilogy is somewhere inside Rygg, who is still inspired by the aesthetics of history and art rather than an ideology, which is why images – such as Bernini's sculpture of *The Ecstasy of Saint Teresa*, and the 'screaming pope' of Francis Bacon's 1953 study of Velázquez's portrait of Pope Innocent X – are found on their album covers or in their booklets. The forces and motivations that got Ulver howling at the moon in the nineties remain, as a remnant. The heaviness is certainly still there, as far as Rygg is concerned: 'I guess there's a sort of underlying minor chord, if we're going for an overarching metaphor.'

In making a pop album with a deep, reverberant sound, Ulver ultimately departed from their roots. When breaking the chains of their past became their modus operandi twenty years previously, Ulver set a new expectation of continual change. They do dwell in the past when they want, but understand staying too long risks self-indulgence ('past redemption, set for nostalgia' as they sign off their acknowledgements in the 2014 trilogy box set). When they cover Frankie Goes to Hollywood's 'The Power of Love' on the *Sic Transit* EP, and live, it is from childhood love, irony-free, and is true to an emotional intensity that is eminently heavy. In one of those pleasing and uncanny ahistorical connections that Rygg likes to make, 'The Power of Love' nods to Ulver's wolfish past and Cradle of Filth's vampiric lusts, when the lyric promises, 'I'll protect you from the hooded claw/Keep the vampires from your door'.

Rygg's rich, sonorous voice is vulnerable, but on 'The Power of Love' is bolstered through the melodious FX and pop prism of the 1980s. It has a similar quality to the late Scott Walker. Walker's journey is particularly relevant here. Even in the sixties, after leaving the Walker Brothers, his songs were infused with heaviness. The grating, discordant strings underlying 'It's Raining

Today' and the depiction of haunted protagonist 'Rosemary' (both from *Scott 3*, released in 1969) demonstrate how the order and lushness of pop is only a hair's breadth away from the heaviest matter. The croon becomes a voice echoing back from the cold distance.

Walker's descent further into the underworld following his sixties heyday was captured in the documentary film made about his life in 2006, *Scott Walker: 30 Century Man*. He forayed deeper and deeper into the cavern still with the avant-garde deconstruction of *Tilt* (1995) and the breathtaking ominousness of *The Drift* (2006). This culminated in his collaboration with Sunn O))) on 2014's *Soused*, working with the hooded proponents of massive amplifier damage in service to a drone that amounted to some of Walker's most accessible (and perverse) late period songwriting. Ulver also made a collaborative album with Sunn O))), *Terrestrials*, released earlier the same year. As such, both artists have closed the circle on heavy music's relationship with pop – an achievement underlined when Walker died in 2019. Like Walker, Ulver have made pop music that is definitively heavy. Heaviness has long been knocking at the door of the mainstream: it sounds like it has finally been let in.

III. Break down this door

Andrzej Żuławski's 1981 film *Possession* is a melodramatic depiction of the dissolution of a relationship. It won Isabelle Adjani a best actress award at the Cannes film festival, even though the film was subsequently banned in the UK as a 'video nasty'. Her character Anna is locked into a mutually destructive downward spiral with her husband Mark, played by Sam Neill. The film has a thread of grotesque, lustful body horror, revolving around a horrific tentacled creature hidden away in a decrepit east Berlin flat. But the real intensity of the film is drawn out of the collapse of Mark and Anna's marriage. One argument in their kitchen sees them take turns cutting themselves with an electric carving knife. The film is perhaps most (in)famous for a jaw-dropping scene in which Anna undergoes a violent paroxysm in a subway tunnel, blood and other liquids seeping from multiple places as she thrashes around the space like a whirling dervish. The scene is both a literal and figurative depiction of a miscarriage.

This sequence was a direct inspiration for the frantic, dissonant climax of Oathbreaker's 'Second Son of R.' video, directed by Jeroen Mylle and Fabrice Parent, a.k.a Maanlander. In it, singer Caro Tanghe lies on her back and is shot from above, her limbs in paroxysms of fevered movement as they create patterns on a layer of black sand. It is a nightmarish performance art piece that is a good approximation of Adjani's movement in the subway scene from *Possession*. 'Second Son of R.' is taken from the Belgian band's third album, *Rheia* (2016). In a reversal of the story at the end of Ulver's *Nattens Madrigal*, the album opens with a delicate, bewitching song called '10:56' that recounts finding a male lover with his head dashed against the cobblestones of the 'back alley to our house' where his 'skull merged with the surface'. '10:56' is a US police code that can mean an intoxicated pedestrian and also a suicide. The 'starving beast within my chest' of third track 'Being Able to Feel Nothing' also portrays a bloody act of self-mutilation, a hollowing-out with a knife by the narrator (not unlike Anna and Mark's mutual self-harming in *Possession*). With blood dripping all over the floor, the subjects of the song are able to walk into the sunlight, the weight gone, finally able to feel nothing.

Oathbreaker was formed in the Belgian city of Ghent by Tanghe and guitarist Gilles Demolder. They both came from Belgian seaside towns before they moved to Ghent as the nearest big population centre: Demolder was from De Haan and Tanghe from Blankenberg. When their music is aggressive it is positively savage – Tanghe's voice is hellishly abrasive, ripping her throat to shreds in the service to her red-raw storytelling. Yet she can also sing cleanly and – with her billows of long brown hair, often wearing a dark cloak onstage – she looks like she has stepped out of the shadows of a Cradle of Filth record, before eviscerating everyone in sight.

On *Rheia*, Oathbreaker took black metal and twisted it back further for their own purposes, until it began to look like something completely different. If Demolder could not make something work on the guitar – if physically stretching his hand to apply the shape needed for a chord became impossible – he would simply retune his instrument to make it doable. Incorporating shimmering, reflective passages and spaces in the onslaught of *Rheia*, Oathbreaker moved from the blackened hardcore of their earlier work to the territory explored by artists like Deafheaven and Liturgy, fellow exponents of 'blackgaze', the term coined to describe a more ethereal, shoegazing form of twenty-first-century black metal. But this description ill serves the violence in Oathbreaker's sound – in the band's eyes, Oathbreaker is not black metal anyway.

Their songs are intimate and savage – take the depiction of the death of a loved one in the hospital scene of 'Needles in Your Skin'. This scours with lightning-fast guitar runs in the full diminished chords that Euronymous defined for the genre, but then pauses to pick out moments of mellow profundity in the melee. As he reflected to me, it is part of Demolder's mission to make black metal somehow more 'gentle' and to make both him as a player and his listener, 'smile in a sad way'. There is a strong current of self-help running through the album, an attempt by Tanghe and Demolder to get to know themselves better in a 'welcoming' musical mode.

Rheia is structured according to the tenets of a theory called the Johari Window, about self-awareness, which Demolder studied as part of a degree in social work. He explained to me that they arranged the album's songs into four sections: the first comprises those things known about the subject that everyone knows (The Known Self); the second, those things known by the subject but that no one else knows (The Hidden Self); the third, what is known about the subject that they themselves don't know (The Blind Self), and the fourth being what no one knows about the subject (The Unknown Self). The sections were used and manipulated by Demolder and Tanghe to drive home the album's key messages about the red thread of fate that tied them together: sex. This compartmentalising of different selves has something in common with the 'disowned' selves that Dr Kate Quinn (from the opening of this book) seeks to honour as part of her voice-therapy mental health work. In both cases these selves are invested into heavy music, and for Oathbreaker particularly, give it structure.

The band recorded a session of the first five songs from *Rheia* for music platform Audiotree when they toured America in late 2016, just after the album's release. Backed by Deathwish Inc., the label owned by hardcore band Converge's Jacob Bannon, *Rheia* broke them out of the underground. Like Napalm Death's remarkable first BBC session for John Peel in 1987, the Audiotree session crackles with the energy of a band on a massive upsurge. But it was after the high of those early *Rheia* shows that things began to fall apart. Demolder felt events began to run out of his control. That worked against his desire for Oathbreaker to be a positive, 'major chord' project: 'I don't like to listen to music which has a negative energy whereas I feel with Oathbreaker that it gets to a positive vibe in the music where you overcome things instead of letting yourself hang.'

Tanghe and Demolder's relationship, the one at the centre of Oathbreaker, one-part lyrics, one-part music, started to break down – drink, drugs and the hardships of touring made the band a brittle and increasingly bitter unit. Demolder questioned whether the layers of guitars and cloak of distortion the band played behind actually provided somewhere to hide. Listening to the stripped-back music of bands like Low and Shellac he was reminded how much power could be found in the acoustic guitar and that all of Oathbreaker's material was written on the acoustic guitar given to him by his mother. Not that acoustic music doesn't feature in their catalogue. From the closing title track of 2011's *Mælstrøm* to *Rheia*'s 'Stay Here/*Accroche-Moi*', they haven't been afraid to peel back those layers. Demolder particularly looked to Mount Eerie, a heartbreaking project from singer-songwriter Phil Elverum that is almost unspeakably sad.

Mount Eerie's *A Crow Looked At Me* (2017) concerned the death of Elverum's wife Geneviève Castrée from pancreatic cancer, diagnosed four months after the birth of their daughter. He recorded the material in the room she died in with an acoustic guitar, one microphone and a laptop. On the song 'Real Death', Elverum addresses the way that songwriting itself is futile in the face of a grief so real and so overwhelming: 'When real death enters the house all poetry is dumb'. The album was released as Oathbreaker were starting to fray at the seams and Demolder was struck by how *A Crow Looked At Me* showed that 'gentle stuff can be way heavier'. Elverum surprised him by showing that 'acoustic guitar and words can be so much heavier than anything I've heard before'. It begged the question of whether metal's lashings of distortion actually *masks* heavy emotional truths. Metal is bathed in a sonic fury that is perhaps also a method for diffusing pain and removing feelings like encrusted dirt: to avoid looking the crow in its black eyes.

Cradle of Filth crossed an invisible line when they suffused black metal with the gothic. Ulver made a defining album of lo-fi cult appeal almost as a meta-comment on the genre's ridiculous adherence to its own strictures. They repeatedly shape-shifted for the next twenty years, reaching further back than their old Norse origins in nineties' Oslo to classical Rome and eighties' pop. Oathbreaker want to strip it all back and disappear into near-nothingness, to recover the essence of heaviness hiding beneath the tyranny of distorted guitars. Gilles Demolder thinks that the only way forward for him (and, who knows, perhaps the black metal genre as a whole) is to 'destroy and rebuild every time', to 'get to the point where you've completely lost it', and, ultimately, to 'kill stuff from the past'. To let transgressions go and to let dead things lie.

5
LEAVING THE WORLD BEHIND

'Smoke went up from His nostrils,/And devouring fire
from His mouth; Coals were kindled by it'– *Psalms* 18:8[1]

'I only went out for a walk, and finally concluded
to stay out till sundown, for going out, I found, was
really going in' – John Muir, *John of the Mountains:
The Unpublished Journals of John Muir*[2]

Sometimes, the Earth is not enough. Who hasn't wanted to get off their heads and find solace in the clouds? Fuelled by a propensity for psychedelic drug experimentation and marijuana worship, as well as escapist science-fiction landscapes and cloying horror narratives, Sleep, Electric Wizard and Elder are creating new pathways to ascend into cosmic bliss. But they are hampered by the gravity of reality. The heaviest band covered in this book, Primitive Man, are testament to the fact that the struggle to escape reality avoids the more difficult task at hand: to stare it unremittingly in the face.

I. Departure

Al Cisneros was finished with music. For five years, he had struggled to bring the hour-long-plus epic he had composed with his band Sleep – *Dopesmoker* – back to the ground. It was a song that wanted to keep going and going and the band had entered the studio at 10 a.m. every day to write, get high and perfect what their producer Billy Anderson has described as 'the heaviest thing ever recorded'.[3]

Now it was done and London Records rejected it: it was too long, the production was too raw, the whole thing was just too much. It didn't help that the band had allegedly blown their $75,000 advance on custom-made 'Green' amplification by guitars and considerable amounts of LSD and marijuana. When they weren't wrestling with the song, guitarist Matt Pike and drummer Chris Hakius would flip beaten-up old cars to high school students for thousands of dollars more than they were worth, do sporadic manual labour and whatever else they could to keep it together.[4] Cisneros did screen-printing on the side, but the psychic toll exerted by the project became too much and when the label suggested getting in a high-profile mixer to improve the sound and suggested slicing the song into segments – renaming it *Jerusalem* in the process – the band's relationships began to strain. By the time *Jerusalem* was released in February 1999, they had split up.

That is when the song's journey really begins and with it the legend of its recording: over the years, it has gradually acquired the status of a narco-sonic masterpiece of heavy art without parallel. Music as ceremonial ritual, it imagines a distant planet where – as Cisneros describes in thunderous prayer-chants – a 'caravan migrates through deep sandscape'. This caravan is

populated by 'weedians', or 'lungsmen', who follow the creed of
the 'Hasheehian'. They are on a journey to the 'riff-filled land' as
the lyrics collide Judeo-Christian prophecy with a wide-eyed,
delirious stoner-religious zeal. It is a syncretic vision that shares
a lot with the 'grounding' ritual of Rastafarianism.

Damian Marley has put weed's spiritual significance thus: 'For
Rastafarians, herb is our sacrament. I'd compare it to incense in
church, or the body of Christ in a communion.'[5] In a refinement
of the grounding ritual's communion with Jah while burning the
herb, in *Dopesmoker* the marijuana plant is the object of worship
itself: 'Earthling inserts to chalice the green cutchie/Groundation
soul finds trust upon smoking hose'. The overriding message is
one of escape from the toil of the quotidian. The opening line is
the key to it all: 'Drop out of life with bong in hand'.

The song is structured into a series of movements, themselves
containing slow, quasi-oriental melodic patterns. The intention
behind *Dopesmoker* is to convey the hypnotised state the band
would go into while playing it. It is a meditative act driven by the
drums, but powered by the guitars. The structure has its own
written guide. As a flavour – it opens with 'DEPARTURE MATT
4X', works through 'SONIC TITAN ALL 4X', 'HOTEL ROOM
ALL 4X' and the excellently named 'HOT LAVA MAN 4X ALL
SLOW (VOCALS)', etc. This document was printed to resemble a
weathered, religious parchment on the back of a new line of
T-shirts after the record was remixed and remastered in 2012.

Dopesmoker is a masterwork in heaviness and one with some
similarities to long, powerful symphonic works. Professor John
Deathridge points to this as an example of heavy music's 'unusual
alignments of the vertical – dense-sounding instants – and hori-
zontal lines': 'If you compare the opening of [Wagner's] *The Ring*,
for example, with Sleep's *Jerusalem*,[6] the provocative thing about

them both is the fixation on a single pitch/chord/sound – E flat and C respectively. Wagner's only lasts a mere 137 or so bars, while Sleep's goes on for over fifty minutes. But the effect is similar in the sense that they both give a sense of "security", firm base, etc., but also with variation of texture around the base that give an increasing sense of insecurity. The listener begins to lose him or herself in the sheer sound.'

When *Dopesmoker* was revived in 2012 in its definitive version, it was given new artwork by Arik Roper, who visualised the weedians with their elaborate smoking headgear, leading camel-like pack animals across the orange sand of a distant planet. The artwork strongly evokes Frank Herbert's 1965 novel *Dune* and the barren planet Arrakis, where its chief commodity, the spice 'melange', is a drug that increases your life force and prescience: the spice is life. For Sleep, marijuana is their spice.

In the battle that the making of *Dopesmoker* represents – between a band's craft and what record companies perceive as a product they need to sell – *Dune* has further resonance. The Mexican director Alejandro Jodorowsky attempted to make an adaptation of *Dune* in the mid-seventies that remains one of the greatest near-misses in cinema: Salvador Dali to star; Pink Floyd to soundtrack; Moebius, Chris Foss and H. R. Giger provided concept art. The documentary about its failure, *Jodorowsky's Dune* (2013), is an essential document of ambition and folly. The parallels with the science-fiction settings of *Dune* and *Dopesmoker* are also intriguing, with the main difference between the two works being that the Jodorowsky version of *Dune* can only be experienced by reading one of the few copies of the thousand-page book of elaborate storyboards the director commissioned from Moebius. *Dopesmoker* can be experienced in three different recorded forms and when the band still plays long excerpts of it live. In addition, Sleep's previous album (*Sleep's Holy Mountain*) was named for an earlier Jodorowsky film, the psychedelic fantasy *The Holy Mountain*.

When a song is as long as *Dopesmoker* it forces you to make time to listen to it. This is unusual for the twenty-first century, when music is squeezed into the interstices of people's lives. The song demands its own headspace. Its heaviness lies in its message of outward escapism and the journey inward that follows, as the listener slowly synchronises with the undulations of its drones, which slowly evolve to describe the mountains of the mind. The onslaught on, and of, the senses is paramount here. Professor Deathridge told me that Wagner's own idea of sonic overwhelmingness came out of a dream about rushing water from which he awoke with a sense of fear. Deathridge's view of *Dopesmoker*'s form of heaviness is that 'you get caught up in the sound and its unfolding, lose your bearings, intentionally not defined by the absence of predictable cadences, the mesmerising repetitions, the sheer spaced-outedness of it all'. When you awake from this deepest of sleeps, the plotted mesmerism of *Dopesmoker*, have your anxieties been assuaged? Did you manage to escape them for ever? Or is the risk of inhaling such a heavy sonic strain actually total psychic overload – the risk of not being able to return? For many years, the 'marijuanaut' members of Sleep were drifting in space, ploughing their energies into other musical projects which could not capture the massive ambition and journeying of their sacred, resin-soaked magnum opus.

When the band eventually reformed and later toured the *Dopesmoker* reissue, they played the All Tomorrow's Parties festival at Alexandra Palace, London, on 25 May 2012, headlined by Slayer (playing their own classic *Reign in Blood* in full – a whole album under half the running time of *Dopesmoker*). I watched

Sleep take to the stage of the grand hall of the building in the late afternoon. The sun streamed through the high windows to the side of the stage as the band launched their set with the opening sixteen minutes of the song, culminating in Pike's sprawling first solo. The venue is situated on a prominent hill overlooking the city and was the location of the first television broadcasts of the 1930s. I imagined the palace's still-operational giant masts broadcasting the departure of the sonic pilgrimage up into space, reaching a far-flung, dune-swept planet, promising what the song calls the 'caravan's stoned deliverance'.

II. Return

Two decades after recording *Dopesmoker*, Sleep surprise-released a new album called *The Sciences* in 2018 on 20 April, otherwise known as 4/20, a date associated with the celebration of smoking marijuana. *The Sciences* also contained a new epic recording, albeit only fourteen minutes long this time: 'Antarcticans Thawed'.

This shifted the band's view from outer space, and the sun-blemished sands of another planet, to the polar regions of Earth. Depicting an 'Antarctic legion' freed by the warmth of the sun's rays – 'Blood thaws throughout the unused veins' – the unspecified subjects of the song then travel in thrall to a 'stoned priest/Hierophant' as the icebergs around them rise 'as war machines'.

When Sleep originally reformed in 2009, Cisneros declared onstage that 'Antarcticans Thawed' was 'a new song from a long time ago'. As such, it is a companion piece to *Dopesmoker* which warns us about the human urge for exploration and the heavy consequences of journeying into the unknown. It is a powerful allegory for climate change and man's meddling in the balance of nature. The awakening of 'Matterhorn's children' is played out in the encroaching menace of the song.

The track begins with Cisneros's insistent, single-note bass motif, pulsing with the slow heartbeat of life buried under many metres of ice. Jason Roeder (drummer since their first two reunion shows) paradiddles into the gaps and Pike's guitar wraps itself around the beat like an enveloping ice-fog. When the song yawns out to a slow descending chord sequence it amasses the weight and heft of *Dopesmoker* in its loose, droning hypnotism. It echoes out in a sparse and glacial sense of unfamiliarity – its musical patterns exerting the monstrous, deadly slow pressure of pack ice locking the listener in its grasp. Pike's solo is pure free-form, elliptical brilliance. He draws heaviness from the melting permafrost, encased for millennia and surfacing in a tumult that delineates the Antarctic landscape: his guitar lines form seracs, drifts, pressure ridges and glittering ice pinnacles. It melts away to a truly chilling conclusion.

Antarctica was long one of the great unexplored regions of the Earth, with the most significant incursions into its territory happening in the early twentieth century (including Roald Amundsen reaching the geographic South Pole in 1911). It was a subject of fascination for writers who imagined the awakening of unknown, supernatural forces there. One famous example is *At the Mountains of Madness* (1936) by H. P. Lovecraft, with its uncovering of the ancient cities of alien Elder Things and their monstrous, protoplasmic servants called 'shoggoths'. But a more recent book about a fictionalised expedition to the other end of the Earth depicts the collision of European explorers with the reality of survival in the frozen wastes.

The Terror by Dan Simmons, published in 2007 (and turned into a television series by Ridley Scott a decade later), is a reimagining of Sir John Franklin's doomed expedition in the mid-1840s to find the Northwest Passage. It was known as a treacherous, often ice-locked waterway that ran from the Atlantic Ocean to the Pacific Ocean, via the Arctic Ocean, across the top of Canada. The two discovery ships charged with the mission were the *Erebus*, captained by Franklin, and the *Terror*, captained by Francis Crozier. In the historical accounts, the ships were trapped by pack ice after they made their way through the main access point of the Lancaster Sound. They were stuck on the ice for several years in abominable conditions, with the temperature regularly bottoming out at 100 degrees below freezing: no one returned.

In the novel, Simmons heaps on the misery by also imagining them being stalked by a ferocious and gigantic bear-like creature that proceeds to wreak havoc and kill many in the crew. At almost a thousand pages in length, Simmons's novel is a huge, harrowing portrait of the extreme attrition of those freezing conditions, with all its attendant horrors from frostbite to slow starvation to debilitating scurvy.

As the novel progresses, the men abandon ship and make one last pitch for survival. Crozier is rescued from imminent murder at the hands of his mutinous men by an Inuit woman with no tongue taken in by his crew and dubbed 'Lady Silence'. He goes on to be taught about the beliefs of the natives. The white beast is known as a *Tuunbaq*, a 'spirit-animated killing machine'[7] that understands when 'the pale people' invade its territory it will be the end of times. Rather than confront the beast, which he knows he cannot defeat, Crozier elects to become one of the shamans who commune with the spirit world. He undergoes a ceremony in which the *Tuunbaq* bites off his tongue to make an alien form of music by blowing on his vocal cords (!). Earlier in the novel, when one of the other officers sees Lady Silence engaged in this activity with the beast on the ice, he is unable to scream because 'the ceremonial *heaviness* of the moment and his own incapacitating fear kept him silent'.[8]

In *The Terror*, the heavy act is the ceremonial communing with the spirit world, and its foreboding analogue is white people's destruction of the physical world. Sleep's 'Antarcticans Thawed' is another manifestation in art of this truth, drawn out in thunderous, glacial momentousness. It is an old story and will continue to be told as long as humanity continues thrusting into the unknown in the name of scientific progress. That process risks ongoing dislocation from the myths and magic that have been used to understand the furthest reaches of the world by the native people that inhabit them. Sleep's ceremonial stoner-doom metal forces us to reflect on that fact and, by journeying out, allows us to journey in, and maybe reconnect with a primordial knowledge of the world.

Crozier's go-to book when addressing the men on ship is *Leviathan* by the seventeenth-century philosopher Thomas Hobbes. Before he is rescued by Lady Silence, physically and spiritually, Crozier is resolved to Hobbes's conclusion that life (outside society) is 'solitary, poor, nasty, brutish, and short'.[9] What is compelling about Sleep's sonic rituals is that they speak to broader truths than the petty illusions of day-to-day reality, by offering the musical means to celebrate the mysteries of existence. They are part of an ongoing fight against Hobbes's worldview.

However, there is another band who dispenses with any optimism when humanity's place in the universe is concerned. They wrote the line 'I hope this fucking world fucking burns away' on their 1997 album *Come My Fanatics . . .* and have seen little reason to be cheerful since.

III. Let there be doom in Dorset

The Dorset town of Wimborne Minster is unremarkable in some ways. Like similar market towns, its historic centre has seen the encroachment of high-street restaurants and coffee shop brands. But Wimborne, like other parts of Dorset, retains a strong air of the ancient, in its close proximity to villages such as Witchampton and the site of Badbury Rings. Badbury Rings is an Iron Age hill fort that is mooted to be one of the sites of the Battle of Mount Badon between Celtic Britons and Anglo-Saxons. The battle supposedly involved King Arthur, as depicted in *Idylls of the King* (1859) by Alfred, Lord Tennyson. For founding member of Electric Wizard, singer and guitarist Jus Oborn, it is a 'small, weird town' from which the members of his band sought to escape in their music, but which then forced itself into the centre of their hateful vision of the world around them.

In Oborn's eyes the town was 'anti-individuality'; he grew up feeling bullied and alienated. The market square itself was the nexus for the exchange of underground culture – horror films and banned 'video-nasties' were traded under one particular stall, as were transgressive magazines and literature. When Oborn, drummer Mark Greening and bassist Tim Bagshaw were growing up, the town provided a focal point for their stand against mid-nineties' censorship. They asked, 'What's being hidden from me? What am I not being allowed to see?' This way they were exploring the 'occult' in the sense used by David Peace, author of the *Red Riding Quartet* and *The Damned Utd*, who explained in an interview with the BBC in 2004, 'I use the word "occult" to mean hidden – but also as a play on the more grotesque aspects of the word.'[10]

From early forays into gruff, slowed-down death metal, Electric Wizard evolved into presenting a blown-out, cosmically dismal rendering of Black Sabbath's (then reasonably cult) sound. The mindlessness of the everyday in Wimborne lent itself to heavy drug experimentation, particularly weed and acid. Electric Wizard's breakthrough album *Come My Fanatics . . .* was conceived as a story of leaving the Earth behind, in a mission destined to failure. Its second half is a mini-concept album of three songs depicting a spaceship lost in the yawning void of space. As Oborn told me, 'The idea was we'd try and search our universe for another planet to live on, but never find it.'

The billowing weirdness of the harsh, overdriven-to-abstraction guitars, and barely discernible hit-and-miss drums, all amounted to a seething chaos that emulated Oborn's vision of a universe without order, or hope. They wanted to convey an arcane knowledge of our planet heading towards its doom. This was an apocalypse that those 'overground' – people representing authority and 'the man' – were blissfully unaware of. Oborn had read the weird tales of H. P. Lovecraft since he was a teenager. Rather than literalise the horrors of Lovecraft's fiction (most famously the tentacle-faced aquatic cosmic entity Cthulhu), he sought to make music that was as timeless and as dread-laden as those stories.

In seeking to escape Wimborne, Electric Wizard only found themselves drawn further into its vortex. Their masterpiece *Dopethrone* (2000) was an angry, deeply unhappy album with the town at its centre. On the title track, built around a riff of instant-classic immensity and immediacy, 'black amps tear the sky' that hangs forebodingly over 'this land of sorcery'. The album heavily references Lovecraft and the Conan mythology of Ron E. Howard. Howard's character was most famously portrayed by Arnold Schwarzenegger in the 1982 film *Conan the Barbarian*. But *Dopethrone*'s most impactful song is 'I, The Witchfinder'. The album's ten-minute-plus centrepiece, written from the tormentor's perspective, begins with a sample from the 1970 German horror film *Mark of the Devil*. The film was one of the victims of the British video-nasty controversy in the 1980s and seized under the UK's Obscene Publications Act of 1959, before finding itself illicitly traded in places like that market stall in Wimborne.

Mark of the Devil is a brutal, sadistic and misogynistic film, in keeping with the events it portrays – the witch-finding legacy that shames a period of European and American history from the fifteenth to the nineteenth century. The song, even by Electric Wizard's titanic standards, is abominably heavy – its excruciating, chained-to-the-stake sonic oppressiveness is layered with lashings of guitar soloing and juddering bass echoes. It also includes the kinds of experimental soundscapes the band happened upon when they recorded *Come My Fanatics . . .* and started playing around with the sampler left lying around by one of the drum'n'bass artists who frequented the studio.

Electric Wizard fell apart on a tour of the US that followed the next album, *Let Us Prey* (2002), and Oborn was forced to reassemble the band with a different line-up. Rather than the vagaries of malevolent, Lovecraftian Elder Gods, it was Oborn's own legacy that haunted his vision for the band. He found it hard to recapture the lyrical and sonic excesses of the iconic albums Electric Wizard had recorded as a three-piece. To make some extra money, Oborn even surreptitiously sold on eBay recordings of the band's 2005 Radio 1 session. That session boasted a particularly impressive and powerful performance from the band's new drummer, Justin Greaves. Greaves hammered the session recording of 'Dopethrone' into an edifice of towering strength.

Greaves was a muscular but controlled player who had been part of the raging stoner-doom act Iron Monkey before the premature death of their singer Johnny Morrow from liver failure in 2002. He told me he strove for drumming power seemingly beyond his physical capabilities: 'I wanted the sound of two drummers playing at once. I always just doubled up. For drum rolls there was no paradiddling, I played like I was doing one-handed drum rolls, with both hands on one drum at the same time. Big, chunky drum fills. You don't hear me going around the kit. Just banging them, basically. It's heavy music – you play the drums heavy. I wanted to do that.' He takes the view that his lack of compromise equates to authenticity: 'Honesty in music is so important to me. I can't lie to people about stuff, I can't put on a front.' Greaves, calloused by tragedy and hardship, took it all out on the drum kit. 'The amount of sticks and cymbals and pedals and skins I went through. I used to break my hands. I've got scars all over my hands from hitting the drums and them moving about and the next time you hit it you hit the lug nut or the rim. I've got a scar on my nose from hitting the cymbal, it rocking back and slicing into my face. And that was just at a rehearsal. That's the way it is.'

The most memorable (well, maybe 'memorable' isn't the right word here) occasion on which I saw Electric Wizard was in 2005 when they were touring the album featuring Greaves: *We Live*. I went with a friend to see them at the Highbury Garage venue. We might have had some magic mushrooms in the pub beforehand. Just enough to get squidgy. It was at the weekend and a club night followed the gig. Electric Wizard had summoned the Elder Gods into the venue and now the DJ was playing The Killers and Kaiser Chiefs. I remember struggling in my stupor to muster the energy to leave, but I thought it might pick up. My friend didn't agree, so he left. I found out the next day that he spent hours walking aimlessly around north London streets he was usually very familiar with, trying to find the way home. Electric Wizard: not a party band.

After *We Live*, Oborn adhered to a certain way of doing things and their albums became increasingly repetitive representations of occult horrors. They didn't forge new paths as they had with the cosmic hopelessness of *Come My Fanatics . . .* and the eldritch hatred of *Dopethrone*. Life kept coming for Electric Wizard and it was hard to beat it back for much longer.

In a strange turn of events, long after the despondent Greaves left, original drummer Mark Greening found himself back in the band for 2014's *Time To Die*, a (slight) return to form which saw some of the chaos of *Come My Fanatics . . .* and *Dopethrone* seep back into the music. It also obsessed over the figure of Ricky Kasso. Richard 'Ricky' Kasso, a.k.a. the Acid King, was seventeen years old when he shot to infamy for the murder of Gary Lauwers in Northport, Long Island, in June 1984. He was under the influence of powerful hallucinogenic drugs when the murder took place during a reported satanic ritual in the woods and it was alleged he cut out the victim's eyes. The crime lay undiscovered by police for some days. Before he was arrested, Kasso took friends to see his victim several times as the body rotted in the woods, just as Electric Wizard took listeners back to the same sonic carnage of their classic sound on *Time To Die*. It is hard to deny that Electric Wizard wanted to be misunderstood. They wanted to be hated.

Two days after he was arrested (wearing an AC/DC shirt), Kasso hanged himself in his cell. After a number of poor shows during which Greening barely kept the time he barely had to keep, he was out of the band again. Oborn's partner-in-crime, second guitarist and wife Liz Buckingham, referred me to Greening's 'attitude towards women and Americans' as another reason why the band's creative direction was best left to Oborn and herself.

If authenticity makes something heavier, then it follows that dealing with the true face of reality is also a heavy matter. Electric Wizard wanted to escape their hometown, but then got caught in a cycle of expectation of their own making. The acrimony in which the band has lost members, and the personal clashes behind their carefully cultivated mask of universal loathing, points to what some people see simply as poor social skills. As Greaves put it to me, 'They're not misanthropic, they're just rude.' Living up to their own hateful standards has sometimes proved too much of a burden for Electric Wizard. Wimborne always wins in the end.

IV. The floating world

Nick DiSalvo, a slender, youthful man with long, fine, dirty-blonde hair, has the slightly self-conscious air typical of someone who is tall and striking-looking. His head is held slightly lower than it would be naturally because of the posture he has developed in front of a mic stand. Onstage, with Elder, the band of which he is the lead guitarist and singer, DiSalvo is a mesmeric blur amidst tangled effects pedals.

Elder, like Sleep and Electric Wizard, are a heavy rock band with a rumbling stoner bedrock, but have woven a more finely stitched and colourful tapestry with their sound. On 2015's *Lore* they took the dizzying melodic complexity of seventies' progressive rock and blossomed, under the influence of underrated British act Gentle Giant and the US band Cathedral. Cathedral's only album, *Stained Glass Stories* (1978), is dextrous and expansive, and driven by the interplay of bass refrains on a grand, ecclesiastical scale. The genesis of progressive rock can be clearly traced in the albums of Gentle Giant, who (like Jethro Tull) began with two records of heavy blues and then became more unortho-dox and atonal as they forayed further into the seventies.

On their song 'Compendium' from *Lore*, Elder juxtaposed the dancing, delicate runs and movements of progressive rock with the elemental surge and power of their earlier work. On the fifteen-minute-long title track, the song fades almost to nothing before gracefully entering a second half, like dawn light piercing through a storm cloud, only for the storm to envelop it again in a finale that feels like thunderclouds smashing against one another. At this stage in Elder's growth as a band, one musical mode enhanced and bolstered the other, creating an electric magic which DiSalvo told me 'launched us into another world'.

This was triumphantly affirmed on 2017's *Reflections of a Floating World*. When he had started writing the album, DiSalvo found himself questioning the new reality the band found them-selves in. He began asking bigger existential questions – was this the right way to lead his life? And he asked questions of the sublunary world itself: 'I started thinking about this alternate reality thing where I realised a lot of our ideas and constructs about what's right or wrong, what people should and shouldn't do, is a kind of self-imposed reality, a society-imposed reality.'

It was while visiting a Japanese flea market that DiSalvo picked up some prints of Japanese art from the Edo period (1615 to 1868). The art was in the Ukiyo style, representing what was known as 'the floating world': 'an imagined universe of wit, styl-ishness, and extravagance – with overtones of naughtiness, hedonism, and transgression.'[11]

In Japan, the floating world was synonymous with urbane decadence and an escape from the everyday, materialising in real places such as the red-light district of Edo itself (now Tokyo). By the seventeenth century, Japan had opened up culturally and economically. It was developing fast and rapidly increasing in prosperity. Accordingly, the arts flourished. DiSalvo was drawn to the way 'there were a lot of questions about decadence and hedonism in society, and for some reason that struck a chord with me'.

For many people, including DiSalvo, late capitalism seems to have created a world that is unanchored from previous conceptions of reality. The idea of an elite untethered and floating above the dross and the impoverished wasteland of normal people has become embedded in the modern era with the Occupy movement and the detested super-rich – the 'one per cent'. It has recurred in modern Japanese culture, notably in the nineties' cyberpunk manga series and anime *Battle Angel Alita* (remade as an American live-action movie directed by Robert Rodriguez in 2019). The titular cyborg heroine lives in a city called Scrapyard that consists of debris and garbage deposited from the floating elite city of Tiphares. The population of Scrapyard are forbidden entry.

Reflections of a Floating World is an album that poses many questions about the reality we find ourselves in. It explores the boundary of one dimension and another, and often the sense of straining to comprehend a possible alternative: 'Grasping at the edge/Somewhere on the other side' ('Staving Off Truth'). The floating world is a fabulation of reality, and its fringes have the taint of the junkyard: 'Living in a myth, the boundaries of which lie in decay' ('The Falling Veil'). At the same time, this idea of 'staving off truth' and deliberately avoiding the answers to those questions, living in a state of self-imposed illusion, seems to provide a necessary comfort.

There are also warnings on the final song 'A Thousand Hands' about how the past stalks us all and how hopeless it is to try and blame yesterday for present dissatisfaction, even if we want to cast aspersions on the 'thousand hands beyond the light' for the state of things: 'From the past is nothing won/Hail glory to the victors/They will crush us just the same'. This speaks to another influence on DiSalvo and one which is more out of the left field: Leo Tolstoy.

As much as Elder's rich, colourful album artwork indicates a love of science-fiction, DiSalvo actually has little time for it. But the intimidating scale of Tolstoy's major works has equivalence in Elder's long, dizzyingly complex compositions. The human struggles at the heart of Tolstoy's literature are also the basis of Elder's music, reframed in the grandiose image of progressive heavy rock. Tolstoy's *War and Peace* (1869) changed DiSalvo's outlook on life. Tolstoy was a wealthy landowner who went to live with the peasants because, according to DiSalvo, 'he found everything so vapid and he wanted to get to the root of life' (a struggle Tolstoy projected onto the autobiographical character Konstantin 'Kostya' Dmitrievich Lëvin in his 1878 novel *Anna Karenina*). DiSalvo had moved to Berlin from Boston on beginning to write *Reflections of a Floating World*. This act of deliberate displacement, of being a stranger in a strange land – accepted by the native population but with conditions – percolated through the album. Tolstoy's work fits with Elder's mission to interpret one reality with another and their attempts to elucidate the truths at the heart of each.

Reflections of a Floating World is where the band starts to get to that elusive truth. As ornate and filigreed as Elder's music is, there is an emotional density to the album which gives it heaviness. Emotion is generated by its searching questions that weigh the songs down – preventing the album from uncoupling itself from land and floating off into the ether. It asks the big, heavy questions of life and daily experience. Elder don't escape, as much as refract, the experience of living their lives through a pin-sharp prism.

V. No escape

But what if there is no escape? What if the system has you locked in so tightly you can't even breathe? Ethan Lee McCarthy, the singer and guitarist of Primitive Man, from Denver, Colorado, can't write about anything that isn't real, that doesn't have lived experiences in it, as well as the emotions engendered by them. In Primitive Man's music he uses those feelings – in order to get rid of them. He told me he is in pursuit of the heaviest music he can conceive of: 'grim and heavy and disgusting' and 'dissonant, fucked up and aggressive'. In his mid-thirties, McCarthy is not mellowing with age. He only wants to go harder: 'The older I get, the more I crave the heaviest shit.' It's the only thing that feels good.

Primitive Man's music is so intense and suffocating it is difficult to listen to, even by the standards of the bands covered in this book. On 2017's *Caustic*, Primitive Man built a sonic dungeon and locked up the listener. Opener 'My Will' is like being pressed to death, each riff and double-bass drum sequence another boulder added to the wooden board across your chest, in a song that revels in its own malice: 'When the last light/Burns out in your dense skull/I'll inhale the smoke/That comes from your burnt bones'.

On the song 'Commerce', the effect they create is to simulate the abject misery of modern-day working conditions: 'Shackled to/The bottom/Of the bottle/Of the socio-economic slavery/That rules/And runs my life'. McCarthy's and bassist Jonathan Campos's guitars are seemingly tuned to the depths of despair itself. They move in sickened, barely melodic increments, as Joe Linden's drums hammer like the blood throbbing in your skull. Together with McCarthy's preternatural roar they make 'Commerce' the sound of capitalism collapsing in on itself and crushing everyone with it. McCarthy is unequivocal about why he wrote the song: 'If you're not born with money and resource that's beyond the common person, you're a slave to somebody in some fucking way.'

'Commerce' came out of a particularly bad experience McCarthy had working with friends, who he regarded as close enough to be 'chosen family', in Colorado's nascent marijuana industry. Stepping out of the realm of education, where he had worked as a teacher's assistant for much of his adult life, was a risk – one rewarded by being belittled, his monetary worth challenged and by him generally made miserable at the behest of bosses over-promising and under-delivering. His mental health suffered under the strain.

McCarthy is college-educated, but was self-funding, ran out of money and didn't get a degree. The school system offers him some security in a world where he has seen that there are 'people out there who have to do criminal shit every day to live'. Ironically perhaps, marijuana – the drug most celebrated as a means to escape the world in stoner and doom metal – became an instrument of mental torture in the hands of his employers, who denigrated his sense of self-worth.

Why does the workforce tolerate their subjugation? Why don't American workers rise up and organise themselves like they do in Europe? For McCarthy it's simple. It's about guns: 'Because if we go out there and we try to start some shit, they're just going to fuckin' execute us on the street.' McCarthy is hostage to a particular gun problem: he wants to retain the right to carry a gun while the police are able to have weapons, but as a teacher he would simply walk out of his job and into poverty if he was forced to keep one by the authorities: 'Everybody has a fucking gun, the cops aren't afraid to fuckin' use them and with any sort of violent protest – everybody's dead. The guns are what makes us different from everywhere else. Europeans talk all this shit about how you don't do enough [to protest], but do you want to have a bullet in your head? Do you know what the fuck that's like – to have a gun pointed in your face? I fucking do. So don't tell me about that shit.'

Primitive Man's music is as personal as it is political – McCarthy is open that it has been a way for him to negotiate and work through his problems and his past. He also sees the bigger picture. He blames himself in a lyric in the song 'Sugar Hole' that acknowledges 'I pissed my youth away'. But then he recognises the broader structural issues that mean, as he puts it in the song, that 'the adult world has swept me into the gutter'. Playing music since he was twelve years old, he was drawn to the extreme imagery and sounds of death metal bands like Cannibal Corpse and Morbid Angel in his teens and, later, the socially conscious lyrics of punk and hardcore. Until his late twenties, he played in grindcore bands, but then formed Primitive Man just as he considered moving out of town for good. Reasoning that it was easier to find good doom drummers than grindcore speed-freaks, he used the far slower, more emotionally engaged band 'to tackle some really specific issues in my life'. The resulting album, 2013's *Scorn*, drew on extreme metal to accent the claustrophobic doom-to-end-all-doom approach of Primitive Man.

In 2015, Primitive Man released an EP called *Home Is Where The Hatred Is*, a direct reference to the Gil-Scott Heron song of the same name that appeared on his 1971 album, *Pieces of a Man*. Gil Scott-Heron saw, and experienced, the societal problems in the USA first-hand. He wrote witty and scathing songs about addiction such as 'The Bottle'. He satirised a racist America with its priorities all wrong on 'Whitey on the Moon'. He lived the life he wrote about and, in the years before he died in 2011, spent time in New York's Rikers Island prison and grappled with his own addiction to crack cocaine. For McCarthy, Gil Scott-Heron was just too honest and perceived as too negative to get the credit and status he deserved: 'The only reason he isn't any bigger is because he was too real during that time.' For McCarthy, Primitive Man are part of a continuum of protest music that is embedded in personal pain, in the vein of Gil Scott-Heron: 'I'm half-black, so I've got all these specific feelings about slavery in America, too, and how that is continuing through the prison system.'

Primitive Man's music refuses to flinch from the blows of reality. It is not refracted through a psychedelic prism or once removed from the truth by allegory and fictional scenarios. The pain is right there. McCarthy has to psych himself up to watch horror films, because he finds them so emotionally draining. He is interested in extreme behaviour and will watch documentaries about a serial killer like Ted Bundy, if only to confirm what a scumbag he was and how low human nature will descend. He loves the films of Lars Von Trier, but held himself back from seeing Von Trier's 2018 *The House That Jack Built*, after hearing that Matt Dillon's serial murderer character kills children in the film. As McCarthy told me, the rape and murder of children is verboten: 'I've worked with kids – here's the thing: I have fuckin' seen that in real life. So it's not funny. You know, dude, I've had kids tell me so many stories of shit with kids. So that's my line.' People who feel heavy music the most are also more liable to be profoundly affected by art. McCarthy reminds me of the way I have to gear myself up for going through the wringer if I know a film is going to push me with the violence of its imagery: 'If you're so passionately upset about something you must be sensitive. You know, I am. I'm a very sensitive person.'

McCarthy baulks at the idea that Primitive Man are nihilistic. For him, the bleakness of their sound belies a striving for the chink of light in the cellar door: 'We sound fucked up and I talk about fucked-up shit but it's only because I want to get out of it. I believe in too much to be a nihilist. If I didn't believe in anything I wouldn't care about any of this shit. But I believe that people deserve to live well. And I've got all these other personal problems I'm trying to deal with. We believe in a ton of shit. We're the opposite. We feel *too much*.'

Stoner and doom metal provide uniquely wide-eyed visions of other worlds, or ways to see our world through other means. In their differing perspectives of 'reality', Sleep, Electric Wizard and Elder create music which is huge and otherworldly in scope: in extra-terrestrial vividness, or crushing, terrifying horror – and sometimes both at the same time. The intoxicating effect takes you out of yourself and your immediate surroundings, alleviating the boredom or frustration of trivial life pressures, but also allowing you to gain a perspective on your emotional well-being by stirring and swelling the senses.

There is a reason why this form of heavy rock and metal is so closely associated with psychoactive substances more than other subgenres. That is because the music triggers similar chemical reactions in the brain – excitement, euphoria, edginess. The freedom for the listener is you get to choose whether you go on a more or less powerful trip; one that promises to feel good, or one that is distinctly feel-bad.

This is metal music that pulls back from the grey minutiae of life to render the human experience in its most extraordinary and fundamental primary colours. Accordingly, it demands you make the space for it. This is ritualised immersion in sound that you breathe in. It's a hell of a trip – when you return you find it has often left its fluorescence on the world around you, and that something indiscernible within you has changed. By contrast, the revelation to be found under the crushing weight of Primitive Man's music is not one earned by having too much hatred, or too much despair. It's the knowledge earned by remaining under duress, of being chained to the world, desperate to make it better and caring a huge amount about it.

6

THE AGONY AND ECSTASY OF A SUPERMAN

'Will to the conceivability of all being: that is what I call your will!'[1] – Friedrich Nietzsche, *Thus Spoke Zarathustra*

'I broke your fucking mold/Then threw away the cast' – Pantera, 'Living Through Me (Hell's Wrath)'

If the human will is at the core of how we express ourselves – what happens when it fails to deliver? Philip Anselmo, as singer of a band which reinvented conceptions of heaviness, Pantera, has spent his career trying to reach the position of the Nietzschean Superman. His bold, self-defining vision of heavy music, beset by personal struggles with chronic pain and an abuse of opioids, takes us to the highest peaks and deepest valleys that the metal genre has to offer. His music is testimony to the power of the will, as well as its tyranny, in showing us how to live the heaviest of lives.

I. A Vulgar Display

In the early hours of 23 January 2016, the house lights were up at the end of a concert to celebrate the life of Pantera guitarist 'Dimebag' Darrell Abbott. The band's former lead singer Philip Anselmo still had the mic and was drunkenly remonstrating with the crowd. The 2016 edition of the Dimebash event had taken place at the Lucky Strike Live venue in Los Angeles, with a capacity of eight hundred people. That year, proceeds were going to the Ronnie James Dio Stand Up and Shout Cancer Fund. Organised by Dimebag's long-time girlfriend Rita Haney, Dimebash was an annual gathering of musicians. They paid tribute to Darrell, who was murdered onstage by a mentally unstable ex-marine in December 2004.

At the 2016 Dimebash, Dave Grohl, former Pantera bassist Rex Brown and Machine Head frontman Robb Flynn were among the players who jammed on several all-star performances of Pantera songs. It was after a rendition of Pantera's signature anthem 'Walk', involving anyone, it seemed, who could pick up a guitar, that Anselmo loitered. Looking out of shape, deeply drunk, and behaving erratically, he had some words to say about what Pantera represented: 'We were the antichrist of fucking heavy metal.' To this a man in the crowd shouted, 'You were heavy metal, man!', but Anselmo misheard 'were' as 'weren't'. 'You come up on this stage and say it to me to my face,' he replied, 'and I'll say you're not conscious any more – and I'll prove it.'

Just as it looked like a confrontation was going to get out of hand, with Anselmo looking at the owners of phone cameras that were recording him for the 'big mouth', the audience confirmed the fan had been complimenting Pantera. Anselmo replied that he didn't need 'ass kissers', but that, 'I will call other motherfuckers out on their bullshit, for ever, and get used to it because I don't give a fuck about none of ya's' – what he was referring to was unclear. 'Pantera was what we was . . .' he started again, at which point former Type O Negative drummer Johnny Kelly appeared from the back of the stage, said a word in Anselmo's ear and indicated with his hand across his throat that they wanted to close up the venue.

'That's that. Let's go,' he mouthed, taking the mic off Anselmo. Then, as they were about to turn to leave the stage, it happened.

Anselmo threw his right arm out in a Nazi salute and bellowed, the spit spraying from his mouth like a rabid dog, enunciating each word with maximum force, 'WHITE POWER!'[2]

When the video of the occurrence surfaced a few days later on YouTube, the effect was seismic. Initially, uploader 'Chris R' edited out the ending, but then reposted it separately to its full, ugly extent. In response, Robb Flynn posted a video on Machine Head's channel, titled 'Racism in Metal', berating Anselmo and a music scene that turned a blind eye to such behaviour.[3] He accused Anselmo of Sieg-heiling during their performance of 'A New Level' earlier that night. He also said Anselmo had mouthed 'white power' after the song's chorus which speaks to a 'new level' of 'confidence and power', leaving a couple of beats to raise the salute and mouth the words in place of the recorded version's adjunct '. . . such power'. The footage of 'A New Level' from that night confirms Anselmo did just that.[4]

That evening's 'A New Level' had already created a tension between the two frontmen. Anselmo had quickly stopped the performance to encourage the crowd to 'stop standing around like a bunch of pussies' and, when Flynn was slow to cease playing, Anselmo pointed to him and quipped, 'I said, "Stop" – you don't know me.' Philip Anselmo has performed many shows deeply intoxicated but during no other live footage I've seen of this song does he come in too early on the first verse, as he did the second time they tried it. The assembled players had to stop and start it yet again.

In his video, which sailed north of one million views in the aftermath, Flynn described the 'Sieg Heil' incident as 'almost too much to believe'. Initially, Anselmo posted his own comment on the original video of the incident from his Housecore Records account and attributed the gesture to a backstage joke about white wine: 'OK folks, I'll own this one, but dammit, I was joking, and the "inside joke of the night" was because we were drinking fucking white wine, hahaha ... Of all fucking things. Some of y'all need to thicken up your skin. There's plenty of fuckers to pick on with a more realistic agenda. I fucking love everyone, I fucking loathe everyone, and that's that. No apologies from me. PHA '16'.[5]

The comment was soon deleted and Anselmo then posted an apology video. He spoke of it having been 'extremely late at night' and that 'heavy-duty talk' had been exchanged between him and 'those that loved Dime'. He reiterated his line about jokes shared backstage, and that the exclamation onstage was some kind of manifestation of that: 'It was ugly, it was uncalled for and anyone who knows me and my true nature knows I don't believe in any of that. I don't want to be part of any group. I'm an individual. I am a thousand per cent apologetic to anyone that took offence to what I said, because you should have taken offence at what I said. And I am so sorry.' He ended the video asking for another chance.[6]

In the ensuing days he apologised again: 'My biggest obstacle(s) are the over-indulging in the booze and blurting out spiteful, ignorant reductions of the human spirit itself. I will address these issues, head-on. I'm repulsed by my own actions, and the self-loathing I'm going through right now is justified by the hurt I've caused.'[7] The incident led to live dates cancelled for his band Down, who he encouraged to move on without him. He spent much of 2016 in his bunker, his home on the North Shore of New Orleans, not giving interviews.

The incident pointed to the rupture that was happening in America more broadly. On the one hand, it exposed a sharp contrast between liberal metal fans who were disgusted with Anselmo's actions; fans who were generally unmoved either way; and right-wing voices online, who accused offended parties of being politically correct 'social justice warriors' (SJWs). This last contingent saw nothing wrong with Anselmo standing up for white pride. The comments section of metal websites were shut down in multiple cases. It pointed to a division in online discourse that would be ripped wide open with the election of Donald Trump in November that year.

Robb Flynn's video was incandescent and disbelieving: 'Only in the metal community is something like this so . . . so brushed off.' On the night of Dimebash, Flynn recalled that he had approached Anselmo, a musician he had toured with twice in the late nineties: 'Within thirty seconds of sitting down and talking to him, his drunk ass had decided to let me know, in no uncertain terms, that he hated the "nigger era" of Machine Head.' This presumably referred to the nu metal styling of Machine Head's third and fourth albums, 1999's *The Burning Red* and 2001's *Supercharger*, where Flynn incorporated rapping into their songs. Flynn spoke about his fear of speaking out and the fear of appearing a hypocrite for having used the term 'nigger' himself before, while in his twenties. Flynn claimed that he and other bands had been onstage with Anselmo in his Pantera days and witnessed him Sieg-heiling 'like you've done for ever'. Flynn speculated that no metal musicians had previously called Anselmo out on it because any moral outrage was out-muscled by their own love of Pantera as fans. To put it bluntly: Philip Anselmo was scary. Anselmo had built his image through physical strength and intimidation which was hard to contest – repeatedly over the years he either threatened to knock out antagonists onstage (in the crowd or, more often, the venue security overreacting to those fans) or invite them to suck his 'enormous' dick.

Perhaps the most difficult thing to swallow in Flynn's statement was the accusation that Anselmo had been Sieg-heiling onstage 'for ever' and that it had remained unchecked, although the Dimebash incident dredged up another occasion from Anselmo's past when a drunken tirade had landed him in trouble. On 4 March 1995, journalist Mitch Joel was at the Verdun Auditorium in Montreal, Canada, watching Pantera play to six thousand people. In a break in the set Anselmo delivered a speech, which was itself preserved for posterity on a fan's camcorder.

On this occasion, Anselmo also seemed drunk but agitated in a different way – visibly worked up – prefacing his comments with: 'We have friends of all colours and all kinds, we are not a racist band.' He went on, 'The rap bands – the majority of them, the hardcore motherfuckers, are pissing all over your white culture. They don't fucking want your fucking culture at all.' He then lambasted T-shirts with the slogan 'Stop black-on-black crime': 'You know what that means? That means stop black people from killing each other. What does that say to you? That means it's OK to kill white people, don't it? That's what it means to me. It doesn't say stop fucking crime. It says stop *black-on-black* crime. It's OK to kill a white motherfucker – no problem. Well, look. Let me tell you what. Let me tell *you what*. If you walked around with a fucking T-shirt on that said "White pride" you'd be a fucking racist . . .' And the coup de grace: 'When you wake up in the motherfucking morning and you look at yourself in the goddamn mirror . . . Look, hey, have all the fucking pride in your heart, man – have all the fucking pride in the world, man. That's all I've got to say. Because we are the great people. And you know what? Maybe, just maybe, tonight is a white thing and the black [people] would not understand what the fuck I'm talking about – does that make sense to you?'[8]

Joel's letter relaying what had been said was sent to Pantera's manager Walter O'Brien and numerous press outlets. It was printed by *Kerrang!* magazine in their 1 April 1995 issue – but this was no April Fool. It ran under the cover splash: WE ARE NOT NAZIS! PANTERA ON THE ROPES OVER RACIST RANT! The story explained that Anselmo apologised for his remarks at a gig the following night from the stage at the Nassau Coliseum in Long Island, New York, before anyone in the audience even knew what he had said (in a time when news and outrage travelled at the fraction of the speed it does today). In the subsequent written apology that was distributed to the media, Anselmo said he must 'take responsibility for the harmful words that may have racially offended our audience'. In other respects he stood his ground, as he continued: 'On any normal night the speech that I give on the subject of racism goes in the direction of unity. A unity of pride, for in today's society (especially in the USA) white people are basically stripped of any pride, and if any is shown, then in the eyes of others, that white person who has shown pride is labelled a racist. However, if, say, a black or Hispanic person wears T-shirts on the street boasting their pride and heritage, it is seen as OK. Well, my message – especially to the young people who have come to see our shows – is to have pride, no matter what colour you may be. Nobody can help being born any colour. We are all sort of on the same sinking ship when everyone starts pointing fingers, which is what I did, and so I must explain myself. What my mistake was, I was reacting angrily to something that recently happened in my life to someone very close to me. I realise that in Canada racial problems are not as swollen as they are in the USA. Where I live, blacks and whites especially, and unfortunately, do not get along as well as with other races. The speech that I made to the audience in Montreal was so pro-white that even as I made it, I knew it had come out wrong.'[9]

It is clear from the caveats in the apology that the twenty-six-year-old Anselmo in 1995 did not seem to appreciate there was such a thing as structural societal racism. The reason why white and black pride is a false equivalence in the United States is because one side has oppressed the other throughout its history. Nonetheless, he ended the apology letter by begging his fans to go back to the band's first three albums: '. . . for references to how I truly feel. On this particular night, I sunk as low as the people that I claim to hate.'

What had happened that night to the sentiment of 'Rise' from 1992's *Vulgar Display of Power*? Anselmo's lyrics encouraged, 'Every creed and every kind to give us depth for strength'. Anselmo's onstage rant had more in common with a line from the song 'No Good (Attack the Radical)', also from *Vulgar Display*, where Anselmo rapped (no less) in a seeming attack on the criminal elements of minority communities, 'You blame oppression and play the role of criminals'. As he wrapped up his 1995 apology letter, he insisted he made 'a very human mistake'. He concluded, 'And on behalf of the rest of the band (who are mad with me also), I plead for your forgiveness, for this is a mistake I will never make again . . .'

A couple of weeks after the 2016 Dimebash, the Days of the Dead horror festival was held – 'where horror and pop culture collide!' shouted the poster strapline. It was held at the Sheraton Hotel, Atlanta, over the weekend 5–7 February and, as one of the featured attendees, forty-seven-year-old Anselmo sang at karaoke. He performed The Smiths' 'How Soon Is Now?', a song that protests about being only human and wanting to be loved.[10] He had previously described The Smiths as 'heavy in their own way' and long advocated Morrissey as a great lyricist on the subjects of depression, self-loathing and the grimness of life.[11] He performed the song (terribly) with The A League, an African-American vocal group who on their website say they aim 'to be positive role models and prove that everyone can have fun together and succeed regardless of race, age, sex or class'.[12] It seemed to be an act of knowing contrition but one also defined by the self-pity evident in his 1995 apology: that of being 'only human' – did this mean he was only partially accountable for his actions, as a fallible human being?

For Anselmo, attack always seemed to be the best form of defence. Throughout Pantera's career, as a band that professed to be 'Stronger than all', any signs of public weakness were to be avoided. Manager Walter O'Brien recorded Pantera's concerts so he had a full record of everything Anselmo said from the stage, inflammatory or not, for the purpose of defending him against false accusations.[13] Moments of weakness and folly seemed to occur the more they tried to choke them off. They provided the fullest insights into their characters and made Anselmo, in particular, such a compelling, charismatic and unpredictable figure.

When he finally re-emerged in December 2016, Anselmo gave an interview to metal journalist Eddie Trunk on satellite radio station Sirius XM. It was set up partly to account for his side of the story of that infamous night, now that the dust had settled. What emerged was a strange reason for the 'White power' outburst. Anselmo claimed that he had been 'more and more aggravated by just two or three little hecklers' who were calling him a racist during the Dimebash show.[14]

In the footage of the interview with Trunk, it's clear Anselmo is having to keep his temper, and acute sense of persecution, in check: 'See, this word gets thrown around like it's *easygoing* or something, but when people start screaming "racist" over and over and over and over again at me, what I did was show them exactly what the ugliest possible thing that I could think of at the time was.' Anselmo's argument was that he engaged with his accusers – just as he had engaged with thousands of audience members over his career – by giving them what they wanted, and that was his mistake. For him it boiled down to a moment of weakness: 'They were looking for what they got and sadly enough I gave it to 'em.'

This struck me as a misguided and perhaps specious excuse. How far does this logic extend? The following year in Charlottesville, Virginia, on 12 August 2017, James Alex Fields Jr drove his Dodge Challenger into hundreds of anti-fascists who had been peacefully protesting the Unite the Right rally he was attending. He killed thirty-two-year-old Heather Heyer and injured twenty-eight others – was he too giving those protesters the hate and ugliness *they* wanted?

And who were these hecklers taunting Anselmo that he was a racist? It has never been established. So much of that incident, ripping through a haze of alcohol and heightened emotion, does not make sense. In the aftermath, Anselmo certainly had staunch defenders from mixed ethnic backgrounds. His solo band's

Mexican drummer Joey 'Blue' Gonzalez was particularly riled by the racism accusation. There was also Doug Pinnick, frontman of King's X, who Anselmo encountered backstage that night at Dimebash and was supposedly also making wisecracks with him about 'white power': 'I think he was trying to be funny and controversial, but he doesn't have a racist bone in his body.'[15] In the Eddie Trunk interview Anselmo referred to his patronage of the Kronk boxing gym in Detroit (attended by boxers of all colours) and described black boxing trainer Emanuel Steward as 'the last father figure I had in my goddamn life'. He spontaneously referred back to the 1995 onstage rant about the 'Stop black-on-black crime' slogan, saying that looking back, 'I can agree with that shirt wholeheartedly.'

Anselmo became deeply aggrieved at his treatment after Dimebash. The incident seemed to harden his views on the new, highly sensitive liberal agenda online. In an interview with *Decibel* magazine, also from December 2016, he said: 'Let me make it very clear, here and now: I have never written a white power song in my entire discography. Maybe I've said controversial things, but that's the school of music that I come from. If you want safe music and safe spaces and all that type of shit, then run screaming in the other direction, please, and go toward yon safety. Way back when, if you didn't like what someone was saying, you changed the channel. It's not all that difficult.' That invitation to turn the cheek, or walk away, affirms what Robb Flynn said in his video – that if he was forced to accept that metal was harbouring and protecting expressions of racism, 'count me out'. The *Decibel* interview tempered contrition with defiance – second nature to Philip Anselmo and his mouth for war: 'Two words and one hand gesture do not define my fucking career.'[16]

Anselmo has said repeatedly that he comes from a place of love.

He described his detractors' ire to Eddie Trunk: 'It's so much easier to *hate* than to put the fucking effort in to *love*.' Not that he had any love for Robb Flynn. Pushed by Trunk to refer to him by name, Anselmo insinuated that Flynn was not part of the inner circle at Dimebash. In Anselmo's mind, a large part of Flynn's resentment resided in the fact that, as he memorably put it, 'he wants to ride the coattails'. This is partly true: Machine Head have not shied away from showing their love for Pantera. They recorded one of their most successful songs, 'Aesthetics of Hate', as a response to online bile spewed in the wake of the murder of Dimebag. Machine Head have been known to cover other Pantera songs (including 'Fuckin' Hostile' for a *Metal Hammer* Dimebag tribute album), before Flynn vowed never to play another Pantera song again in the video he made after the 'white power' incident.

When he conducted those interviews in December 2016, Anselmo was actually promoting a new album from his band Superjoint, *Caught Up in the Gears of Application*. Superjoint (formerly Superjoint Ritual) had been long dormant but now, as they had before, they seemed to function as Anselmo's reactionary id. On the album, Anselmo clumsily calls out SJWs in 'Burning the Blanket' and on 'Clickbait' delves into the pernicious workings of social media and the cowards of the internet, who he seems to blame for making him a pariah like never before. He was used to being in control onstage and he had none over the internet. On stage in 2014 he mocked online messageboards: ' "This sucks. Phil is fat. I hate the beard" . . . the internet is made for pussies. It is. It really, really, really, really is.'[17]

Playing scabrous hardcore punk, with the woozy sludge metal breaks that puncture its blistering speed, on 'Mutts Bite Too' he points to the 'pale skin' and mixed Italian heritage and how 'Not everything/Is black or white/Wrong or right/Pegged on sight/To realize/Just how opaque we are/We must be/Fucking related some way'.

In January 2018, his solo project, Philip H. Anselmo and the Illegals, released *Choosing Mental Illness as a Virtue*. The album was furious, angular, difficult, ugly. The opening track, 'Little Fucking Heroes', contained a familiar phrase from the Eddie Trunk interview: 'Riding the coattails of infamy/(You) little fucking heroes' and though it is deliberately obscure, it is hard not to think of Robb Flynn when you hear Anselmo bark that his addressee should 'Just finally admit you're jealous/Of the riddle that is me'.

However, in the years following Dimebash, a change in Anselmo was evident. In fact, he seemed to physically transform back into the slim, youthful version of himself who fronted Pantera in his prime. He had stopped drinking and seemed clear-headed and rejuvenated. After the release of *Choosing Mental Illness as a Virtue*, his band toured with mental health support and suicide prevention professionals in attendance at certain dates. At a gig at the Saint Vitus Bar, New York, in September 2018, Anselmo explained that the suicide prevention text-line representative couldn't be there due to illness and took the opportunity to address the subject matter of the album: 'When people ask about the cover and the title of the new record . . .' At this point in the footage, he blows out hard, composing himself, and clears his throat, 'I've said it once on this tour – I'll say it again. You ask me fuckin' twelve months ago if I gave a fuck about waking up the next day, I would have given you every legit reason in my mind about why I didn't give four fucks, it's true. Fast forward to right this very fucking second: I wanna fucking live, man! It's good to be awake, goddamnit! Fuck . . . sorry it took so long. We're dealt the cards we're dealt. Talk to each other. Put love first and go fucking bananas, this is one called "Choosing Mental Illness".[18]

Philip Hansen Anselmo seemed to have had an awakening. What had made this period in his performing life so difficult for many onlookers was seeing a hero stumble, and so inexplicably. The reason this was not his downfall was because his was a career of downfalls: falls as great as the tremendous heights he ascended in his career with, and after, Pantera. The story of his mental and physical struggles, the drugs, the depression, the death of his bandmates, and the chronic pain that defined him for so many years, is also the story of his ultimate struggle: with himself. We cannot know who Philip Anselmo really is. We can only know this public face, as ugly as that has got, and as triumphant and inspiring as he has been for his multitude of fans. There is also, for me, the undeniable fact that he is the greatest frontman heavy metal has produced.

II. Becoming

In his book *Thus Spoke Zarathustra*, subtitled, 'A book for everyone and no one', written between 1883 and 1885, Friedrich Nietzsche introduced the concept of the 'Superman': '*I teach you the Superman.* Man is something that should be overcome. What have you done to overcome him?'[19] With it came his notion of the 'Will to power' – man must exert his will on his environment, so that it bends and accommodates to that will, like the mind's mirror: 'You want to create the world before which you can kneel: this is your ultimate hope and intoxication.'[20] Overcoming in this sense means exceeding the self, but also being subjugated to that self: 'He who cannot obey himself will be commanded ... commanding is more difficult than obeying.'[21]

During his onstage rant in 1995, Anselmo had lost himself and in doing so, lost control of his command. The language he used was Nietzschean in his apology: 'Here I was, standing in command, in front of 6,500 people. I should have felt 10 feet tall, but when I left the stage and the arena, I felt like an ant ready to be squashed. I ruined the night for myself, as well as others. I am only human, and when I have a bad day it's a shame that it has to be in front of vast audiences. I was extremely out of character.'[22]

When Pantera became a force in heavy metal, the great struggle within Anselmo was the striving and pressure to be Superman in the Nietzschean sense, and the extent to which that attempt came to undermine its goal. In *Thus Spoke Zarathustra*, Nietzsche wrote about a specific period he called the 'great noontide' in the transformation to the Superman: 'It is when man stands at the middle of his course between animal and Superman and celebrates his journey to the evening as his highest hope: for it is the journey to a new morning.'[23]

If there was one gig that represented Anselmo and Pantera's basking in the midday sun of this noontide, it was 28 September 1991, at the Tushino airfield, Moscow. They were on the undercard at the enormous concert in front of 1.6 million people, where Metallica also reached a career peak. Anselmo had joined Pantera in 1987, when they were already a well-oiled machine with multiple albums under their belt. He sang on *Power Metal*, released in 1988, with the band displaying backwards-combed hair, spandex and glam stylings, despite an already harder sound that was more in league with Judas Priest. On 1990's *Cowboys from Hell*, Anselmo began to exert his will on the musical direction of the band, while the Abbott brothers on drums (Vinnie Paul) and guitar (Dimebag Darrell), with Rex Brown on bass, embraced and excelled at delivering the new vision, which they agreed on.

When they played Moscow, the band was transitioning towards the new form of brutality that would characterise the following year's *Vulgar Display of Power*.

The songs from *Cowboys*... performed at the gig were tougher, rawer and more confrontational than their recorded versions. Anselmo delivered his vocals in a coarser, barking style, still melodious but with a sandpaper underside. That day, 'Domination' had a booming, Gatling-gun intensity, building to its crushing breakdown outro section; 'Primal Concrete Sledge' saw Dimebag tear at his guitar and deliver mind-bending soloing at the song's denouement as Anselmo exhorted a crowd, newly liberated from communism, 'to let it all out'; he introduced 'Psycho Holiday', with its whirling stomp, as a song 'about getting away from your own mind'. The behind-the-scenes camcorder footage of that day, immortalised on *Vulgar Video* – the second instalment of three Pantera home-video releases that captured the chaos, debauchery and tomfoolery of the travelling circus of band and crew – shows a band in the ascendant, ready to seize their crown. They were making jokes, interacting with and making fun of the locals, and lightly undermining their meagre backstage accommodation.

Looking back, Anselmo told me, he then had a 'chip on my shoulder... any time we were in a live situation or playing live, it was not only competition, it was almost like a fighter's mindset. Like a boxer's mindset: I. Can. Not. Lose. I had to be Superman. I *had* to be Superman. And I had to fly higher. I had to fly higher than your average lead vocalist in a heavy metal band. But still at the same time allow people to understand that my feet are on the ground. Which, to me, was important in Pantera, because I very much did take my love for everything that was hardcore music and the no-bones, stripped down, no-nonsense image and attitude and all that.'

His aspiration was to be the Mike Tyson of heavy metal vocalists, to embody a ferocious, unprecedented explosion of violence ('A prime Mike Tyson is really not that far a cry from the individual that Nietzsche imposes, you know what I'm saying?' he said). In the footage from Moscow, the shaven-headed Anselmo is wearing a T-shirt advertising the first Evander Holyfield–Mike Tyson fight, which was soon scheduled to take place, on 8 November 1991 at Caesar's Palace, Las Vegas. In the run-up to the fight, Tyson had been indicted on the rape charges that would send him to prison the following February, though it was actually injured ribs that postponed the bout. Tyson in his prime was a dangerous role model.

Anselmo to this day, now over fifty years old, believes in the power of what Nietzsche called an 'exalted, robust will'[24] in *Thus Spoke Zarathustra*. Anselmo said, 'Believe me, I'm a one hundred per cent believer in the will, and the strength of the will – to will yourself through situations because that's what I've done my entire freaking career.'

Pantera began to bend the heavy metal scene to that will and change it to resemble them. In *Kerrang!* of 10 April 1993, as *Vulgar Display of Power* smashed through the half-a-million sales mark in the United States, writer Mike Gitter described Anselmo as 'a different kind of rock star. A 24-year-old tattooed thug, schooled in Hardcore etiquette, who's made a career of gripping audiences around the throat and slamming them through the wall.'

That issue of the magazine reported on the ongoing demise of glam metal and the break-up of the Brett Michaels-fronted Poison: the cover design featured a photo portrait of a shirtless Anselmo dwarfing a smaller image of Michaels. Anselmo was heralded as a new kind of frontman who was '[c]harged by confidence, not ego'. The physicality of Pantera was paramount: to exude strength and commit massive levels of energy to their performances. In a video interview with *Revolver* in 2010, celebrating the twentieth anniversary of *Cowboys from Hell*, Anselmo reflected, 'We were made of rubber. We could bounce off the ground. We could walk through walls.'[25] But they did concede some vulnerability in service to showing that they were like their audience. As Anselmo put it to *Kerrang!*: 'Definitely, I feel real human. Vulnerable. Happy. Sad. Angry. In love. Out of love.'

Released in March 1994, *Far Beyond Driven* was a conscious attempt to go further and better than what many saw as the unbeatable record that was *Vulgar Display of Power*. On the contrary, Anselmo, with that fighter's mindset, told *Kerrang!* it was 'very beatable'. On 'Becoming' from *Far Beyond Driven*, Anselmo wrote about achieving a 'godsize' stature. His irascible aggression was imprinted all over 'Strength Beyond Strength' and 'Five Minutes Alone' – the latter sounded like the proclamations of a tyrannical king over one of Pantera's signature locked-in, high-tensile-steel poundings: 'You've waged a war of nerves/But you can't crush the kingdom'. But something was different on *Far Beyond Driven*. The song 'I'm Broken' with its offer to 'inherit my life', wound tautly around a grinding power-blues riff, hinted at a mental disturbance and a deeper vulnerability.

The source of this was an emerging injury to Anselmo's lower back, brought on by countless shows leaping from the drum riser, stomping around the stage and attempting to match the intensity of twelve rounds in the boxing ring. Around the time he found out that *Far Beyond Driven* had gone to No. 1 in the US, he got the results of an MRI that revealed he had ruptured two discs in his lower back. He told me, 'It felt like I had everything and more until I was about twenty-four years old and then it was a different battle. And so all of the equipment, I guess, that I used in stage presence and the attitude that I would bring into either a live or recording situation or if I was going to sit and write lyrics about overcoming – when I was injured it definitely tilted the view, so to speak.' Anselmo doubted whether his will would be enough to get him through what was demanded of him as Pantera exploded: 'I was a very young man when I was injured and the popularity of Pantera was going through the roof when I found out there's no way I should be doing any shows of these sorts at all, especially with the physicality and the toll that that takes on the body and whatnot. I had to make some very rash decisions about what I was going to do.'

In *Thus Spoke Zarathustra*, Nietzsche warned about exceeding your strength in a situation that defies your will: 'Do not will beyond your powers: there is an evil falsity about those who will beyond their powers.'[26] Soon, Anselmo realised that in his eyes, as he put it to me, 'it made for a different type of fight' to preserve the 'indestructible image' he had cultivated, and that the rock press had propagated: 'I can't say that I was well-equipped for that fight, despite being a proponent for the strong will, but then again at the same time I wasn't unequal to it either.' The following years would take a huge toll on Anselmo, but his struggle would also deliver some of the most important heavy music ever created.

III. Never Died Before

On 16 March 2009 Anselmo gave a talk at Loyola University, New Orleans, about his life as a heroin addict. After his injury diagnosis, he was faced with a non-choice. Giving up everything he had achieved was not an option and he had to find a way to carry on. 'In order to be that Superman the media had built me up to be, I had to quell that pain,' he told the students. What that meant was climbing a ladder of painkillers, starting with those containing the opioid hydrocodone, inexorably leading him to heroin. He continued to push himself to be that juggernaut onstage, but struggled to simply 'hang out . . . that's when you close the door and the needle slides in. From that point on, you are on your own. You are on a ride.'[27]

The ride came off the rails when he overdosed on 13 July 1996, after a show in Dallas, Texas. In an interview with MTV's *Headbanger's Ball* in Kalamazoo a few days later, Anselmo sat next to drummer Vinnie Paul. He said he was regretful and embarrassed but also appeared contrary: 'It didn't really shake me up. I overdosed and killed myself for about four minutes. I think it shook everybody else up. I was in bliss, actually. I was gone, don't remember anything.' He vowed he would keep 'that particular light switch off in my life, for ever.'[28]

The embarrassment was reinforced by being paraded on MTV's flagship heavy metal show. The frontman and his band-mates would often bemoan the lack of support from MTV, though this is not really substantiated by the number of times they have subsequently popped up in archive footage from the channel. Even today, Anselmo is riled by how heavy metal was positioned: 'It seemed like even when glorifying heavy metal, they had to humiliate it at the same time by making something like *Beavis and Butthead* synonymous with heavy metal. I thought it was stupid as fuck. I did – I thought it was a slight. It felt like a slight. And to call the show *Headbanger's Ball* – it's fucking silly, man.'

As he told it at Loyola, Anselmo wouldn't give up heroin until the early 2000s after the near overdose of a friend he had injected with what he thought was a 'pussy shot'. The overdose in 1996 was the first time he had publicly faltered since the 'white pride' speech the previous year but, rather than appearing bull-headed, this time he appeared vulnerable and under the control not of his will, but of addiction itself. As he reflected in Loyola, he felt under attack from the media: 'Once Superman trips up, they will judge your talent, your accomplishments and your trip-ups, and solidify your entire life in one paragraph. And it hurts, jack. It hurts. Because you know: they don't know you. They don't *really* know you. They don't know the struggles. They don't know what it's like.' He went on to describe a day in the life of a heroin addict – stuck in bed, smoking copiously and making his way through bags of heroin, 'waking up with a vengeance', craving the next fix. To 'stay safe in your unmade bed' was a situation he had described in the Down song 'Lysergic Funeral Procession'. The life he described at Loyola was far more harrowing than the fantastical demons of heavy metal fantasy.

In the *Headbanger's Ball* interview Anselmo spoke about how he used to 'wake up and dread the day'. Alongside physical pain and his addiction to heroin came depression, which he attributed to the narcotic 'depressants' he was consuming. But depression would turn out to be a shadow that would stalk him for the rest of his career. The way in which Anselmo wrote about addiction, depression and the spectre of suicide in his music contributed some of the deepest introspection and strongest emotional intensity the metal scene had witnessed. Onstage at the Donington Festival in 1994, flush with success, he had altered the spoken word refrain of *Vulgar Display* favourite 'This Love' from 'I'd kill myself for you/I'd kill you for myself' to quip 'I wouldn't kill myself any more, I got way too much money.'[29] Over a year later, in September 1995, touring with his side project Down in Dallas, Texas, he introduced a song called 'Losing All' by stating, 'It's a song about suicide.' He paused briefly as the song sprang into motion before adding, 'but aren't they all?'[30]

On Down's first album *NOLA*, released in September 1995, and Pantera's fourth Anselmo-fronted album, *The Great Southern Trendkill*, released in May 1996, Anselmo reached a vocal pinnacle, which married soulful passages with an excoriating ferocity. On Down's 'Losing All' he transitioned between the two with insouciant power, screaming, 'My wrists are slit, I'm losing all!' These albums were the height of the realist metal of the nineties.

The Great Southern Trendkill continued the musical scope and lyrical bent of 'Hard Lines and Sunken Cheeks' from *Far Beyond Driven*, on which Anselmo ironically boasted: 'I've done it all but tap the vein.' *Trendkill*'s centrepiece is a two-chaptered song, 'Suicide Note Parts 1 and 2'. The first part is washed out with keyboards and chilling lyrics about whether the narrator might try to take their own life again, amidst consuming 'The pills that kill and take the pain away'. 'Part 2' is the most savage song in the Pantera discography. Anselmo howls like a wounded animal and transmutes the melancholy of the first part into a frightening rage of self-harm, about an 'addict of misery'. Elsewhere, Anselmo dug into the addiction consuming him on '10's' and '13 Steps to Nowhere'. 'Living Through Me (Hell's Wrath)' has a trippy interlude of overlapping whispers and voices, simulating a mind in derangement, before the band powers in again. Throughout the album, bludgeoning rhythm and contemplative melody are locked into a perpetual arm-wrestling competition. Anselmo recorded the vocals in Nine Inch Nails frontman Trent Reznor's Nothing studios in New Orleans separately from the rest of the band, while in the grip of his heroin addiction. According to producer Terry Date, 'Phil and I would work every day for four hours. Trent's studio was in an old funeral home – we were in the "viewing" room.'[31]

It was all based on genuine personal experiences, as he told me: 'I guess I knew that artistically there was something there. It was a thousand per cent real. I was being more honest probably than I wanted to even be when we wrote songs like "Suicide Note Part 1 and 2".' In 1995–6, as Anselmo began to physically suffer he also creatively thrived – he had begun to succeed in that other battle he was fighting, driven by the will that had propelled him from the earliest stages of his life: 'There's no way I can say I was sane during my most damaged years, as far as the injury goes. Once again, touching on all the booze and drugs and all that shit, I was definitely me, myself – I was just off-kilter, man. But still there was that chip on my shoulder, that would not allow me to just lay and cry. I had to be creative at the same time.'

The Great Southern Trendkill also seemed to contain prophecy. 'Floods' wrapped together Pantera's past, present and future. Dimebag Darrell's extraordinary solo and outro parts weaved in passages that he had been playing live in an onstage solo spot since the late eighties. Musically, it incorporated the shades of night that made *Trendkill* the band's most ambitious and atmospheric album. Anselmo's lyrics seemed to presage the devastating upheaval of Hurricane Katrina's impact on New Orleans in 2005. Prophetic lyrics extended to *NOLA*, as well: 'If you listen to the first Down record – and I wasn't injured and I wasn't going through deep drug problems quite yet in my life – that to me reads like prophecy when I go back over it and go, "Goddamn!", so I'm with you on that.'

The potential for prophecy in lyric writing is not to be underestimated. Nick Cave wrote 'Jesus Alone' for his 2016 album *Skeleton Tree*, starting the lyric with the line 'You fell from the sky'. It was written before his son Arthur's tragic death, aged fifteen, when he fell from a cliff near Cave's hometown of Brighton and Hove.[32] The fact Cave had written the lyric prior to his son's death did not lessen its relevance. In a way, it collapsed time. Anselmo sees it that way too: 'It's either that or we create a bit of it. I'm not saying Nick Cave created that at all, no way. Not at all. It is tough to even fathom that we have this innate ability to create our own fate through previous works [and] writings. When I say freestyle writing that is how most of my stuff comes to me. It's a little weird. For a lack of a better word: supernatural. And I'm an atheist, y'know.' For Anselmo, Nick Cave remains a paragon of heaviness, 'a never-ending fount of genius lyrics that are absolutely heavy. I mean, look no further than Nick Cave. Genius.'

Cave put forward a robust case for separating art from the artist when a fan wrote to ask him his opinion of the 'newer, more ugly persona' of Morrissey. He replied, 'Personally, when I write a song and release it to the public, I feel it stops being *my* song. It has been offered up to my audience and they, if they care to, take possession of that song and become its custodian. The integrity of the song now rests not with the artist, but with the listener.'[33]

Despite, or maybe because of, the struggle with drugs, depression and death, Pantera entered an imperial phase playing live in the two to three years that followed *Trendkill*. Anselmo had grown his hair out, wore sleeveless T-shirts depicting Charles Manson and underground extreme metal bands – he was often heavily inebriated but still able to exert an iron-willed control over the stage, even as he ripped his throat to shreds with the vocals. The only time I saw Pantera, at the Ozzfest in Milton Keynes Bowl on 20 June 1998, he threw himself around with terrifying abandon, seeming to lean into the pain, enveloped in a cloud of rage, totally in command.

The set Pantera played at the Dynamo Festival earlier that summer, on 31 May 1998, was released as a live recording in

2018, and it shows a band at a savage peak with their deranged powers, as each song is delivered in unbridled fury. Anselmo was still Superman, but Superman after his death, somehow existing on the other side of the veil. 'Fuck everything like I always tell you. Don't think about nothing but you!' Anselmo instructed the audience as they closed their set with a version of 'Domination' that excerpted the song's breakdown instrumental and fused it to the take-off riff from another song, 'Hollow'. 'Hollow' was a song from *Vulgar Display of Power* where Anselmo addresses a 'shell' of a hospitalised friend, and here the lyric could be directed at his junkie self, a hollowed-out version of the Superman, seemingly present and correct onstage. But Pantera could only hold it together for so much longer.

IV. A lethal dose of American hatred

On 8 December 2004, Dimebag Darrell was playing alongside Vinnie Paul in their new band Damageplan at the small Villa Alrosa venue in Columbus, Ohio, when Nathan Gale stormed the stage and shot him five times in the head, killing him. Gale killed three others and injured seven more amongst the audience and band's crew. He had John 'Cat' Brooks – Vinnie Paul's drum tech, famous amongst Pantera's fanbase for the wild energy of his cameos in their home videos – in a headlock with a 9-mm Beretta M9 pointed at his head, when a police officer called James Niggemeyer shot Gale in the head, killing him. Dimebag Darrell Abbott was murdered on the anniversary of the assassination of John Lennon. For the metal community, the death of the greatest guitar player of his generation was just as significant.

Grieving and angry, fans and family members sought some-one, or something, to blame for the murder. Gale was mentally unstable. Friends testified that he had been deeply upset by the dissolution of Pantera and also believed the band had been stealing lyrics from him. Reports at the time said that witnesses in the audience claimed that Gale had screamed at Dimebag, blaming him for the break-up of Pantera.[34] As the acrimony between the former members of the band came under scrutiny, a lot of the fans' anger began to coalesce around Philip Anselmo.

After Pantera released *Reinventing the Steel* in 2000, they embarked again on extensive touring, supporting Black Sabbath. By the time the band reached Seoul, Korea, and headlined the Olympic Tennis Center on 6 May 2001 – the gig professionally filmed and released as the bootleg *Killing in Korea* – Anselmo seemed demonically dishevelled on the stage. Nonetheless, he declared that Pantera were 'going to be ageless and timeless' before an overwhelming performance of 'I'll Cast A Shadow' from the new album. The band was still remarkably on point, despite Anselmo's alarming appearance. Now sporting long, lank hair and voluminous beard, thinner and drawn, he resembled one of the 'slippies' of the Manson family, embodying what he calls the 'low culture' he still loves to this day: 'Everything from Robert Crumb comics to Charles Burns comics to Anton LaVey, Charles Manson, the films of Richard Kern, it's all low-culture stuff.'

The set was still ferocious – Vinnie Paul's snare sounded like a cannon going off – but Anselmo was certainly 'off-kilter'. That night's rendition of the rarely performed 'Floods' was bathed in deep blues and greens, then hellish red light for the monstrous breakdowns, as Anselmo introduced Dimebag's solo by telling the audience, 'Everybody smoke heroin.' His vocals, which he pushed to the limits of intensity in previous years, were ragged and flat in places, but he still had that compelling command of the stage. Off stage, the Abbott brothers had concerns about whether their on-point 'pitbull' of a frontman would materialise each night, or someone high on heroin who didn't know what to do.[35]

By the end of the summer, it was over. The band were in Ireland for a September co-headlining run of British arenas with Slayer, billed as Tattoo the Planet, when the terrorist-flown planes hijacked by Al Qaeda hit the World Trade Center in New York on 11 September. I never got to see them as planned at Wembley Arena on 15 September. The tour was postponed and while Slayer returned to fulfil the obligation in October, Pantera did not. The band's estrangement had begun.

Anselmo immersed himself in new projects. In doing so, fans started to become concerned that an irreparable division had emerged within Pantera. He reformed Down, who released *Down II: A Bustle in Your Hedgerow* in March 2002. Touring their album that summer, Anselmo recorded a radio interview with shock jocks Gregg 'Opie' Hughes and Anthony Cumia backstage at Ozzfest. The pair took every opportunity to make fun of an incredibly stoned-sounding Anselmo, who at this point denied he had left Pantera: 'I'm still playing with Pantera, I guess, unless they're against me.' Having recently turned thirty-four years old ('the stupidest age ever'), Anselmo suggested his inner state had slowed to the tempo of pill-popping doomers Saint Vitus: 'I feel like one walking Saint Vitus concert. When I was fifteen, I felt like a walking Slayer concert. Now it's Saint Vitus, for crying out loud.'

He also spoke frankly about his methadone use, in a rare moment of lucidity in the otherwise mystified air and non-sequiturs of the exchange: 'There is a drug called methadone that saves . . . your . . . ass. It saves your ass. If you want to get your life back, if you want the ability to leave your home without multiple paranoias and sickness and just the worst psychosis you could ever imagine . . . you feel like inside of you that the messages your body is giving your brain are: "I am killing you. You are killing me." [36] At his Loyola University talk seven years later, Anselmo described coming off methadone itself as 'falling from a fifty-storey building every three minutes'. It sounded like his body and his mind were locked into an eternal conflict and recalls a haunting sentence of *Thus Spoke Zarathustra* in a section titled 'Of the Afterworldsmen': 'And this most honest being, the Ego – it speaks of the body, and it insists upon the body, even when it fables and fabricates and flutters with broken wings.' [37]

Seemingly forming a primal twin with Down was Superjoint Ritual, who released *A Lethal Dose of American Hatred* in July 2003. Anselmo was in a very bad way physically in these years, but his musical focus seemed to be a necessary remedial activity, as he later reflected: 'At the same time when you're feeling that negative, that low, when it's my job to write songs and make records and everybody's always brought up, "You're injured but you started this band, that band, the other band." It's like, "Yeah, I did." I guess I was doing what I felt was a natural progression, and playing it by ear. It's not like going through the motions, it's pushing for these bands and giving these bands everything that I have and at the same time, no matter how different the music genres may have been between bands, it was all coming from the same broken place, if you feel me. Or the same off-kilter place.'

A Lethal Dose of American Hatred is a deeply angry record with that pain woven into its fabric. There is full recognition of Anselmo's new manifestation as a Manson-style acolyte on 'Dress Like A Target'. 'Destruction of a Person' is one of its most upfront and graphic songs, about being an addict amongst a bad crowd 'with syringes hanging out of our arms'. The album was also polit-ically reactionary in a way that was rare for Anselmo, but he was swept up in the hurt and hunger for retaliation that followed 9/11 with the subsequent wars in Afghanistan and Iraq. On 'Personal Insult' he declares Americans to be 'the most pissed-off mother-fuckers in the world', labels jihad 'a joke' and characterises the US itself as the 'great Satan'. Conflating the freedoms of America with the freedoms of the satanic self is a uniquely perverse way of twisting the crusader image of the USA post-9/11. Anselmo doubled down on his viewpoint as Superjoint embarked on yet another Ozzfest, speaking to *Metal Edge* magazine in August 2004: 'But I'm just saying, if you fuck with the US, no matter what we do, you're going to have to pay at one point or another.'[38]

Satanism has long been attractive to Anselmo as a code for living according to your own rules: 'Satanism has this great free-dom,' he says. As was the teaching of the occultist Aleister Crowley: 'Crowley with the, "Do what thou wilt, that shall be the whole of the law, love is the law, love under will." That's always made a lot of sense to me. It's kinda like the golden rule. "Do unto others . . . ", it's very similar to that. That's how I look at it.'

As this was a band in which Anselmo was only supposed to play guitar, the lyrics for the Superjoint Ritual project came from him improvising vocal melodies while the band wrote the music. It was a stream-of-consciousness approach that blended the most direct with the most obtuse of his lyrical themes: 'When I wrote the lyrics it was almost like a bizarre freestyle writing situation where words just started coming to me and I started scribbling them down. And whether they made complete sense with each other or not, it didn't matter really at that point in time. But then you go back and look at it and there *is* something there. There is a lot of layers of things that I guess came out, but without me even understanding or knowing, man. And then you can look at a song, you can look at the lyrics, and completely think that I was purposefully going for something because there is something there, but in all truth, it's kinda like it just fell out of me.'

Dimebag Darrell and Vinnie Paul released the debut Damageplan album, *New Found Power*, in February 2004. When they swapped slots with a delayed Slayer on the mainstage at Download Festival at Donington Park in the UK that June, they concluded their mainstage set with Pantera's 'Walk'. Introducing it, Dimebag acknowledged the Pantera shirts in the crowd: 'I got one thing to say about that whole fucking situation. Vinnie Paul and Dimebag Darrell never fucking ever once turned our fucking backs on you people, ever!'[39] I was there that day: as great as it was to hear the Abbott brothers perform the classic, vocalist Patrick Lachman simply didn't have the same level of performance and command of the audience as Anselmo did. Anselmo's influence on how metal frontmen conducted themselves onstage, and even looked, was prevalent for years. It emphasised that any performance of Pantera songs by other vocalists was mere karaoke.

Looking back, Anselmo acknowledges now that he struggled with the talent and perfectionism of the Abbott brothers. Anselmo's rise to prominence was at least partly propelled by a sense of inadequacy – of being an outsider in the self-styled Cowboys from Hell: 'Because being in Pantera, I guess it was a challenge for anybody, or would have been a challenge for anybody, because the Abbott brothers in particular were so hardcore about perfection. They were perfectionists, they were workaholics, and they pushed and pushed and pushed. So there was always that pressure there. And there was always that slight feeling that I was the guy on the outside, in a way. I was the guy from New Orleans. I was not a Dallas/Fort Worth native. I came from a different place and a different city, a very different city – a very different atmosphere and climate. So there was always pressure there. Always, always pressure there. And I guess I took that pressure to heart and I guess I allowed it to both annoy me and impact me negatively. But at the same time, I guess it added fuel to the fire of what was going on around me, y'know. So it was a little bit of both.'

Dimebag's murder in December 2004 coincided with the publication of the Christmas edition of *Metal Hammer* magazine (printed before the murder) in which Anselmo stated that Dimebag 'deserves to be beaten severely'. Taken out of context, an already incendiary comment spread like wildfire. In its original context it still shocks, although Anselmo had been talking about how Dimebag would attack him in the latter days of Pantera: 'There was never a point when he could not get drunk.' Anselmo was using heroin, so the frustration was mutual between the junkie Anselmo and the alcoholic Darrell. As he told the magazine: 'He would attack me, vocally. And just knowing that he was so much smaller than me I could kill him like a fuckin' piece of vapor, you know, he would turn into vapor – his chin would, at least, if I fuckin' smacked it. And he knows that. The world should know that. So physically, of course, he deserves to be beaten severely. But of course, that's criminal and I won't do such a thing . . . Really, I just let him prattle on. I grew very tired of it very quickly, and whenever it came up, like it has come up today, I just chose to wish them the best of luck. And in all honesty, I really wish that they would be men, which is very hard for them, figuring that they were living in their mother's house until they're thirty years old. In comparison, I was on the street by choice at the age of fifteen, living anywhere I could – but living, and successfully living, through my will.'[40]

When Anselmo called Darrell's long-time partner, Rita Haney, to offer his condolences soon after Dimebag's death, according to Rex Brown – who handed her the phone – she told Anselmo: 'If you even come close to Texas, I'll fucking shoot your ass.'[41] Anselmo, asked to stay away from the funeral, stayed in a nearby hotel, knowing he had to keep his distance but harbouring some hope of being allowed to grieve with friends, family and fellow musicians. In a video message recorded after Dimebag's death, a desperate Anselmo, in tears, seemed full of regret: 'I never got a chance to say goodbye in the right way and it kills me,' he said. 'I wish to God I could've gone to his funeral, but I have to respect his family's wishes, and they do not want me there. I believe I belong there, but I understand completely.'[42] He went on to dig into that feeling of isolated grief on Down's song 'Mourn', from their third album *Over the Under*, released in 2007.

The police found no reason to suspect Anselmo was implicated in Gale's actions in the 627-page investigative report that followed the murder, but it remained a toxic and divisive issue for fans[43] and for family, with Haney telling *Guitar World* magazine in January 2008: 'The bottom line is Phil's actions led to what happened. The guy wouldn't have been after Vinnie and Darrell if Pantera had not broken up. It was all due to Phil's stupid, stupid actions.'[44]

Time healed the wound with Haney – that process started after they bumped into each other at a concert in London.[45] It was at her invitation that Anselmo performed at Dimebash in January 2016 and she even defended him in the aftermath. But Anselmo and Vinnie Paul were never fully reconciled. Vinnie Paul died on 22 June 2018 of a heart condition, leaving Rex Brown and Anselmo as the only surviving members of Pantera. Anselmo recorded a brief message for Paul's memorial, telling him to 'rest in peace'. Anselmo had said in a VH1 *Behind the Music* about Pantera from 2006 (which went into Dimebag's death in a programme that Anselmo later criticised as 'biased'[46]) that 'he needed' Vinnie Paul in his life. In an updated version of the programme broadcast in 2013, he even pledged to let Paul beat him up if that was what it took for them to both sit down and talk. The Abbott brothers had long complained that Anselmo never returned their calls or reciprocated their attempts to speak to him after the break-up.

On the morning of the day Dimebag was murdered, Anselmo had discussed a dream his wife (then girlfriend) Kate Richardson had had the previous night in which she was babysitting the guitarist. Anselmo began reminiscing and pledged to call Darrell that day. But they got distracted by other matters and instead, that night, received the phone call to say Dimebag had been shot while Richardson happened to be on another line to Rex Brown.[47] Pantera's members had found it somehow impossible even to reach out to each other on the phone to resolve their differences at the best of times – and this was the worst possible way to reconnect.

With both the Abbott brothers gone, Philip Anselmo and the Illegals performed multiple shows in 2018, most often at smaller club-sized venues where they played multiple Pantera songs. At a show in September 2018 in Dallas, Texas, Anselmo introduced their rendition of the 'Dom/Hollow' edit: 'This goes out to the un-fucking-touchable memory of both Abbott brothers, Vince and Dimebag.'[48]

V. The will to survive

In J. D. Vance's memoir *Hillbilly Elegy*, about his family and the white, working-class Appalachian communities of Kentucky and Ohio, the author laments, '[A]n epidemic of prescription drug addiction has taken root'.[49] Vance's mother was embroiled in a downward spiral of opioid drug use. His book is testament to the power of family to support and raise you up, but also stymie your chances when the wounds of one generation are passed on down the years.

As far back as the *Kerrang!* interview of April 1993, Philip Anselmo spoke about how his family were negotiating his success. 'They want to know if I have any deep-buried resentment for them, for having me too young in life, for not being able to give me everything. Y'know what? I don't think about it. Till it surfaces, y'know. It's really strange when it does.' He went on to tell a story about going for a drink in his dad's bar with friends, when his father laid into him about not connecting with his paternal, Italian side of the family. Anselmo destroyed a bar stool out of frustration and left: 'I can rest every night without a guilty conscience about the old man.' But the event clearly stayed with him. In the lyrics to '25 years' from *Far Beyond Driven* he wrote about a 'splintered chair' that was aimed at the head of his 'old man'. In the song, he describes himself as a 'bastard father' to the thousands of disenfranchised youths that made up the Pantera audience.

I asked Anselmo if he felt responsible for his fans: 'When I was younger I didn't understand that people looked up to me. By all means I could have been a role model, should have been a role model. Things that I do really matter, because I was in a popular band. I didn't take it seriously. But at the same time, I did want to get across to the audiences that I was no different than them. That me, myself, I'm just a music fan following my dreams, just like everybody in that audience is a music fan. I'm really no different. I guess I wanted the audience to feel as close to me as possible. But as far as feeling responsible when I was younger – I didn't see it.'

He is now over fifty years old, double the age of the narrator of that song, and has spent half of that period struggling with pain and addiction in one form or another: 'The torture that I have gone through for twenty-five years, with the lower back damage and the nerve damage that comes with it – it's torture, man. It is plum torture, from the second you open your eyes and the waking moments of the day 'til the second you fall asleep. That's how it felt, especially back when it was a whole lot worse.'

After writing the 'berserk and absurd' *Choosing Mental Illness as a Virtue*, Anselmo chose to delve deep into his family history: 'I had come off a big stint of really trying to understand where this deep depression I had been going through came from, besides chronic pain. Chronic pain for me, I would say, is a great catalyst for a lot of the more struggle-filled lyrics. But then when I started looking into my past – you know, I've got dad issues, big time. I've got trust issues because of my father. And then on my mother's side – her mother, my grandmother on my mother's side: mean as a snake. And it's interesting, because I take these two personalities, my father and my mother, I look at the blood-line: my mother's sister – my aunt – and her mother, my grand-mother on my mother's side. There's some abrasive tempers right there. Very, very crass, rough around the edges, and abrasive. It was interesting looking at that and it made me look at my own situation and things that I've done, things that I've said, things that I've struggled with my entire life. It almost made sense to me.

It does – it makes sense to me, don't get me wrong, it's just I never really looked that deeply before.'

J. D. Vance's story is one of cutting the shackles of inhibited social mobility, a large part of which was accepting that his parents' mistakes were not his own. Anselmo doesn't wholly blame his parents, but there's little doubt they were part of the mix, along with chronic pain, narcotics and the tragedy of what eventually befell Pantera.

There is footage of a soundcheck from May 1989 in Fort Worth, Texas, in which Pantera play through Judas Priest's version of 'The Green Manalishi (With the Two Prong Crown)' with Slayer's Kerry King sitting in on guitar. Out of nowhere, Dimebag Darrell transitions into the second part of 'Victim of Changes', which Anselmo sings perfectly.[50] Today, Anselmo is not a victim of the events that befell him and Pantera. For better or for worse, he drove himself through them, retaining that sense of the chip on his shoulder, that iron will, and a determination to change the world around him, which makes his impact so considerable to this day. And, finally, he is 'the happiest I've been in my life, maybe since I was in my early twenties'.

Did Anselmo adjust to circumstances and grow enough as a person? Does it matter? He sees himself as relatively unchanged. 'There is a connection between every little thing because I've been the same guy my whole life, it feels like. It feels like I've always been into music, boxing and horror films, and all of them have contributed I guess thematically to my music and my lyrics.'

Alongside his frenetic work leading The Illegals, Anselmo has a project called En Minor, described as gothic pop: 'A band that's always been there. There are certain songs that are older than anything anyone's heard, that's been released. I've had a few of those songs since I was probably a pre-teen even. Early guitar-playing stuff. That's a band that I'd always fall back on, even when I was in the heaviest bands.' For a man who redefined sonic aggression several times over, he agrees that 'heaviness can come from a ukulele and a guy singing, it just depends what he's singing about'.

It was at a horror convention that Anselmo sang karaoke 'How Soon Is Now?', in February 2016. That coincided with the early seeds of a process of profound awakening: 'The best way I can describe it is I feel like that guy that you see in the horror films, or the girl that you see in the horror films, that was possessed by the devil, didn't know what the fuck was going on, and then all of a sudden I'm exorcised and I'm sitting back here. And the story has been explained to me about what I went through, but it just doesn't feel – don't get me wrong it feels real, everything's real – I just . . . it feels like I have woken up from a cloud of *possession*.'

A question remains as to whether the world around Anselmo will also allow him to leave his troubles behind. In March 2019, two New Zealand venues cancelled The Illegals playing in the immediate wake of the Christchurch mosque white supremacist terrorist atrocity. A gunman killed fifty-one people and injured forty-nine at two mosques in the country. The shows were cancelled due to Anselmo's controversial actions at the 2016 Dimebash.[51] As 9/11 proved definitively, a national tragedy can change the mood and tolerances of its people overnight. After the New Zealand attack, Anselmo and his band were suddenly not welcome.

Anselmo once sang about how his kingdom could not be crushed. It is within his gift to banish the demons that once drove him. 'Like I say, I can't put it all down to drugs but I can say, without a doubt, here I am a year away from any of those medicines or anything like that, whatever you want to call them, nar-*fucking*-cotics is what they are: narcotics. Just away from all of it. I couldn't be more pleased with being away from them. I still have some. I have a bottle of the motherfuckers that I still don't touch, that I have there symbolically. I'll never take one of those fucking pills again. I know that they're there and there they sit. Symbolically banished, absolutely banished.' Perhaps now, without them, Anselmo will be able to overcome himself for good.

1
THE ALL-PERVADING

'When the phenomenal ego transcends itself, the essential Self is free to realise, in terms of a finite consciousness, the fact of its own eternity, together with the correlative fact that every particular in the world of experience partakes of the timeless and the infinite' – Aldous Huxley, *The Devils of Loudon*[1]

'So crucify the ego, before it's far too late/And leave behind this place so negative and blind and cynical/And you will come to find that we are all one mind/Capable of all that's imagined and all conceivable' – Tool, 'Reflection'

Our journey has now turned inwards. The promise of self-transcendence is tantalisingly close – but can it ever be reached? The songs of Tool dig into the mysteries of consciousness through highly crafted musical geometry, but what do those patterns reveal and how close do they take us to the heavy truths of existence?

I. Compton calling

The All-Pervading by George Frederic Watts is a painting that hangs in Watts Gallery, just outside the small village of Compton, near the town of Goldalming in Surrey. Its subject is a foreboding angelic presence shrouded in billows of material, holding a huge orb – perhaps Earth itself – in its hands. Its face is blank and eyeless but seems to be female (is this Mother Earth?) as huge wings arch up and join over its head. It sits, as if suspended in time and space. The sepulchral gloom of the painting makes it less a benevolent guardian of mankind than an unnerving, powerful arbiter of our fate.

The painting hangs in the main public art gallery, but another version forms the centrepiece of the altar in Watts chapel, a little down the road. A small but ornate and lavishly daubed structure, the chapel seems impenetrable to light on a gloomy day. It is less a place of structured religious worship than a private, arcane space to meditate on existence and reflect on the system of the universe.

It is appropriate that the ashes of author Aldous Huxley are interred in a gravesite just beyond the chapel. Huxley died in Los Angeles in 1963 aged sixty-nine but his ashes were later returned to his British ancestral birthplace to be buried along with his parents and wife. The leafy surrounds of Compton, Surrey, and the urban sprawl of Compton, LA, could not be more different.

Over a two-year period in LA Huxley wrote both a non-fiction work about the possession of a nunnery by demons in the seventeenth-century town of Loudon, France, and the subsequent burning of the town's Jesuit priest Urbain Grandier – *The Devils of Loudon* (1953) – and a hugely influential essay about his experience taking mescaline, *The Doors of Perception* (1954). The former was the source text for a highly controversial film adaptation in 1971 by Ken Russell called simply *The Devils*.

An excellent book about the scandal and dangers of religiously motivated mass hysteria, *The Devils of Loudon* is also a fascinating text in which Huxley begins to work through the theme of humanity's urge for self-transcendence, via religious devotion or debauchery, or both. *The Doors of Perception* is a practice-led exploration of self-transcendence through the taking of hallucinogenic drugs.

In 1993, thirty years after Huxley's death, an LA-based band called Tool released their debut album, *Undertow*. The music was sinuous and hypnotic. It enacted a journey from the depraved to the spiritual. It reached for an understanding of the divine in all things but was delivered with the force and pummelling rhythmic patterns of physical reality.

Huxley's writing is a fascinating prism through which to view Tool's music and examine how – in their highly crafted vision of heavy rock – they progress Huxley's notions of an ecstatic response to consciousness.

II. Wings of desire

Tool is an immigrant project. Its four members – Maynard James Keenan (vocals, from the midwest via Boston), Danny Carey (drums, Kansas), Adam Jones (guitars, Illinois) and Paul D'Amour (bass, Washington state), later replaced before their second album by Justin Chancellor (London, UK) – were drawn by the creative pull of the city. The band were formed from a close-knit community of musicians and artists and practised in a squat, white building on Hollywood Boulevard that was once Cecil B. DeMille's production studio.[2]

Tool was birthed in the hedonistic mire of Sunset Strip. Their name signified something utilitarian and suggested something carnal and they grinded their way to being signed by a label after only seven shows.[3] The set of early, confrontational songs from their first EP, *Opiate* (1992), and the following album, *Undertow* (1993), emphasised bodily exertion and excretion: 'Sweat', 'Crawl Away', 'Jerk-Off'. Their songs were vulgar, profane and funny. 'Swamp Song' jabs you in the chest: 'This bog is thick and easy to get lost in/'Cause you're a stupid, belligerent fucker.'

Like the big hog on the back cover of *Undertow*, the band's earliest work wallows in filth and degradation. Sex is an excursion from the mind, or at least a temporary form of release. In '4 Degrees' (which *might* be a reference to the anus being four degrees warmer than the vagina), the penetrative act enables release that 'brings us out'.

Urban Grandier, the Jesuit Priest at the centre of Huxley's *The Devils of Loudun*, was first accused of marshalling the devils who sent its convent into a frenzy, then was found guilty of being a sorcerer and burned at the stake. His comeuppance was a result of the political and religious enemies he had made through succumbing to his sexual instincts: he had numerous affairs and conceived a child out of wedlock. Just as Maynard Keenan's protagonist of '4 Degrees' is encouraged, over a juddering rhythmic pulse, to 'Free yourself from yourself', Grandier sought what Huxley terms a 'downward self-transcendence',[4] by means of sexual depravity.

Huxley distinguishes an 'elementary sexuality which is innocent' from one that is 'morally and aesthetically squalid'.[5] Keenan was fascinated by the aesthetically squalid, and created extreme, lurid imagery to make a bogus liberation through down'n'dirty corporeal submersion.

Tool's most spectacular musical and lyrical foray to the bottom is 'Stinkfist', the crushing, and yet almost stately, opener to 1996's *Ænima*. The album name is a conflation of *enema* and the Jungian word for feminine force and spirit, *anima*, and a nod to John Crowley's novel sequence *Ægypt*, which was organised around the twelve astrological houses – all of which sums up the Tool project nicely.[6] In 'Stinkfist', the protagonist for whom 'nothing seems to satisfy' succumbs to a fisting which is first 'finger-deep' then 'knuckle-deep' then 'elbow-deep inside the borderline'.

The song speaks of the numbing effects of 'over-stimulation' pushing its participants to be 'desensitized to everything'. The message is delivered in layers of thick, cloying guitars over a slow, constricting drum pattern which insists mercilessly on its progression. There is an elasticity and stretching of the bass and guitar fingerings that amounts to a heady intoxication. The song breaks down and builds to a euphoric pre-finale climax in which Keenan laments the way desire has to become so obvious, so spelled out: 'What became of subtlety?'

Huxley might call the act of bodily transgression it depicts 'the sexuality of the sewer',[7] doomed to leave the participants as hollow, if not hollower, than when they started. This theme returns to Keenan throughout his work, most baldly on a song by his other band, A Perfect Circle – 'The Hollow'. As Huxley would have it, this kind of sexual act 'takes those who indulge in it to a lower level of sub-humanity, evokes the consciousness, and leaves the memory, of a completer alienation'.[8]

'Sober', from Tool's debut album describes a 'stalking butler' shadowing its protagonist. This butler is a symbol for addiction – it might be alcohol, it might be sex, it might even be religion, but it describes this hollowing out beautifully in one of the band's most straightforward songs.

Strung together by a cable-taut bassline that gives way to a plaintive chorus ('Why can't we all be sober?'), the song buzzes with the fidgety energy that marks early Tool from their more transformative later work. The song literally bows and scrapes in bassist D'Amour's rough picking and tearing at his instrument. It yearns for the possibility of a new start and the compulsions that make it an impossibility.

The footage of the band's performance of this song at the 1993 Reading Festival shows Keenan's ability to sacrifice himself to a song. His body is tensed and knees locked together like he might wet himself, but his vocal delivery is extraordinary, as is the intensity of his interactions with the audience, locking eyes in a trancelike state. He can reach the high A and B flat necessary for the drama of the 'Mother Mary won't you whistle' section of the song but his vocal control means that the tonality and vowel shapes in his voice are consistent. At this stage in Tool's career, when Keenan sang high he retained the rich intensity and mood of his lower register, only pitching it higher, keeping the song's mood of a deep-seated fear and yearning under control.[9]

After _Ænima_, Keenan began positioning himself at the back of the stage, parallel with the drums – he claimed it was to get enough space to perform without getting overwhelmed by bass and guitar amplification bleeding into his mic on his flanks. He also often elected to perform without spotlight. This seemed to be more a theatrical gesture than a reaction to competing noise levels, but it was also a form of subjugating the position of the egotistical frontman to the needs of the music – denying the vainglorious positioning of 'lead singer' entirely, preferring to be 'just part of the story'.[10] In doing so his absence from front of stage made him a subject of curiosity and sometimes derision, arguably undoing the good work he might be attempting in making himself a bit-player in the onstage drama. The singer is the singer, after all.

III. 'Real fucking high on drugs'

If *Ænima* opens with the bogus liberation of self-transcendence in sex, then 'Third Eye' closes it in emphatic mode, with a violent prying open of consciousness via hallucinogenic drug use. The song opens with a sampling of comedian and band contemporary Bill Hicks aping a newscaster: 'We are all one consciousness experiencing itself subjectively. There is no such thing as death, life is only a dream, and we are the imagination of ourselves . . . Here's Tom with the weather.'[11]

Live, they turned to the lysergic prophet Timothy Leary, as captured on the *Salival* box-set performance of 'Third Eye': 'To think for yourself you must question authority and learn how to put yourself in a state of vulnerable open-mindedness – chaotic, confused, vulnerability – to inform yourself.'[12]

Timothy Leary and Aldous Huxley were friends. The only known photograph of them was taken in Copenhagen in 1961 at the Fourteenth Annual Congress of Applied Psychology, where they both spoke. Huxley had earlier participated in Leary's Harvard psychedelic research programme as 'subject No. 11' in a group psilocybin session.[13]

'Third Eye' is a remarkable song. It opens with the sound of a dull heartbeat, stretches over thirteen minutes in length and collides a torrid visionary drug experience with a steady stream, and then overflowing, of tribalistic musical surges. It is a rough, overwhelming concoction and Tool's most sprawling and deceivingly structureless song, but it powers through with a meticulous rhythmic propulsion. For such a perfectionist band, they fucked it up a few times live too.

The divine is confronted in an up-close manner: 'Dreaming of that face again/It's bright and blue and shimmering'. This could be Vishnu, but it's also the Self, bifurcated in the transcendental drug experience. 'So good to see you again' is a recurrent refrain in the song, as its protagonist seeks to reassemble a shattered alternative identity.

This experience is encountered by means of 'phosphorescent desert buttons'. This is a canny description of the flower-like desert cactus known as peyote. Keenan once participated in an American Indian peyote ritual which he described in his book *A Perfect Union of Contrary Things* as 'an extended, concentrated moment, a path that opened to the mirror image of discord and anger, opened to a rhythm, a harmony. That was all.'[14] In the song, the 'withered' third eye of psychedelic vision is not opened voluntarily but instead is violently forced: 'Prying open my third eye!' Keenan screams over hyper-distorted guitars, driven home by Carey's seven-time bass drum hits.

Mescaline is the psychedelic alkaloid that occurs naturally in peyote and which Aldous Huxley famously experimented with, recording the effects of an afternoon spent taking the drug in *The Doors of Perception*. His view in the book is that it impairs the 'cerebral reducing valve' that is able to regulate and organise what we perceive as the 'real' world, governed by the laws of physics and codified in language. Psychoactive drugs weaken 'the under-nourished ego', the mind's third eye is opened and the finite mind is able to become one with the universe. Self-transcendence is achieved through what Huxley describes as 'the glory, the infinite value and meaningfulness of naked existence, of the given, unconceptualised event'.[15]

Tool do not insist that their audience join them in this naked existence, but they do invite them to look at matter in a new light, as if for the first time. On the live version of 'Pushit' from the *Salival* box set – an insistent song about coercion – Keenan

requests the audience's help and their 'permission' as he intro-
duces the song: 'We need you to find a comfortable space, that is
not only comfortable, but vulnerable. To just shut your eyes and
go there, and we'll meet you on the other side.'

If this sounds like new age pretension, perhaps it is, but the
band was also capable of ridiculous humour when it came to the
transcendental drug experience. On 'Rosetta Stoned' from 2006
album *10,000 Days*, Tool begin with a wavering sustained synth
line and sonorous, arpeggiated chords. The voices of a doctor and
nurse consult in the backdrop as to the nature of a patient's condition after which the song bursts into piston-pumping life, mani-
cally recounting the narrator's story about a drug-fuelled alien
encounter 'just outside of Area 51'. Open, mentally and physically,
to an alien visitation ('The blotter got right on top of me. Got me
seein' E-motherfuckin'-T!'), under the influence of these powerful
drugs it is revealed to the narrator that he is 'the chosen one . . .
And I didn't even graduate from fuckin' high school!' A typical
Grateful Dead Head ('Please believe what I just said, see the Dead
ain't touring/And this wasn't all in my head'), the protagonist
pleads to be believed but ends up with his mind blank in a hospital bed: 'Can't remember what they said/Goddamn. Shit the bed!'

The protagonist suffers profound mental degradation from
overwhelming substance abuse and ends up externalising himself
as an alien entity in a manic tall tale. The song also boasts one of
Tool's most slippery time signature changes: the breakdown
section at the six-minute mark is in 3/4 but the accents on the
bassline make it feel as wonky as the mindset of the protagonist.
(Drummer Danny Carey has spoken about his love of King
Crimson's *Discipline* (1981) album – the way that the drums
pursue one time signature and the guitars another: they only sync
on certain rotations of the riff sequence.[16]) After this off-kilter

section, the song reaches a wider, panoramic musical refrain before tightening up as it reaches its outer limits.

There's something uncanny about this song, set in the desert of Nevada, speaking about 'that time Dave floated away', the fact that the alien had 'Isabella Rossellini lips' and an exclamation of 'Bob, help me!'. The 2017 series *Twin Peaks: The Return* posits that the Trinity nuclear test in 1945 in New Mexico was the unleashing of the evil spirit BOB. Director David Lynch (the 'Dave' of the song?) set much of this third series in the encroaching nightscape of the desert and he also directed Rossellini as Dorothy Vallens in *Blue Velvet* (1986), one of the most controversial depictions of screwed-up sexuality in cinema. As a proponent of storytelling that fractures time and space in such a way that there is no definitive version of events – which are in any case often just plain weird – perhaps Lynch would allow that this song, written some ten years before the eighteen-hour instalment of *Twin Peaks*, might have unconsciously had some of its threads drawn together in his series. Or maybe not.

'Rosetta Stoned' is draining and exhausting: drugs do not necessarily let the user achieve the Godhead and indeed, 'Opiate', from the band's debut EP, compares a malicious, rapine God with sedative drugs. The protagonist of 'Rosetta Stoned', one of Tool's most complex compositions, is pulled this way and that by drug overstimulation. Rather than seek to do the work and reach a self-transcendence through the discipline of religion, they opt for what Huxley calls one of religion's 'chemical surrogates'[17] with disastrous results: an *alienation* manifesting in the evacuation of the self from the anus in an existential diarrhoea ('Goddamn. Shit the bed!').

IV. Water, water everywhere

Another route to self-transcendence is via the destruction of the self, be it the quasi-martyrdom of Urbain Grandier, burned at the stake, or some other apocalyptic scenario beloved by heavy music. Tool, a Californian band, after all, have a thing about that most biblical of apocalypse events: the great flood.

On *Undertow*, the doomy 'Flood' closes the album, with images of the waters rising up, promising to 'purge' and 'cleanse'. Keenan joked with an audience in Tulsa in 2016 that 'all those people on the west coast, when the big one hits, and they become fossil fuels, people from Oklahoma are going to hitch onto a tornado and ride on over to the beach, because you're some tough motherfuckers . . .'[18] This ingratiating witticism introduced Keenan's strained, almost tantric breathing that kicks into 'Ænema' (the not-quite title track from *Ænima*). It is as direct and caustic a condemnation of LA anywhere in music: 'Here in this hopeless fucking hole we call LA/The only way to fix it is to flush it all away'. The song was Keenan's response to Bill Hicks's vision of California collapsing into the sea because of an earthquake from his *Arizona Bay* performance (posthumously released in 1997) and Keenan's own dream visions of the city being engulfed by a tsunami.[19] The song's appeal is directly to Mother Earth ('Mom's gonna fix it all soon/Mom's comin' round to put it back the way it ought to be') and all the ridiculous constructions of humanity, from lattes to Prozac to hairpieces, with particularly strong fuck-yous for L. Ron Hubbard and 'his clones', 'gun-toting hip gangster wannabes', 'retro anything', tattoos, 'junkies with short memories', 'smiley glad-hands with hidden agendas' and 'dysfunctional, insecure actresses'.

'Ænema' revolves around one particularly menacing refrain: 'Learn to swim'. The burn-it-all-down sentiment makes for one of their most accessible songs. When they played their first live show in the UK for thirteen years at the Download Festival, Donington, in 2019, they started with 'Ænema', wrenching their fans ecstatically back into their world. Listening to a song that has more currency now than ever, I felt a cheap thrill shouting 'Learn to swim!' along with everyone else.

Keenan would return to those who would watch and implicitly endorse death and destruction from a distance in 'Vicarious', the opener to *10,000 Days*, in which 'drowned by the ocean' is one of the tragedies that thrills the participant-viewer. 'Vicarious' explores another strain in their lyrics – that of technology's tendency to externalise our inner thoughts and dislocate an aspect of humanity from knowing itself. This is part of Tool's message of connecting to wider consciousness and the inner-spiritual, which can also be understood through Huxley's writings. As Huxley says in *The Devils of Loudon*: 'The fundamental human problem is ecological: men must learn to live with cosmos on all its levels, from the material to the spiritual.'[20]

Man's inability to do either has brought us teetering at a climatic turning point: 'As a race, we have to discover how a huge and rapidly increasing population can go on existing satisfactorily on a planet of limited size and possessed of resources, many of which are wasting assets that can never be renewed,'[21] Huxley wrote in the 1950s, far ahead of the first half of the twenty-first century, which scientists say is the juncture beyond which there is no turning back.[22]

Tool's music might revel in that turning point, see it as a form of natural selection that should be welcomed head-on for its purgative effects. But this is part of a sly, self-abnegating tendency to fly in the face of any orthodoxy. Ultimately, they are more interested in making *useful* music and it is on the meticulous constructions of *Lateralus* (2001) that they achieved a successful mass-psychic breakthrough.

V. The life of the mind

Aldous Huxley acknowledged the power of the creative arts as a means of self-expression that could lead to transcendence. The act of singing itself, in which singers tend to breathe out more than they breathe in, leads to the increase of carbon dioxide in the bloodstream. This has a similar effect to that of psychoactive drugs – lessening the ability of the brain's valve to inhibit the onslaught of the universe: 'The concentration of carbon dioxide in the alveolar air and the blood is increased and the efficiency of the cerebral reducing valve being lowered, visionary experience becomes possible.'[23] Throughout history, chanting and incantations have been modes of praying and of engaging with the 'mind-at-large'. Writing before the electrification of rock music, what would Huxley have made of metal, with its primeval bellowing and sonic force?

Tool have gone beyond what J. G. Ballard described as Huxley's attempts to 'understand the mystery of human consciousness'.[24] Working in the medium of music, in the verbal realm of Keenan's lyrics, as well as beyond, Tool have pushed the craft of modern rock music to new limits. They have deployed occult practice to demarcate zones for casting their sonic spells, using geometrical patterns that adorn their stage sets and mathematical techniques for the construction of the songs themselves. This work reached its apogee with 2001's *Lateralus*. It sounds now like a prelapsarian and giddying work of arcane transportation, released only a few months before the horrors of 9/11 and the West being dragged into a much more actively hostile physical and spiritual era.

Mathematics is the science of patterns and Tool turn this into an artform. The song 'Parabola', named for a mathematical plane curve of mirror symmetricality, is itself pleasingly symmetrical in structure. The song moves down the curve in surging power, its mid-section anchored by arcing and bowing guitar lines, and then climbs out in a funk-driven groove, before finally petering out in a pure doom crescendo. It describes a 'holy experience', a 'holy reality' where the body is unified with the mind: 'This body, this body holding me, feeling eternal/All this pain is an illusion'.

Keenan builds on the sanctity of this union on the title track, 'Lateralus': 'Over-thinking, over-analysing separates the body from the mind/Withering my intuition, leaving opportunities behind'. The core metaphysical theme is the spiral: 'To swing on the spiral of our divinity and still be a human'. And it's this sense of spiralling that resounds at the song's conclusion: 'Spiral out. Keep going'. The main riff of the song ended up being in a measure of 7, 8 and 9: 987 is the sixteenth integer in the Fibonacci sequence, an expanding fractal in its numerical form that underpins design in nature (for example, the number of petals on a flower tends to be a Fibonacci number). The pattern of Keenan's word placement and syllable metre in part of the lyric follows this sequence. The progression of this ratio is the 'golden ratio' – the larger side of a rectangle made up of a Fibonacci number is divided by the shorter side, which is also a Fibonacci number (1.618034), something that has been used to determine the construction of pieces of fine art.[25] Keenan said on the *Joe Rogan Experience* podcast that making this Fibonacci influence so obvious is the equivalent of a musical 'dick joke' since so much music is based on these sequences and alchemical composition anyway.[26]

The physicist and saxophonist Stephen Alexander, in his book *The Jazz of Physics: The Secret Link Between Music and the*

Structure of the Universe, delves into the relationship between saxophonist John Coltrane's mathematical approach to jazz and the quantum theories of Albert Einstein. Coltrane gave a complex geometric diagram reflecting his musical process to musician and University of Massachusetts professor Yusuf Lateef in 1967. Alexander recognised that 'the same geometric principle that motivated Einstein's theory was reflected in Coltrane's diagram'.[27]

It is this higher, organised thinking around music – the union of form, content and intent – that makes *Lateralus* the artistic achievement it is. Though, for me, it lacks the rawer, harsher psychedelia and subversion of *Ænima*, an album created by its interludes and digressions as much as by the quality of its song-writing. On *Lateralus*, Tool pulled themselves away from the sex, drugs and apocalyptic visions towards a grander statement of their struggle for enlightenment.

As full-blooded in its arena-rock progressive tendencies as it is, *Lateralus* also contains a mini-trilogy of a more introverted nature: 'Disposition', 'Reflection' and 'Triad'. Played as part of their live shows touring the album, often in the third quarter, 'Disposition' carries a message of passive participation in nature, letting it transform without the need for intervention over a mantra – 'Watch the weather change' – that serves to neutralise and settle the distracted mind, to open it up to the cosmos.

In 'Reflection', a low-key tabla (a conscious nod to the oriental form of mysticism that suffuses this song cycle) casts a spell as the bass dances around the beat and a Moog synthesiser layers the song with a retro-futurist ominousness. Keenan's voice is small and delicate here, distended like he is singing backward and as if it is coming from within the narrow confines of *Twin Peaks'* Black Lodge: mind and body splicing and returning back to one.

The narrator is 'fetal and weeping', at their lowest ebb, before succumbing to the light of the moon, allowing its light to penetrate the darkness where those without hope are rehabilitated. There is something almost approaching Romanticism here, of nature triggering a personal epiphany, edging closer to the oneness of all things. Or, as Wordsworth put it: 'a sense sublime/ Of something far more deeply interfused'.[28]

'Triad' rounds off this sequence in pummelling fashion, bereft of lyrics and vocals. It is locked into an undulating waveform of the interplay of drums, guitar and bass. Each new polyrhythm has a unique identity of accents and emphases as the trio transition, sometimes in gaps of only a few seconds. It is like a snake charming itself. If the body is one with the mind, here Carey, Jones and Chancellor show that the body's own unconscious actions are as thrilling and transporting as any of Keenan's hymnals.

This holy trinity of songs is the closest Tool come to facilitating a mesmerising and transcendent music. The trilogy provides the key to unlock each person's capability, according to Huxley's words in *The Doors of Perception*, 'of remembering all that has ever happened to him and of perceiving everything that is happening everywhere in the universe'.[29]

VI. Mind's mirrors

Tool's rendering of music is intrinsically useful and makes their name particularly apposite. They offer themselves as a tool to unlock the mysteries both within and without. This is a long way from the illustration on their demo CD, of a phallus-like spanner: a tool with a baser physical function. Tool's peeling back the layers of the self – the cravings for the distractions of sex, drugs and broader self-annihilation – let them uncover mystical forces and make orisons freed from the constraints of religious dogma. What could be heavier than communing with the vibration of the universe?

Tool channel a form of mysticism that Aldous Huxley explored at length in his non-fiction. The central mystical tenet is dying to your selfhood in an act of devotional self-annihilation and, in doing so, becoming united with the (wider, infinite) reality from which that self has been separated. When Tool released the long-awaited album *Fear Inoculum* in 2019, Keenan reminded us we are born of 'one breath, one word' on the song 'Pneuma'. The album's fifteen-minute-plus climax, '7empest', is a throwback to the angular aggression of their first two releases. It is a whirlwind of riffs, in which the tempest is a metaphor for sweeping away self-delusion.

Tool's music is a key to understanding and unifying inner and outer mystical forces as 'God' presents itself to us as whatever we want it to be. Their music can be usefully explained in terms of mysticism and through the more structured sciences of mathematics and physics. Looking hard at the replica of *The All-Pervading* in Watts chapel serves as a reminder that these are mysteries that are not solved, at least not in this lifetime.

Even if Tool's mission can be dismissed as being wilfully esoteric and pompous, the carnal urges and thrusting violence of their early work saw them digging into our deepest impulses in a confrontational manner. Tool's music urges us to be honest with ourselves. Existence is a sorrowful thing and Tool make their listeners face up to it, cope better with the challenges it presents and heal the wounds it inevitably inflicts.

8

EVERYTHING ENDS

'You are wrong, fucked, and overrated/I think I'm gonna
be sick and it's your fault/This is the end of everything/You
are the end of everything' – Slipknot, 'Everything Ends'

The end of history coincided with the end of metal and heaviness as we knew it. Then out of nowhere, metal was reborn *and* topping the charts. An age of anxiety had ushered in heavy music which boiled with personal grievances. It also articulated its rage at the injustices of the world better than ever. It had died to be reborn in one of the most spectacular bands of the twenty-first century, who shared their trauma with a generation waking up to a frightening new world order. The new millennium came with new wars without, and within. Nothing would be the same again.

I. At the gates

On 17 August 1996, on a baking hot day in the English county of Leicestershire, the revolution that had been fomenting in metal reached its citadel. Donington race track had hosted the Monsters of Rock festival since 1980, but this was to be its final year. The

1996 festival was co-headlined by Ozzy Osbourne and Kiss – the original line-up of the latter had reunited in full makeup after years of bare-faced mediocrity. However, it was down the bill that the sea change was happening.

This was my first full-blown festival. I was fourteen years old and had taken a coach from London with my school friend Ash, who accompanied me to the vast majority of the metal gigs I went to during those years. Ash was Ashir Pattni – a brown-skinned, second generation Hindu whose family was from Kenya. I mention this because metal audiences are predominantly white, although I never gave his background a second thought at the time. This was the nineties – the era of En Vogue's 'Free Your Mind', when it was cool for people of all backgrounds to listen to whatever music they wanted. In theory. Today, I can see how unusual it was. There was never any issues at gigs – metal audiences tend to be incredibly chilled, placid even. Frustration is vented through the music and the controlled chaos of the mosh-pit. By contrast, did you ever see Oasis live? If so, you'll understand what an aggro audience was really like. Ash works in Singapore for a large bank now. I wonder if he kept the drumstick he caught when we went to see Slayer at the London Astoria?!

That August Saturday in 1996, I felt self-conscious boarding the coach with my backpack and its packed lunch with plenty of water. We were young and entering an unknown, adult world. Donington was a hall of kings from the eighties: Iron Maiden, AC/DC and Whitesnake. I was conscious of some smirking from older passengers as we boarded. What no one realised, including me, was that my generation of fans were the agents of change that were going to blow the established heavy metal order apart.

We were nervous, but mostly we were excited. We'd been blooded at our first proper metal gig at the Kentish Town Forum on the first May bank holiday weekend that year, where we were slammed against the barrier in a performance by Fear Factory. They were opening the main stage at Donington in the August heat of eighty-plus degrees. Fear Factory's *Demanufacture* was released in 1995, its Dave McKean cover artwork depicting a spine and ribcage transforming into a barcode. The image represented the band's interpretation of a world that was moving towards the apocalyptic dystopia of James Cameron's 1991 movie *Terminator 2: Judgment Day*. The music, like that film, was high-gloss and mechanical – the guitars and double-bass drum locked together in a synchronised death grip. The songs were given a synthetic sheen with keyboards, but were principally articulated by the drums, drilling out the riffs as if they were describing them. Vocalist Burton C. Bell barked and roared during his verses and then let his voice soar in clean, melodious choruses. This was one of the true innovations of the nineties. The overall impression was of an artificial intelligence reaching self-knowledge. It was metal music for the rise of the machines. The genre had stepped into the future.

When Fear Factory played Donington, the crowd was crushed together, heaving itself up and down. Attempts at pogoing were countered by the pressure of hundreds of bodies bearing down on each other. This was some years before festival crowd crushes were alleviated by better barrier design, following some high-profile tragedies.

Fear Factory were followed by Paradise Lost, whose *Draconian Times* (also released the previous year) was so good that it could have propelled their gothic-tinged metal much higher up the bill. But it was the group that went on after a set by New York's Biohazard that made it evident where the power centre was shifting in metal. As the crowd dusted themselves down, an announcer said that newcomers Korn were about to begin their set on the second stage. The burly brawlers of the Biohazard mosh-pit promptly turned their backs and started *running* up the hill towards the second stage.

The footage of Korn's performance that day makes it plain how they single-handedly steered metal onto a new course and created a schism which is looked back on darkly today. There is the style, of course: the baggy trousers, skate shoes, worker shirts and hair in tight braids or dreadlocks, not to mention singer Jonathan Davis's bespoke, sequinned Adidas tracksuit. But then there is the music itself: the churning riffs from (some still say sacrilegious) seven-string guitars, weird doodle-like verse sketches, the hip-hop interludes (most notably Snoop Doggy Dog's 'Lodi Dodi' from his album *Doggy Style* during the performance of 'Ball Tongue'), and Jonathan Davis's bagpipes (deployed for the nursery rhyme-mangling 'Snakes and Ladders' with an excerpt of War's 'Lowrider' to bring it in).[1]

Korn's self-titled debut album brought personal mental and physical injury into the mainstream: the intimidation of the playground and the abuses of the family. It was filled to the brim with a raw energy and an emotional volatility that, when aligned to the dynamism of the capture/release format of their songwriting, made their power undeniable – especially live. The billowing storm cloud of the opening of 'Faget' had an intensity which was insistently ratcheted throughout its remorseless self-reflection, exploding with the refrain that bulldozes after a remarkable, muttering spoken-word section and final crescendo, spiralling into the relentless Californian sun burning down on Castle Donington: 'All my life who am I? I'm just a faget'. It was clear there were few bands who could pulverise an audience like Korn did that day at the Monsters of Rock festival.

Their onstage dynamic was unusual too: Jonathan Davis looked like a rag doll having his strings violently pulled this way and that by the mudslide guitars of James 'Munky' Shaffer and Brian 'Head' Welch. They were doubled over their instruments in painful-looking contortions as bassist Reginald 'Fieldy' Arvizu stalked the stage, using his instrument's percussive ability to slap the drastically loosened strings. As the crowd swelled and receded, in thrall to the onstage outpourings, you could begin to see metal changing before your eyes: the sections of long-hairs bouncing against people with close-cropped, dyed hair. Korn weren't even headlining the second stage. That honour fell to Type O Negative. But it was very much Korn's festival for the taking. And they took it.

There were other prime movers behind the scenes who were orchestrating the revolution – its Robespierre was Ross Robinson and its Danton was Monte Connor. Ross Robinson produced Korn's debut in a fraught, emotionally intense process of recording-as-catharsis. Meanwhile, Roadrunner Records, and the bands signed by A&R man Monte Connor, were leading the charge for this new wave of metal (although their roster did not include Korn). Metal had been changing radically for a couple of years: it was becoming more streetwise, tougher and, in a sense, more *real*.

The festival had been captured in a similar way two years previously by a band signed to Roadrunner, from São Paulo, Brazil. Sepultura's *Chaos A.D.* (1993) was a tank of an album taking aim at injustice all over the world. They stripped metal's excesses down to the bone, just as singer-guitarist Max Cavalera stripped strings off his guitar, playing with only the four rhythm strings. Their deceptively simple riffs, and the roll-and-tumble of brother Igor Cavalera's drumming, made their music punishing, groovy and loved by American and European audiences. The song

'Territory', from *Chaos A.D.*, and its accompanying video is an incisive breakdown of the Israeli-Palestine conflict, from the track's battering-ram introduction through its pounding chorus that skewers the reasons for armed confrontation at its simplest level: 'War for territory'.

Sepultura's determination to go to different parts of the world and dig into different culture and rituals was well documented on the home video they made after *Chaos A.D.*, called *Third World Chaos*. It also reflected how they wanted a street-level view of the world, unmediated. They had been living in Phoenix, Arizona for some time when they decided they needed to see Brazil 'with different eyes' and headed to the centre of the country to visit the Xavante tribe. By this time they had already recorded most of what would become *Roots* (1996) in the Indigo Ranch, Los Angeles, with producer Ross Robinson jumping and screaming along as his reputation dictated. Guitarist Andreas Kisser and bassist Paulo Jr. recorded an interview with Andy Cavanagh for the BBC Radio 1 *Rock Show* in December 1995. They spoke about their journey into the heartland of Brazil, the scorching land of red dust south of the rainforest that the tribe had made their home.[2]

Musically, *Roots* was already a departure for the band. They tuned their guitars down several steps to A sharp and gave the bass tones of the music more room to breathe. Paulo locked into the steadier rhythmical beating heart of Igor's drumming, significantly slower than the tremolo-picked guitars of their thrash origins. Max Cavalera had been practising hard at the berimbau – an instrument associated with the martial art of capoeira and developed from the musical bows brought to Brazil by African slaves. It features in the introduction to the pulverising song 'Attitude'. The band brought in a percussionist, Carlinhos Brown, who layered native instrumentation and even Japanese drumming styles into 'Ratamahatta'. The hypnotic drumming also marked out the psychosis-tinged paranoia of 'Lookaway' featuring Jonathan Davis from Korn and Faith No More's Mike Patton, providing a disturbing simulation of the moaning, groaning and shrieking of the voices in a fractured mind. On 'Straighthate' it sounded like Sepultura were sculpting songs from the distortion itself, rather than filtering their songs through it.

When Sepultura ventured into Brazil's interior, the Xavante tribe took three days out to welcome the band. The encounter was documented by photojournalist Michael Grecco, who was more accustomed to shooting for *National Geographic* and *Time* magazines than *Kerrang!* Daubed in red paint, feathers decorating their hair and wearing tribal necklaces, Sepultura were pictured with acoustic guitars and drums on the *Roots* sleeve and in publicity shots. After a 'very scary' ninety minutes aboard a biplane on the last leg to visit the tribe, according to Kisser, 'by the time we got in with the tribe, everyone was happy and friendly. It was great. The whole environment was very peaceful and was perfect for us to work.'

But Sepultura were outsiders in their own country. The band felt that, in general, youth culture looked too much to Europe and America for musical inspiration. Sepultura, too, had lost touch with what it meant to appreciate the freedom that comes with what Kisser described on Radio 1 as the Brazilian 'street way of living': enjoying some beers and playing football on the streets. It was a freedom with costs: a crazy, confused social mix that was exploited by the government.

This was not the first time the band had explored the Brazilian side of what was anyway perceived by the vast majority of the metal world as a determinedly Brazilian band. On *Chaos A.D.*'s

Electric Wizard's Jus Oborn and Liz Buckingham keeping it underground.
(© Metal Hammer Magazine/Getty Images)

German 'video-nasty' *Mark of the Devil*, sampled at the beginning of Electric Wizard's abominably heavy 'I, The Witchfinder' from their album *Dopethrone*. (© Courtesy Everett Collection/Mary Evans)

Three beauties by artist Chobunsai Eishi from the Edo era of Japanese history, an inspiration for Elder's album *Reflections of a Floating World*. (© Gift of William Green/Bridgeman Images)

The 'great noontide' period of Pantera in 1991. *(left to right)* Dimebag Darrell, Philip Anselmo, Vinnie Paul and Rex Brown. *(© Ron Galella Ltd/Getty Images)*

The *Kerrang!* front cover that followed Anselmo's 1995 onstage rant in Montreal. *(Author's Collection)*

Anselmo performing at the peak of his onstage powers with Pantera in the late nineties. *(28 © Mick Hutson/Getty Images)*

nselmo resembling one of Charles Manson's lippy' followers onstage in 2001, complete with 'elter Skelter T-shirt. *(© Scott Harrison/Getty Images)*

Off-kilter: Anselmo performing with Down at Ozzfest in 2002. *(© Scott Gries/Getty Images)*

nselmo onstage at the fateful Dimebash 2016, as Rex Brown looks on.

The Devils, directed by [...]
Oliver Reed, had its so[...]
of Loudun by Aldous [...]
story that had much t[...]
drive for self-transcen[...]
(© Courtesy Everett Collecti[...]

Maynard James Keenan, daubed in Vishnu blue,
onstage with Tool in 1996. (© Patti Ouderkirk/Getty
Images)

Shawn Crahan, aka Clown, onstage with Slipknot during the *Iowa* era. His mask was never more grotesque. *(© Hayley Madden/Getty Images (above), © J Shearer/Getty Images (right))*

Pieter Bruegel the Elder's *Landscape with the Fall of Icarus* which has uncanny similarities to the lyrical imagery of System Of A Down's song 'Jet Pilot' from *Toxicity*. *(© Bridgeman Images)*

Tonehenge: Sunn O))) searching for the resonant frequency of London's Royal Festival Hall at the 2015 Meltdown Festival, curated by David Byrne.
(© Maria Jefferis/Getty Images)

Francis Danby's painting *The Upas, or Poison-Tree, in the island of Java* is portentous of a dying world and a portrayal of isolated despair.
(© Victoria and Albert Museum, London)

The poster for *Over the Edge*, a film about violent high-school rebellion, enthused about by Kurt Cobain and Buzz Osborne in Brett Morgen's documentary *Montage of Heck*. *(© Orion Pictures Corp/Courtesy Everett Collection/Mary Evans)*

ayne Staley *(left)* and
rry Cantrell of Alice In
hains performing live
1993. *(© Tim Mosenfelder/*
etty Images)

Chris Cornell
of Soundgarden
assuming his
Jesus Christ Pose
during a gig in
1992. *(© Gie Knaeps*
Getty Images)

ly to Live: Iron Maiden perform 'Aces High' during their *Legacy of the Beast* tour in 2018.
© *PYMCA/Getty Images)*

The severed head of a Japanese soldier propped up on a tank in Guadalcanal in 1942, by photographer Ralph Morse. Its desiccated visage was an anatomical reference point for artist Derek Riggs when he created Iron Maiden's mascot, Eddie. *(© Ralph Morse/Getty Images)*

Where Eagles Dare inspired Iron Maiden's song of the same name and stands as a partial allegory for the Brexit process. *(© Courtesy Everett Collection/Mary Evans)*

The Green Man, Peter Steele, performing at the London Astoria with Type O Negative during their *October Rust* period. Neither the venue, nor the man, are with us anymore. May he rest, or rust, in peace. *(© Photoshot/ Getty Images)*

acoustic jam 'Kaoiwas' (named for another tribe), they recorded in the open air of (perhaps incongruously) Chepstow Castle in Wales. It is probably the only time seagulls have been captured on a metal recording. On *Roots*, the song they recorded during their sessions with the Xavante tribe was called 'Itsári' and was one of the ritual dream songs with which the tribe communed with the spirit world, a song for the 'healing of the world'. Elsewhere, the tribe's chants break up the heaving groove of 'Born Stubborn', their communication with the dream world interleaved with the metallic torrent.

Sepultura reinvented thrash metal and, with it, Anglo-American notions of what constituted 'world music'. The culture of interior Brazil was as new to them as it was for much of their listenership. They shone a light on atrocities and injustice at home and abroad and were able to point out the human cost of rapidly accelerating globalisation, even as they themselves formed one of its positive cultural products.

Sepultura previewed *Roots* on a selective ten-date run of shows in Europe, which they described as 'terrorist' gigs. But tension was starting to emerge between their insurgent outlook and growing prosperity as a band. They had already parted ways with the major label that had distributed *Chaos A.D.*, Epic Records, and preferred to work with Roadrunner, who let them retain full artistic control of their work. They were fast becoming one of metal's big-ticket bands: a globally minded band with global appeal.

At Donington that summer in 1996, flush from their triumphant return with *Roots*, the day would have been theirs were it not for the death of Max Cavalera's stepson, Dana Wells. The son of his wife and band manager Gloria, and only twenty-one years old, Wells had died in a car accident in Los Angeles in the early hours of the day of the festival, meaning that Max and Gloria flew home before the band's set. Sepultura decided to play the gig as a three piece with lead guitarist Kisser taking up vocal duties as well.

The performance at Donington would be an augury of the demise of this line-up of the band, which came at the end of 1996. On 16 December, the band played the final date of their UK tour at Brixton Academy. I was there for what was a superb concert, but also a strange one. On the excellent live recording that documented the evening, *Under A Pale Grey Sky* (released in 2002), you can hear what seems to be an off-mic dispute between the Cavalera brothers. On the night it was clear that this conversation came as a result of the repeated stage invasions mounted by two particularly 'roided-up muscle-heads the security staff were unable to deter. During a protracted pause in the second half of 'Territory', when the band would customarily take a breath before building up to their thundering conclusion, you can hear Max shouting 'Fuck off!' at the stage invaders. The disturbance continued after the song ended, as Andreas Kisser took the mic to thank the audience.

A year before, in that BBC Radio 1 *Rock Show* interview, when John Cavanagh asked the band what image they took away from their time with the Xavante, Kisser spoke about the 'unity in the tribe . . . Everybody's aware of what's happening and everyone has a right to give an opinion and speak up. It's great: no one dares do stuff on their own . . . it's a very united and democratic way of doing things.' This was the basis for 'Sepultribe', the term that the band used to describe their fans when they were promoting *Roots*. In the interview, Paulo Jr explained that, after hunting, all the rewards were divided equally amongst the Xavante. Cavanagh signed off the interview with the quip, 'Sounds like the same ethos that has kept Sepultura together to me.' The comment was met with no discernible acknowledgement from his interviewees.

After the fractious Brixton Academy gig, Sepultura imploded. Max and Gloria walked out on the band. A pall of grief had shrouded Sepultura following the death of Dana Wells, and Paulo Jr and Kisser had put pressure on Max to fire his wife, unhappy with the arrangement of Gloria managing the whole band. Unable to reach a compromise between the two sides of the band, Max – widely recognised as its leader – left. The much-vaunted stable line-up of Sepultura, that had survived for more than a decade, fell apart that cold winter's night in south London.

II. Future breed machine

Though 1996 saw metal adapting to the end of an era, it also promised new beginnings. I had gone to Sepultura's Brixton gig with my friend Chris Page, who went on to DJ and produce drum'n'bass as part of DC Breaks, signed to Andy C's RAM records. I asked him what he remembered from the night. He said, 'I think we were only about fourteen at the time and going to a metal gig in Brixton felt pretty edgy. That was half the appeal of course, but what struck me was that although the crowd and mosh-pits were full of much older, bigger, crazier guys and girls, there was a certain – almost tribal – camaraderie amongst the people in the crowd. If you fell someone always scooped you up. At the end of the show, Max Cavalera brought his family and kids out on stage and they were there all drumming along with them which was pretty cool.'

For a generation of teenagers who were starting to dabble in the crossover rock and dance of the mid-nineties, this era of metal sat at the extreme end of music in different fields that fed off the same hi-octane raw energy – what Chris describes as a 'sheer wall of power': 'I was also really into crossover metal and dance music at the time. It was like the best of both worlds. The Prodigy were massively influential, of course, but also bands like Fear Factory who fused dance elements and effects into their sound. I think that's one of the reasons why, when jungle evolved into drum'n'bass and it started becoming dark and techy in the late nineties I lapped it up. It was dance music but with the power, darkness and energy of metal.'

The techniques used to create drum'n'bass mirror those of metal music. Soft synths, like clean guitars, are processed through distortion plug-ins that are modelled on the physical hardware distortion units used by metal bands. Tunes revolve around an all-or-nothing drop, and drum'n'bass evolved with producers creating breaks from scratch using software with sampled drum kits. This is where Sweden's Meshuggah comes in.

Meshuggah came from Umeå in north-east Sweden and, in 1996, released *Chaosphere*, a truly revolutionary album in terms of how it used unorthodox rhythm in the forefront of its song-writing. Drummer Tomas Haake created a rhythmic foundation that putatively adhered to a regular 4/4 structure, but also incorporated polyrhythms and challenging, if not downright awkward metrical deviations from standard rock'n'roll forms. They created a sound that was completely their own, one that even became a subject of a 2007 academic paper by Jonathan Pieslak, 'Re-casting Metal: Rhythm and Meter in the Music of Meshuggah'.

In this paper, Pieslak summarises Meshuggah's approach: '[T]he guitars, bass, and pedal bass drum are based on a large-scale odd time signature and mixed meter while the cymbals (or some other instrument of the drum set, usually a hi-hat) maintain a steady quarter-note pulse that expresses a symmetrical, hypermetric structure.' Pieslak notes that the melodies of the guitars in *Chaosphere* are usually arranged in a tight chromatic framework – up to a minor third above the tonal centre – and the riffs move in semi-tonal increments.[3] The overall effect is of music deliberate in its rigidity, with challenging dissonance and unstoppable momentum.

The track at the vanguard of the *Chaosphere* album is 'New Millennium Cyanide Christ', which launches itself like an off-balance, giant mechanised monster into the fray. The hilarious video Meshuggah made for the song was captured on a grainy camcorder with the band sat in a shitty tour bus, nodding their heads and playing air parts to the song.[4] Its budget over-exaggerates the term 'made on a shoestring'. Even so, Haake demonstrates the metrical rigidity of the track with faultless air-drumming, sat on the top bunk of the bus. For all of the song's juddering magnificence, it's when the band lock together in passages of more regular groove that the power of this emergent breed of heavy metal modernity is affirmed. The breakdown at the end of the song is terrifying in its alien intensity.

This angular, uncompromising quality is found elsewhere in Scandinavian music. The Cheiron Studios production team in Stockholm, led by Denniz Pop, defined the sound of pop music in the late nineties. They worked with Britney Spears, Backstreet Boys and NSYNC. One of their producers, Andreas Carlsson, was featured in the BBC documentary *Flat Pack Pop: Sweden's Music Miracle*, where he talked about co-producing NSYNC's 'Bye Bye Bye'. 'Does that sound like R&B? No. It sounds like something da-da-da-da-duh-duh . . . duh-de-duh. It's got that Swedish rigid, everything perfect . . . it doesn't have a natural, laidback R&B feel to it. It's something else.'[5] That 'something else', as far removed from pop music as Meshuggah stands, also underpins *Chaosphere*.

Meshuggah's influence on metal has been huge (Devin Townsend on the song 'Planet of the Apes' baldly states, 'We all rip off Meshuggah!'), and they came to have a direct impact on the evolving sound of drum'n'bass. In 1999, Haake entered a studio with Meshuggah engineer Daniel Bergstrand and guitarist Fredrik Thordendal to record his drums for a new piece of drum machine software developed by the company Toontrack, called 'Drumkit from Hell'. The band loved the software so much that they used it on their 2005 album *Catch Thirty-Three* and a remastered re-release of their 2002 album *Nothing* the following year.

Nik Roos of drum'n'bass act Noisia also used the software. 'To be honest, growing up I didn't really get into metal. I got into the fringes of it, but only later on when I was already deeply enveloped in electronic music I started exploring it. I especially like Meshuggah. Because of their use of cross-rhythms, the tonality of the riffs and the guitar sounds. Also the video for "New Millennium Cyanide Christ" is awesome.' Roos has used Noisia to develop new forms of heaviness, propelled by the innovation of Meshuggah and led on by their own thirst for the new: 'Not all our music is "heavy" in a classical sense, I think, but a lot of it is pretty intense. I think in the electronic world there's lots of different ways things can sound "heavy", meaning we're not reliant on the sound of mainly guitars and acoustic drumkits. This has always been an exciting area for us to explore – creating new sounds that are visceral and intense but not based on traditional amps/stomp boxes, etc. but on synths and their myriad parameters and effects. Sounds maybe no one has ever heard before.'

Paul Harding, a.k.a. El Hornet, DJ of crossover act Pendulum (who themselves played Donington's main stage in 2009 and 2011 after it was resurrected as Download Festival), sampled directly from Machine Head and Megadeth: 'The power of metal wasn't something I could compare to anything else and when I started to become interested in electronic music, it seemed that drum'n'bass was really the only genre that held my interest in the same way.' The blend of organic and electronic sounds is a part of an ongoing evolution of heaviness that Paul Harding and Pendulum see acted out in the group's music. For him, the earth-shattering hugeness of the resulting sound acts as a kind of personality test to find out who is open or closed to the ways of the heavy: 'Heaviness occupies a time and place in one's life journey if you're programmed in that way and not everyone is. That's what makes it great, I think. It's not for everyone, thankfully. I love heavy music because I view it as an evolution from organic sound. It's like man harvested the destructive power of nature and turned it into sounds that don't exist naturally. Either that makes goose bumps stand up on your neck or it makes you run a hundred miles away from it. Either way, the extremity of human reactions to heaviness complement the weight of what you're hearing perfectly.'

This notion that a taste for heaviness is pre-programmed and is not for everyone makes it feel like a secret society – a tribe with a shared code that is impregnable from the outside. Let's face it – a lot of heavy music fans like it that way. And if you don't like it – then you can fuck off. But what happened when new forms of 'heavy' music emerged that *lots* of people liked?

III. Do you call that heavy?!

Though Meshuggah became a totem of a new era of metal, this period of the mid-to-late nineties was also a problem for the genre's relationship with heaviness. It was coming to terms with another kind of self. Between the Monsters of Rock of 1994 and the final festival in 1996, a distinctly 'new' brand of metal – as represented by Pantera, Machine Head and Sepultura – transitioned into the 'nu' metal of which Korn was at the vanguard. A slew of bands followed. Sepultura were caught at the intersection of this change and it is debatable whether Sepultura at the time of *Roots*, with their downtuned riffs, streetwise aesthetic and Ross Robinson at the production desk, were now a nu-metal band. They were snuffed out before the debate properly began. But *Roots* was a landmark heavy album either way.

Many of the bands that followed Korn – Papa Roach, P.O.D. (with the added ignominy of being a *Christian* metal band) and Alien Ant Farm – were merely simulating heaviness. They made pop music with distorted guitars. They asked challenging questions about heaviness being absent from metal itself. There were, and still are, metal bands that simply were not heavy, who were going through the motions, merely *performing* heaviness. One of the reasons nu metal came to be so detested was that a lot of the nascent genre's 'heaviness' was purely cosmetic.

A case in point was Limp Bizkit. I don't think the band's first two albums are without their merits, particularly the adamantine guitar playing of Wes Borland on 1999's *Significant Other*. Limp Bizkit summited the British charts during the campaign for their third album, the abominably titled *Chocolate Starfish and the Hot Dog Flavored Water* (2000). They reached UK No. 1 in the singles chart on 27 January 2001 with 'Rollin' (Air Raid Vehicle)' and sat there for two consecutive weeks. Limp Bizkit took a nu-metal single platinum. It reached the broadest possible audience with a twenty-first-century variant on the rap-rock formula that had proved so successful for Beastie Boys in the eighties and Rage Against the Machine in the nineties.

The video for 'Rollin' . . .' saw Limp Bizkit performing on top of the south tower of the World Trade Center. When the twin towers were destroyed later that year, the video became an artefact of an era lost for ever in the rubble, debris and dust.

Lostprophets – a Welsh band that enjoyed huge success amidst a late nineties' wave of loosely connected British bands who in turn seemed to despise each other[6] – sold millions of albums, supported Metallica and enjoyed mainstream adulation. In a *Kerrang!* tour report as they mounted an assault on the USA ('America's most wanted!' read the cover tagline), singer Ian Watkins said, 'Our song ['Last Train Home'] is on the radio but we're still a touring band, a working-class band and people here are seeing that. We want people who turn into real fans – not just music that turns into dollars.'[7] Watkins went on to betray what 'real fans' they acquired. Just as behind the mask of 'heaviness' they were found wanting, so behind the good-looking veneer of Watkins lurked the worst kind of behaviour imaginable.

Who knew that Lostprophets harboured a monster like Ian Watkins? His conviction as a paedophile in 2013 and sentencing to twenty-nine years in prison – and the gut-churning details of his crimes – have turned the band's legacy into pure poison. The sentencing remarks made by Justice Royce in December 2013 revealed that Watkins 'plumbed new depths of depravity'. His example is extreme but he embodied the shadow side of a male rock star's power. As Royce recorded in his judgement, 'You had many fawning fans. That gave you power. You knew you could use that power to induce young female fans to help satisfy your apparently insatiable lust and to take part in the sexual abuse of their young children. Away from the highlights of your public performances lay a dark and sinister side.'[8] Watkins' actions were indigestible to the metal community, as well as wider society.

IV. Slipknot in the shadow of 9/11

Towards the end of the eighteenth century, a pantomime clown called Joey, a.k.a. Joseph Grimaldi, was reinventing the conventions of the harlequinade on London's theatre stages. He became famous for slowing down performances, increasing audience anticipation and incorporating his own short utterances into the routines, including one when he came onstage: 'Here we are again.'[9]

On 'People = Shit', the opening track of Slipknot's second album, 2001's *Iowa*, it is singer Corey Taylor who roars a bastardisation of the same salutary welcome: 'Here we go again, motherfuckers!' Slipknot was a band run by a member known simply as Clown (real name Shawn Crahan) and not unlike his Regency-era antecedent, Crahan brought a loutish, chaotic sense of threat to the already frenetic live performances of the band, as one of its two percussionists. In the live setting, when not beating his assortment of keg drums with a baseball bat or using the hydraulic riser to balance precariously above the melee, he regularly conducted altercations with the band's other freewheeling members, particularly turntablist DJ Sid – scuffling and roughhousing each other onstage.

Like another game-changing group, the Wu-Tang Clan, Slipknot had nine members. 'The Nine' wore overalls and individually designed masks that one journalist thought gave them the appearance of an 'army of psychotic mutants'.[10] By the time of *Iowa*, Crahan's mask had morphed from a standard party clown look to a grotesque, gnarled visage with part of its brain exposed and an inverted pentagram scarred on its face. Crahan liked to drench his mask in fake blood before shows. Slipknot's already extreme pantomime was being taken to its darkest place during modern America's darkest era.

Rather than make their second album lean on the huge success of their self-titled 1999 debut, rather than ensure it moved forward with a more accessible sound in the vein of its singles, the band wanted (in Taylor's words) to 'set fire to the sophomore curse'. They did the opposite of what they were expected to do and wore the stigma of coming from Iowa as a badge of honour. The album's naked aggression and its aphotic view of both their home state and the USA as a whole turned it into one of the heaviest albums of all time. As Taylor later put it: 'We shot for the moon and blew it to smithereens.' He saw it as the final foothold on their mountain climb to megastardom.[11]

'People = Shit' kicks off *Iowa* with blast beats, which have been the calling card for sonic extremity in metal since the emergence of grindcore. Joey Jordison's drumming throughout the record sends the band into hyperdrive, blending extreme metal with a modern groove that pushed Slipknot's sound into the red again and again. The rest of the album pivots on the extraordinary vocal performance of Taylor, pushed in the studio once again by the mercurial Ross Robinson. With the singer on the cusp of a serious alcohol problem, the album helped focus much of the poison and pent-up aggression Taylor was storing inside. The recording became a release valve. He temporarily quit smoking and drinking for a few weeks and then started up again, his voice returning in an even rawer tone so he could 'barrel through' the screaming parts. Replicating this unbridled performance on subsequent tours, he almost destroyed his voice for good.

On second song 'Disasterpiece', as well as beginning the song with the album's most arresting lyric ('I want to slit your throat and fuck the wound'), Taylor pitches his voice down to a guttural tone that sounds like it has been wrenched from the pit of his stomach. The message is clear: he is taking on the death metal greats. The song mirrors the shape and dynamism of 'Eyeless' from their debut album. It explodes into an out-of-control-train main verse section, then later reduces down to a subdued build-up that culminates in an explosive breakdown, following which the band bring it all down again to Taylor crooning, in the vein of a lullaby, 'All I have is dead, so I'll take you with me/I feel like I'm erased – so kill me just in case'. The band collectively lash out the final beatdown with even more violence. Rollercoaster songwriting like this proved an addictive formula.

Elsewhere, Taylor was outstripping his nu-metal contemporaries with the searing choruses and melodies woven into tracks like singles 'Left Behind' and 'My Plague'. On *Iowa*, he delivered a perfect execution of the blueprint laid out by Fear Factory's Burton C. Bell on *Demanufacture* six years previously. Slipknot took the nu-metal project to its logical conclusion, with an aesthetic that saw them infiltrate provincial town centres all over the world. Everyone knew who they were. Between 2001 and 2002 they were the greatest live band on the planet and, to my mind, the best band on the planet full-stop.

When the planes slammed into the World Trade Center on 9/11, Corey Taylor was up early in his apartment in Des Moines. He was packing for the first date of the band's tour for *Iowa*, which had been released two weeks previously. On the tenth anniversary of those attacks he reflected, 'Everything got really weird after that, especially with heavy music and music that's a little more in-your-face.'[12] Metal bands faced an interesting quandary after 9/11 – there were concerns over security and also a harder-to-define cultural sensitivity around heavy music. It had been felt before, when Marilyn Manson became a displaced target for anger after the Columbine high school massacre in 1999. In the immediate period post-9/11 it was falsely reported that Louis

Armstrong's 'What a Wonderful World' was banned from American airwaves, along with a host of heavy rock songs.[13] For the story to seem credible, it reflected an edginess in the air around heavy culture – the intense outpouring of emotion sequestered in metal music seemed to be overwhelmed by the American public's sense of grief and anguish. Maybe it was also the case that heavy artists felt they themselves were somehow vulgar, or playing too lightly with fire, in this new era. Stranded by this dilemma, Slayer and Pantera were in Ireland at the same time as Taylor was packing his bags, poised to begin a series of massive co-headlining gigs under the banner Tattoo the Planet. The tour was postponed, before Slayer returned to headline on their own in October. As we know, Pantera were then effectively finished.

Slipknot's eerily (and perhaps aptly) named Pledge of Allegiance tour, by contrast, went ahead. Dan Silver from *Kerrang!* magazine reported on an incident at the Great Western Forum, LA, where Corey Taylor took the radical step of holding a minute's silence for the victims of the terrorist atrocity. It was a tactic to calm the crowd, who were getting out of control. The trouble had begun when the singer commanded, 'Get the fuck down on the ground' for 'Spit It Out'. Getting the crowd to crouch or sit on the floor before exhorting them to 'jump the fuck up' for the song's finale was one of the dictatorial theatrics that were an innovation of the band and copied by many others since (see also DJ Sid crowd-surfing and lashing out at non-compliant fans during their London Docklands Arena show in 2002 on their *Disasterpieces* DVD). In this instance, 'the maggots' (as the band called their fans) in the seats took this as an order to storm the standing part of the venue. The fire marshall demanded Slipknot pull the plug and it was then that Taylor came up with his piece of quick thinking that not only saved the show but also tapped into the profound hurt felt by the country. An intense sense of the USA being on a renewed, continual war footing had emerged – an atmosphere that the band themselves exuded. The 3 November 2001 issue of *Kerrang!* contained the report of the incident at the gig, with a cover photo of Clown pointing his fingers in a gun sign at DJ Sid's head emblazoned with the headline 'Slipknot. On tour. At war.'

On meeting Clown, the writer Dan Silver was immediately asked whether he wanted to fight ('This is one of his good days,' shrugged the publicist), before setting Jordison off on a prolonged rant about what *Iowa*'s struggles represented to the band: 'A lot of our songs on *Iowa* are about the press, how people think they've figured us out, that they think they have the right to say things about our personal lives in the press in front of millions of people when they have no fucking clue what it's like to wear that fucking shit every night and go out there and kill each other and do that for two years straight while trying to support an album and still maintain a homelife.' As their country was being drawn into more divisive conflicts, each night Slipknot seemed to be simulating a war of its own. And as it was for the troops that came to flood into Afghanistan and later Iraq, the physical and mental stresses took their toll for years afterwards.

In an interview conducted backstage in 2008, on the band's tour of their fourth album *All Hope is Gone*, Crahan's fellow percussionist Chris Fehn spoke about the band like a veteran with PTSD talking about his last stint in a theatre of war.[14] In a conversation with a quietly penetrating Dutch journalist, Fehn related that when he sat at home off-tour, come 7 p.m. he started to feel anxiety in anticipation of the gig and adrenaline release that would not be happening. He described how he went to bed late and slept into the afternoon. At least he had better rest than he got with the twenty-minute naps he grabbed on tour. It used to take him a month to acclimatise to life back home: being able to shop for, and feed, himself, and to experience the sunlight denied to the band so often during their nocturnal existence on extensive stints in Europe. He spoke of Slipknot's periods off-tour as 'time to heal' and the downtime between shows while travelling as an attempt 'to try everything we can not to fucking lose it' before they eventually got to 'throw that darkness out' onstage.

Killing time on these tours of duty was spent gambling, playing computer games, and trying to speak to family and friends back home, just like any other soldier. Then there were the hazing rituals of being in the band itself. For years, Fehn was a peripheral member of the band. This was despite the fact that, alone with Crahan, when he donned his bondage-style 'liar and hat' mask, and thumped out the introduction to '(sic)' – the first song on the band's debut album – Clown announced that Fehn was the one. Each member identifying himself by a number, for a long time he was denied no. 3 – the only vacant position between 0 and 8 that each member was assigned. At the same time, he was held hostage to the band, worried about breaking up that number sequence to which he was being denied ownership. He craved the love and support of his bandmates and for years was refused it, only feeling he had truly ascended to his role some ten years into his tenure in the band. 'I finally came to a time in my life where I'm no. 3, man, and no one else can do what I do. If someone else tried to imitate me it wouldn't be the same.' Fehn eventually left the band in 2019 citing issues with how the business of the band was conducted and around imbalances in pay and compensation.[15] Ultimately, his complaint was the same as ten years previously: he wasn't treated as an equal.

Slipknot acknowledges that the *Iowa* period was the most difficult and fractured of their career. However, the record reaching
UK No. 1 showed that, like the traditional pantomime which
they mimicked, they were successfully reflecting the mood of a
generation back at itself. When they played Reading Festival in
August 2002 I saw a band at the peak of their savage powers,
playing a blitzkrieg set in the early evening. The whirling mosh-
pits erupted everywhere as they dragged in the curious bystand-
ers, who must have seen those Slipknot hoodies in the shopping
centres of towns just like Reading and been curious enough to
enter the fray. The television footage of the performance was
given a particularly strange introduction by the presenter, and it
is hard to know whether he is speaking about the band or its
rabid audience when he said, 'They're the kids that Bush and
Clinton forgot. Be afraid, it's Slipknot.'[16]

It was actually another nu-metal band that was at the top of the
album charts on 9/11 itself. System of a Down's *Toxicity* is the
other crowning achievement of the subgenre. It was a further
indictment of the malaise in pop and the waning power of MTV
that nu metal's modern take on heavy guitars was now storming
the charts just as it had taken Castle Donington.

The LA-based band, famous for all its members having
Armenian heritage, drew attention to the heavier parts of
Armenia's history when they highlighted the Armenian genocide
at the hands of the Ottoman empire, from 1915 for the best part of
a decade. It was a forgotten past of a forgotten region. Hitler cited
it when Germany invaded Poland in a speech of 22 August 1939:
'Who, after all, speaks today of the annihilation of the Armenians?'[17]

System of a Down were not as psychotically enraged as
Slipknot, but they were politicised and keen to engage their
fanbase on the state of things. Their anger burned in a controlled

and pointed way, and often relented in favour of wacky, subversive subject matter. In a typically mordant article about going to Reading Festival with his son in 2014, the novelist Will Self described System of a Down 'as straight outta Yerevan and . . . a hellishly professional racket'.[18]

Toxicity veers from the detailed breakdown of the injustice of mandatory minimum jail sentences on 'Prison Song', to the joys of group sex on 'Bounce'. In the wake of the fall of the twin towers, their single 'Chop Suey!' was on the fake banned song list (supposedly because it mentioned the word 'suicide'). The song 'Jet Pilot' also stood out on the album, not only because it featured some of guitarist Daron Malakian's chunkiest and fastest riffing. It seemed Serj Tankian's lyrics were oddly prescient of 9/11: 'Wired were the eyes of a horse on a jet pilot/One that smiled when he flew over the bay'. They invoked New York's Hudson Bay in 2001 coincidentally, but also painfully.

The song recalled the painting *Landscape with the Fall of Icarus* (*c*. 1560s) by Pieter Bruegel the Elder. The painting depicts Icarus's legs disappearing into the bay as an almost unnoticed detail in the bottom right of the canvas as a farmer ploughs a furrow with his workhorse in the centre of the foreground. It is unknown whether the horse noticed Icarus's fall. W. H. Auden in his 1939 poem 'Musée des Beaux Arts' (which he wrote after seeing Bruegel's painting in Belgium) noted 'how everything turns away/Quite leisurely from the disaster'. The poem begins, 'About suffering they were never wrong,/The Old Masters', and neither were System of a Down, even if the lyric of 'Jet Pilot' contained unknowing prescience.

As nu metal itself died out, Slipknot and System of a Down thrived. But Slipknot also continued to suffer for their art, and did so in the most self-conscious way possible. They really *performed* it, and injected metal with a sense of showmanship that had been largely driven out during the early-to-mid-nineties, surviving in the live shows of Marilyn Manson. They pushed a shocking theatricality at the time of a terrorist act that itself was larger than life: 9/11 begged to be interpreted as a surreal disaster movie or some other form of representation, to drive it somehow away from its own reality. I found it hard to cope with the footage captured by a documentary crew who happened to be accompanying the fire department that day: the sickening, explosive sound of glass smashing as people fell hopelessly to their deaths.[19] I was distressed to learn recently that the audio in the footage had been altered so that the explosive impacts of falling people occurred less frequently.[20] Slipknot's larger-than-life nihilism exploded at just the right moment to accompany it. Cold comfort it might have been, but their music was also a pressure-release valve for us as much as for them. Their reward was to become one of the biggest bands in the world. 'This is the end of everything/ You are the end of everything!' Corey Taylor screamed at us on 'Everything Ends', and we screamed it back at him – entwined in a too-tight embrace as we fell together at the start of the twenty-first century.

9

UNDER THE SURFACE

'Thunderous resonant sounds call from beyond the
depths/And the winds of gravity change/Into memories
of the consciousness of ancient rocks/Nature's answer
to eternal question' – Sunn O))), 'Aghartha'

Averting its eyes from a reality that was getting all too real, heavy music started to excavate the ancient tones and primitive identity of our history and even pre-history in 'archaeo-sonic' drones. As well as pursuing the white whales in our lives, the gossamer-thin veil between life and death continues to be the stalking ground of the magical realm and the promise of immortality. The search for life beyond death: this is where heaviness connects us to the centre of the Earth and our real and imagined ancestors.

I. Going underground

In 1658, the famed physician and writer Sir Thomas Browne published *Hydriotaphia, Urne-Buriall, or, a Discourse of the Sepulchral Urnes lately found in Norfolk*. The short text was a rumination on the uncovering of around fifty ancient urns in a field on the outskirts of the village of Great Walsingham in Norfolk, near where Browne lived. The urns contained human ashes, pieces of bones and funerary objects, which Browne assumed were the ashes of Romans, or of a Romanised burial practice carried out by ancient Britons. It was later established that the urns were Anglo-Saxon, from around 500 CE. Only one remains today, and even that has been hard to verify – it resides at the Ashmolean Museum in Oxford.[1]

As Browne puts it, '[T]he treasures of time lie high, in Urnes, Coynes, and Monuments, scarce below the roots of some vegetables.'[2] Just beneath the surface of the modern world lie the remains of our forefathers. Uncovering these enables a form of communication with our ancestors and their ancient practices. In *Urne-Buriall*'s meditation on mortality and what it means to be remembered after we die, Browne makes a grim assertion that the record of our lives, if one is made at all, is transitory – but that death is for ever: 'The number of the dead long exceedeth all that shall live.'[3]

At the turn of the new millennium, two American musicians – Stephen O'Malley and Greg Anderson – began deconstructing metal in their project Sunn O))): experimenting with drawn-out, overdriven layers of sound that felt massive in a new way. They made music on a tectonic scale and their 'songs' took the form of meditative excavations of the sonic underworld – enabling a reconnection with a primitive dream of the past, which prefigured music itself. There is very little overt rhythmic architecture to their sound; but the timing between shifts in the drone is important in a broader, maximal sense: in the same way that a planet slowly revolves on its axis.

As O'Malley said in an interview for their 2019 album *Life Metal*, 'Sound energy is basically what our music is all about.

Besides the human aspect, I think it's the most important element of what Sunn O))) is: creating this, or channelling or enabling this . . . energy. And it's exciting to be inside of that and to experience that when it's happening.'[4] Like any loud, heavy music, this 'sound energy' elicits an initial, physical response of primitive alarm in the listener (pupils dilate, heart rate increases, digestion slows). It is the sound of ancient worry; standing-stone blues.

Sunn O))) (pronounced 'Sun') were named after a particularly powerful form of amplifier favoured by the heavy rock acts of the sixties and seventies. Their name is a transcription of the logo and the glyph, 'O)))', represents the soundwave itself emanating outwards. The name was also a tongue-in-cheek reference to the band Earth, whose second album *Earth 2*, from 1993, was one of the first serious forays into drone metal. The message was that Earth could now revolve around Sunn O))).

In England, former Teardrop Explodes frontman and psychedelic specialist Julian Cope had also begun experimenting with drone. In 2001, he released *L.A.M.F Ambient Metal*, after which he was contacted by a German reviewer who commented that Cope must really love Sunn O))). As he told me, Cope was initially confused. 'I'd never heard Sunn O))). But what amazed me was that it was ploughing exactly the same furrow. It was clearly poetically truthful because I got there without knowing they existed. And I found in that case the evidence is in the music itself. That it's necessary.'

Cope had just spent eight years travelling Europe, researching his books *The Megalithic European: The Twenty-First Century Traveller in Prehistoric Europe* (2004) and, before that, *The Modern Antiquarian: A Pre-Millennial Odyssey Through Megalithic Britain* (1998). He speaks of maintaining two parallel selves to research the books: 'I've always considered myself to be visionary. And the only reason I've considered myself to be visionary is that I'm informed by rock'n'roll. And to such a degree that it takes me into the underworld. What is essential when you're travelling in the underworld, for somebody who is a writer, is to be able to keep a parallel, intellectual Self running across the top to see what's going on, or you can't report back.'

By touring the megalithic monuments of Europe, Cope was exploring what he calls 'archaeo-sonics': features of ancient temples that conjured intimidating sonic effects. Monuments like West Kennet Long Barrow near his home in Avebury, Wiltshire, as well as sites in Sardinia, Scotland, Malta and Armenia, confirmed to him that placing yourself in certain positions within them created a bottleneck for flowing air. These produced a low, droning aural effect. He imagined it was an intentional device for the shamanic elder to intimidate the initiates brought into the structure: 'It would make initiates suddenly think, Oh fuck, the god is in here with us. And it would give the priest incredible authority. So, however clever they were – I'm not doubting that they weren't just trying to create some phenomenal effects, but I've no idea what the reasons were. And I always suspect priest-hoods – rather than think, Ooo, isn't that nice?'

In the music of Sunn O))) he identified the 'interface with the total barbarian self' which unifies heavy rock and our pagan heritage. As such he found it 'useful' music for active meditation.

The times I have seen Sunn O))) – in the crypt of the Oran Mor church, Glasgow, in 2004 (the diners in the restaurant upstairs got refunds when the vibrations from below caused debris from light fittings to land in their meals),[5] the Royal Festival Hall, London, in 2015, and the capital's Barbican Centre in 2017 and Roundhouse in 2019 (where someone passed out in front of me)

– the extremity of the volume and sheer pressure of the sound they generate has initially felt oppressive, like a poisonous gas billowing out over the audience. After ten minutes or so of immersion in that sonic magma, and only then, have I been able to settle into that meditative state, and the music's union of the primitive and modern that Cope sees as otherwise 'psychically lacking in the northern hemisphere'.

In *Urne-Buriall*, Thomas Browne wrote, 'Oblivion is not to be hired: The greater part must be content to be as though they had not been, to be found in the Register of God, not in the record of man.'[6] For Cope, the state that Sunn O))) enables is a route to oblivion that bypasses notions of God as well: 'It's a kind of psychic meltdown that I call "eternal cuntedness". And it's really sweet, because it's an oblivion that's at one with the underworld but it's also of the stars at the same time. And it would totally bypass religion if you could get people to just interface with a certain amount of sonic experiences every week.'

Cope was deeply impressed with Sunn O))). He became close friends with O'Malley (who is also known by the anagram SOMA, *soma* being the ancient Greek term for the (dead) body or life in the physical world) – 'He is sonically experimental but he is also obsessed with understanding the mythical side to it.' Cope held Anderson in similarly high regard as O'Malley's facilitator but also something more: 'He's one of the most open-minded musicians I've ever met, is Greg, because in some ways you'd think he'd be the less forward-thinking of the pair but he's always open to going, "Yeah, I'm playing Moog tonight. I've never played it in my life." That's completely brilliant.'

When they played live together, Cope discovered that Sunn O))) tuned to the resonant frequency of the venue they were playing in, creating an architectural sonic reverberation much in the manner of the shamans of ancient long barrows and stone temples. As Cope recalled, when they played at the Lyric Theatre, Hammersmith, the agitated manager of the Victorian structure rushed up to them during soundcheck and said, 'You've got to turn it down because this theatre is from 1893 and all the plaster is coming off the ceiling.' The band used forward-facing and unconventional means of creating the drone – at the time fellow instrumentalist Rex Ritter was using a G4 powerbook for the bass frequencies. Cope was impressed: 'It's not just a Luddite thrash, it's very alchemical, forward-thinking – let's use digital technology to remove the best part of our brain.'

In October 2018, Steve Goodman, founder of the Hyperdub record label, a.k.a. dubstep pioneer Kode9, did the sound design for a new installation for Cuban artist Tania Bruguera. This involved installing a massive 40,000-watt sound system in the turbine hall of the Tate Modern gallery in London. Using it to produce unsettling low frequencies, the project was about getting a physical and emotional response to the migration crisis on the doorstep of Europe.[7] Just as Sunn O))) have long deployed vast amounts of dry ice to establish an atmosphere at their performances, Bruguera also released an invisible gas that triggered visitors to cry.

Goodman is a kindred spirit of Sunn O))). He seeks to use the technology available to him to move his listeners, with discomforting and dread-inducing subsonic power. Goodman also takes an academic interest in this practice. In his book *Sonic Warfare: Sound, Affect, and the Ecology of Fear* (2012), he explores how low-frequency sound moved from the realm of hearing into an affected, felt experience that could be used to produce literal bad vibrations. In one section of the book he cites the use of infrasound in Gasper Noé's 2002 film *Irreversible*. If the movie's graphic depictions of sexual violence were not nausea-inducing enough, Noé added 27 Hz of infrasound, which on a good cinema subwoofer could push the audience over the edge. As Noé put it in an interview: 'You can't hear it, but it makes you shake.'[8]

Sunn O))) and Cope collaborated on the song 'My Wall' from 2003's *White 1* album. On the song, Cope invokes the landscape of Wansdyke, otherwise known as Woden's Dyke, a Roman earth-work that runs west through Wiltshire and Somerset for about sixty miles towards the Bristol Channel. Unaltered for several miles at a time, it consists of a steep bank and trench on its leeside. It was a defensive structure and a means of controlling passage, marked with forts along it. As he intones on the song: 'And I do walk upon Wan's Dyke/And I do survey the land/And I did become the reaper with my own bare hands/For I am Woden'.

In Cope's spoken word, summoning ritual, the earthwork is described as an interzone where all shall 'stand in the thrall of my tidal wall'. The wave of monotheistic religions is literally broken against its ramparts and usurped by a Norse pantheism: 'Not Abraham/Not Moses/And not Christ/Neither Jove to who we sacrificed/Not Altis/Not Mohammed/But to hilltop Thor'. The individual and the archetypal gods of myth are usurped to nature and the hilltop, in a setting where the landscape commands all. In his lyrics, Cope playfully alludes to the band's drones being at one with nature: 'Play your gloom axe Stephen O'Malley/Sub-bass clinging to the sides of the valley/Sub-bass ringing in each last ditch and combe/Greg Anderson purvey a sonic doom'. He ends with an exhortation to join the primordial party and to get down like it's the end of the world: 'For I am Doom so Ragnarock [sic] with me'.

Over eleven minutes of the track features Cope's pagan anti-sermon, with subtle licks and melodic gestures on the guitars responding to Cope's words. Eventually, language relents and Cope asks the guitars to 'play on' and overwhelm the last fifteen minutes of the piece in total sonic obliteration. As 'heathen motherfuckers', as Cope said to me, the northern European peoples have always been resistant to the influence of the world religions, putting the 'protest' into 'Protestantism'. The Greeks turned images of Jesus into a 'blonde, bearded Zeus', but for Cope it set up inner rebellion in the northern mindset: 'And that's also why the term pagan became so heinous, because pagan is often described as meaning "of the countryside", but in actual fact it meant "civilian", in other words: not one of Christ's soldiers.' The drone of 'My Wall' is an act of resistance but also enacts the sounds of religious practice, with the refrain, 'Those meddlesome meddlesome meddlesome bells/And the heavy metal of the heathen bells'.

For Cope, the musical modes that were useful to the ancient people are transferred into religious music and then into heavy metal itself: 'One of the reasons that heavy metal occasionally sounds like religious music is because most religious music was inherited from heathen times. And so when you reduce music to its lowest common denominator, it goes down to those modes that were most useful to the ancient people.'

But, if anything, the Abrahamic religions are pulled asunder on Woden's Dyke. One telling passage of Cope's states, 'There be the ditch that you shall die in/Here be the wall that I shall cry on/Ditch dug with antler and ox bone shovel/This rising wall that shades our ancient hovel'.

Adam Thorpe's 1992 novel *Ulverton* recreates the lost voices from history of a fictional village set in the chalk downs of what might be Wiltshire. There is a chapter set in 1689 in which the village priest Reverend Crispin Brazier ventures out into a blizzard with his clerk and curate. Blasted by the snowstorm, they take shelter in the lee of a hummock called Devil's Knob, a site of heathen practice known for dubious practices such as mass copulation – an activity like the one Cope describes in 'My Wall' that might have 'spunked the vegetation into being'. In Thorpe's novel, relaying the story in a sermon to churchgoers, Brazier boastfully reminds them how he has destroyed such places in the past – 'Yea, who was it but he whom ye now see stood before you that rooted up and broke upon a great fire the seven stones of Noon's Hill?' But on this occasion, the place overwhelms his companions, who both die in the blizzard, one gripped by an inner religious ecstasy that causes him to berate the reverend's ecclesiastical teachings that 'only stuff their mouths with the serpent's food'.[9]

The ancients have a hold on the land and it is literally embedded in the upper strata of the landscape. The energy that manifests there can be channelled: it was by the shamans of old and it is in the music of Sunn O))), who arrange their amplifiers like standing stones into their own heathen configurations. Ancient sites of pagan ritual have long represented the promise of primeval violence. In Ben Wheatley's 2012 film *Sightseers*, murderous protagonists Chris and Tina are berated by a haughty walker because the dog they've just kidnapped has done a shit in a stone circle: 'If you don't pick up this excrement immediately, then I'm going to have to inform the National Trust.' After concocting enough reasons to do so with the impressionable Tina, Chris staves in their hopelessly middle-class aggressor's head with a large, ancient-looking tree branch he had been using as a walking staff. The National Trust is no protection.

With Sunn O))), ambient metal is sunk into the landscape itself. The reduction of the heavy sound to basest metal has a useful function, edging us closer to what psychoanalyst Carl Jung called 'an unknown psychic life belonging to a remote past'.[10] When Thomas Browne wrote about uncovered urns during the interregnum in England after the beheading of King Charles I, he used it to meditate on how mortal men might (or might not) be remembered posthumously. If the elemental drone of Sunn O))) imparts any heavy lessons, it is to agree with Browne that our bodies will be subsumed by the landscape itself, in one form or another: 'Since our longest Sunne sets at right descensions and makes but winter arches, and therefore it cannot be long before we lie down in darknesse and have our light in ashes.'[11]

II. Crossing over

Dan Nightingale was staying at friend and bandmate Brady Deeprose's house when he woke one bleak Sunday morning, sat up in bed and, through the window framed by curtains he prefers to keep open when he sleeps, noticed a lone tree on a hillock that gently rose into view amid the grey. It was such a desolate sight that it immediately evoked a musical atmosphere in Nightingale's head. He grabbed his laptop and tumbled down a rabbit hole, ultimately resulting in the song 'The Mire', the centrepiece of the 2018 debut album *Mire* from his band Conjurer.

Nightingale and Deeprose are the twin-headed attack line of Conjurer, both armed with guitars, and respectively, a deep, guttural roar and higher, searing scream. Conjurer blend different forms of extreme metal to describe dramatic landscapes that climb and plunge, all clinging to the appetite Nightingale has for a strain of sickeningly heavy riff that, he told me, 'just makes me want to pull the skin off my face'. *Mire*'s first song, 'Choke', shows there is more sophistication to their music than that. Its opening chords are an overture of what is to come, beginning in the pomp of a major key but shape-shifting into a minor key dirge, like a creature resplendent in the sun and then cowering from the light – preferring to skulk in the shadows.

Based in Rugby, Warwickshire, their music takes them out of their hometown and into the moors, bogs and heathland that lie beyond. On 'The Mire', and in the woodcut-like illustration of the album's cover, Nightingale shows a fascination with corpse roads traversing the landscape and the 'Lyke-Wake Dirge', a fourteenth-century chant sung by those who had accompanied such coffins. The poem originated in north Yorkshire and was used as the basis of a song by folk band Pentangle in 1969. It describes the soul's arrival at purgatory: if you, the deceased addressee, have performed charitable deeds in the form of sharing 'meat or drink', your soul will be received by Christ, but if you have not: 'The fire will burn thee to thy bare bane.'[12]

Conjurer's reinterpretation of the poem in 'The Mire' centres on a lost soul beset by the elements on the marshland, preparing for whatever torment that its creator deems necessary. The song is a blast of heathen black metal, with drummer Jan Krause driving the guitars along the corpse path in furious bursts, as they cajole and buffet the poor soul who, as Nightingale envisioned, 'didn't know it was dead, and was wandering around, terrified and confused'.

This excruciating suspension between life and death is also beautifully portrayed by Sarah Moss in her 2018 novel *Ghost Wall*. In the novel, a teenage girl called Silvie is pushed by her father to take part in an Iron Age re-enactment camp in Northumberland, as part of an experimental archaeology project. The events of the novel are haunted by the spirit of a bog girl, sacrificed by her tribe in the distant past setting of its prologue. Moss describes her murderers-to-be, 'holding her in the place she is entering now, on the edge of the water-earth, in the time and space between life and death'.[13]

The lonely tree Nightingale noticed that Sunday morning is another symbol of this suspension, being neither of the Earth nor of heaven. As one character puts it in gothic classic *Melmoth the Wanderer*, which we explored earlier in relation to black metal: 'I stand a blasted tree, struck to the heart, to the root, – I wither alone, – but you are the Upas, under whose poisonous droppings all things living have perished, – father – mother – brother, and last yourself, – the erosions of the poison, having nothing left to consume, strike inward, and prey on your own heart.'[14]

Francis Danby's painting *The Upas, or Poison-Tree, in the Island of Java* (*c*. 1820) hangs in London's V&A Museum, a vast canvas that depicts an exiled criminal in the depths of despair as he comes upon the poison tree surrounded by the corpses of other condemned men. The legend of the tree decrees that, if the criminals successfully bring some of the poison back, they will be absolved of their crimes. But it is evidently a hopeless enterprise, doomed to failure and death. The scale of the piece – towering edifices of stone take up three-quarters of the canvas, receding into a descending night – diminishes this man's plight and belittles his suffering. His fate is ultimately inconsequential faced with the immovable longevity of his surroundings. Today, as a representation of the poisoned earth, it is portentous of a dying world.

So much for land, but Conjurer also portray a place further below the surface of the Earth. The song 'Hadal' refers to the hadal zone of the ocean – from six kilometres down – or as the lyric puts it, 'A hell closer than Hell'. Switching musical modes to a terrifying, relentless form of abyssal doom, the album ends with a riff cycle that Dan Nightingale described to me as evoking the pressure of being drowned under the weight of a mountain of water:

'For the end of that album we literally wanted the feeling of being crushed and crushed and crushed. Pressure crashing down, and then just cut off, implosion – that's it, you're gone. End of.'

III. Pulled under

The sea is a vast expanse in which to be lost. You can gaze into the depths and see a version of yourself reflected back. In art, it has been treated as an arena where self and soul are wrenched apart, in the turbulence of the water, and where the end of the Earth is pursued but never gained.

The greatest novel of the madness of the ocean is Herman Melville's *Moby-Dick* (1851). The novel's anti-hero, Captain Ahab, pursues his nemesis, the titular white whale – a sperm whale with supernatural presence and a superhuman capacity for malice against its pursuer, whom it has encountered before, when it took Ahab's leg.

The book is the source material that the band Mastodon used to create their 2004 album *Leviathan*. Its opening track's title, 'Blood and Thunder', takes the phrase spewed from Ahab's lips as he roars at his men to row as hard as they can once they have dropped the whaling boats in pursuit of their quarry. The song has one of the best opening lines in all heavy music: 'I think someone is trying to kill me', predicated on Ahab's acute paranoia. 'Blood and Thunder' has long closed Mastodon's live sets, propelled by its main riff with the urgent bristle of the straining sinews of the rowers and insistent rhythm of the oars taking water.

The song is lean but still strives for more and more musicality in its complex harmonised mid-section, as the guitars weave in and out of each other like choppy waters. There is a penultimate depth charge, gripped tight with the bleeding fingernails of rowers and guitarists alike, and finished off by the death blow: a half-paced final section written to boil the sea of the mosh-pit. It's little surprise that, when invited to play a tiny venue as part of *Kerrang!* magazine's K! Pit video series, Conjurer chose to end with a cover version of this, the song that set the pace for a new generation of metal musicians pursuing their white whales into an uncertain twenty-first century.[15]

One of the key lines of 'Blood and Thunder' – 'I no longer govern my soul' – speaks to a passage from *Moby-Dick* that illustrates how the intensity of the mad passion that has gripped Ahab's mind has, in fact, created a division within himself: 'Therefore, the tormented spirit that glared out of bodily eyes, when that seemed Ahab rushed from his room, was for the time but a vacated thing, a formless somnambulistic being, a ray of living light, to be sure, but without an object to colour, and therefore a blankness in itself.'[16]

The whale holds a special place in the human imagination as a fellow mammal. Hunting them has been a symbol for pursuing what you want to come about in your life, but their condition also represents an ever-growing ecological crisis. Mercilessly hunted over the nineteenth century, their numbers are recovering and French band Gojira used them as a cipher for climate change on the song 'Flying Whales' from their album *From Mars to Sirius*, released the year after *Leviathan*. That song imagines abandoning the 'sinking ship of men' that is planet Earth in favour of escaping entirely to find the whales that have taken up residence in space.

In *A Wizard of Earthsea*, the titular wizard Sparrowhawk, otherwise known as Ged, travels to the end of the open seas beyond Earthsea's East Reach. He is hunting down the shadow he unleashed when he tore a hole in the fabric of the world, in a moment of competitive madness at his wizarding school on the island of Roke. It is only when the sea turns to a kind of black sand on which his boat is beached, that he can confront the dark being and, in a world where names are everything, call it by its proper name: his own. The sea becomes a place where he unites life and death into a complete self.

> And he began to see the truth, that Ged had neither lost nor won but, naming the shadow of his death with his own name, had made himself whole: a man: who, knowing his whole true self, cannot be used or possessed by any power other than himself, and whose life therefore is lived for life's sake and never in the service of ruin, or pain, or hatred, or the dark.[17]

In 2018 the Wigan band Boss Keloid released their album *Melted on the Inch*, an album of monstrous waves of riffs with a sea-shanty-esque approach to its songwriting. On opening track 'Chronosiam', the undulating melody lines are a means to reach out and explore turbulent seas in a more joyous mode: 'Let's sail, rhythm of waves. We shine, we discover/Let's sail through barriers. In sight the lights still breathing'. Even if the song has an undercurrent of insecurity, it is in the striving for stability and self-worth on stormy seas: 'I'm alone, all alone, king of my own island/All the negativity has grown. Be myself, by myself. Try dislocating from the hollow/I'd never be who I'd be, if it wasn't for me/Digging up the pieces from the dirt. Now I know what I know/I'm . . .'. They leave that final self-identification inconclusive but the dry land, the island of self in the sea of life, is the important thing to cling on to.

Alexander Hurst, the band's singer and rhythm guitarist, uses music as a way of projecting positivity and a settled sense of that self: 'It's very important and I find myself writing about this kind of thing a lot. It helps me persuade myself to get in that mindset and steer myself towards PMA (Positive Mental Attitude). I think positivity and self-belief is important in such a negative world. I love music, it's my only hobby and the only thing that keeps me from going mental, so positive music is the only way. You can have positivity in anger as well though, if you direct the anger in the right direction, if you get me.'

Boss Keloid's previous album, the brilliantly named *Herb Your Enthusiasm* (2016), was a surreal and loose concept album about smoking weed and the various chambers of the mind that it opens, and the distortion it exerts on reality. For example, the sinister creep of 'Cone': 'I'm in control/A psychedelic conversation can become so difficult'. For *Melted on the Inch*, Hurst says the songwriting was allowed to flow in the direction of the strongest creative currents: 'We really don't set out to create a certain type of music or a certain type of vibe. We sort of just roll with the flow and let it take us where it wants to. Every album we have created is a different beast to the last. I think it's just down to us letting our musical flavours evolve and not being scared to try anything. Freedom of creation is really important, I think. I would hate to have to write songs a certain way because people expect it. Paul, our guitar player, comes up with some amazing riffs and we just jump on the riff snake and ride it into the creation jungle where nothing is dismissed. If it sounds good then we use it.'

For me, the album's unique, almost jaunty, salt-in-the-beard sound means its title is an empty vessel for listeners to fill with their interpretation of what the band means. Hurst stressed the importance of that process to me: 'I suppose it can mean to the listener whatever they want it to. The same goes for the track names and the artwork. Let people connect with whatever they wish was the idea and it's beautiful to hear what each song means to different people and what people think the album title means. That's what we wanted.'

Thus, heavy music's depiction of the churning seas is one of challenge and turbulence that contributes to obsession and the sundering of the self. This reflects the ebb and flow of life. Cling on to whatever you can. Try to settle wherever life disgorges you.

IV. Don't let me be misunderstood

Dan Nightingale always has a guitar to hand, whether he's watching a film or playing *God of War*, the visionary 2018 video game about the character Kratos and his journey with his son to place his wife's ashes on the highest peak of the mythic realm of Midgard. It's while relaxing in this way that inspiration often strikes Nightingale. A corny, overdubbed lightning strike sound effect from Sam Raimi's *Evil Dead II* (1987) previously inspired a riff for his old metalcore band: as soon as he heard it he wrote it on the guitar with some necessary adumbrations, which he calls 'the *School of Rock* way of doing it'.

By contrast, Nightingale had to watch Ken Russell's banned 1972 classic *The Devils* (based on Aldous Huxley's book *The Devils of Loudon*) several times before it resonated with him. Long commercially unavailable in any decent quality, it wasn't until the BFI put out a special edition DVD of the original X certificate version in 2012 that Nightingale rewatched it. He ended up turning it off again during a strange and hilarious scene where a clearly fake apothecary crocodile is thrown out of a window. But, on the third attempt, Nightingale was floored: 'I love the dialogue, I love the performances. The set pieces are just magical – everything about it I love.'

When Nightingale began writing what would become the first song on their EP *I* – 'Behold the Swine' – he soon realised that *The Devils* was the right way to frame the lyrical theme of the song. 'The one thing I've always been really scared of is being misunderstood and people not getting me and getting where I'm coming from.' Oliver Reed's portrayal of the Jesuit priest Urbain Grandier found a man with flaws – a chauvinist, who pushed the bounds of decency to the limit, but also a man who Nightingale says, 'did not give a shit about being misunderstood. He knew he was clear: his conscience was clear.' As the flames lick higher and higher in the film's climax, in which Grandier is burned at the stake, he requests permission to pass over to the afterlife in the face of his accusers screaming for a confession: 'Give me the kiss of peace and let me die.'

Conjurer used this sample over the introductory clean melodic guitar lines that begin 'Behold the Swine'. It works like a veil being lifted before the main faith-shaking riff and chopped-up rhythm comes down on our heads like the walls of Loudon's fortifications in the film. Grandier is not the wandering soul of 'The Mire' but instead represents a confidence and self-assurance that many lost souls would want to be remembered for. Conjurer might be their guide.

18

ALIVE IN THE SUPERUNKNOWN

'Down in a hole and I don't know if I can be
saved' – Alice in Chains, 'Down In A Hole'

'Only first and second persons matter (I and
thou). And by all means forget dreams' –
Thomas Ligotti, 'Dream of a Manikin'[1]

Kurt Cobain died with Nirvana at their height – before I'd even
heard of them. 'Nirvana' in the Buddhist tradition means
'extinguishing' or 'blown out'. Layne Staley died long after Alice
in Chains's albums had cut deep into my musical life. Chris
Cornell died while Soundgarden were consolidating their place
in the pantheon. Somehow, grunge is all about dying.

The ghosts of grunge haunt an often unsettled intersection
in terms of the evolution of heaviness. Incubated in the mid-
to-late eighties, and exploding in the early nineties, grunge
announced the turn of that decade. Remembered for smashing
the empty china dolls of glam metal that dominated the heavy
rock scene, grunge's sound was itself pulled three ways: fuzzy,
feral punk; downer, slow-motion drone; and titanic, Sabbathian
metal.

Hard to pin down, grunge was thrown in with other hard-to-categorise musical styles as 'alternative music'. It came to punch through into popular culture more effectively than any of the musical styles that formed its key ingredients. It was so popular that its unprecedented emotional intensity was taken as a given. Almost thirty years later, and beset by so much tragedy and lost lives, it stands as an undeniable monument in the story of heaviness. It is not surprising that it is being re-filtered through musicians who have grunge in their DNA.

No other heavy musical movement looked at drugs, depression and self-abuse with such unflinching intensity, or took it to such a vast audience. Its ability to enthral and empower its listenership is also hard to touch.

I. Humiliation

In *Kurt Cobain: Montage of Heck*, Brett Morgen's 2015 film about the Nirvana frontman, part of the myth of the late singer is dismantled and part of it is rebuilt. The film unpeels a layer of emotional 'truth' that is painful to watch. Assembled mainly from an assortment of audio tapes that Cobain created during his life, it is the documenting of his teenage years – tall tales of sleeping with a mentally handicapped woman, attempting suicide on a train track, etc. – which drew the ire of high-school friend and Melvins's frontman Buzz Osborne. There before the beginning of Cobain's fame, and there at the end (the Melvins played Nirvana's last show), Osborne tore the documentary down in a piece for website *The Talkhouse*: 'People need to understand that 90% of *Montage of Heck* is bullshit. Total bullshit. That's the one thing no one gets about Cobain – he was a master of jerking your chain.'[2]

If we aren't to take Cobain's words at face value, then what about those of his parents? The first half hour of the film portrays his childhood through the sadness and regret of his mother Wendy and the glassy-eyed detachment of his father, Don. The home footage of Kurt as a young boy, overlaid with Nirvana's version of the Meat Puppets's 'Oh Me' from their 1994 *MTV Unplugged in New York* set is difficult to watch, since it prefigures how badly the boy's teenage years were handled. It returns the plaid-shirted, ripped-jeans icon of Cobain to a white-blond, smiling, hyperactive, hard-to-handle boy and suffuses the film with the more common experience of a childhood turned upside-down. It foreshadows the later struggles with fame, heroin, a rock-star wife and the vision of the 'I Hate Myself and Want to Die' poster boy for the faux-glamour of suicide.

A twin-headed snake of emotional pain becomes clear: ridicule and embarrassment. Wendy Cobain cites her divorce from Don when Kurt was nine years old (saying that divorce in the mid-seventies was still rare) as the wellspring for the emotional self-torture that was to follow: 'It just embarrassed him to death that we had got divorced.' When his father remarried, as his current wife Jenny remembers, Kurt struggled with not being the 'most loved' in a new family dynamic. He had already been sent to live with his father due to unruly behaviour, which then spiralled, and Kurt began to pinball around other members of the wider family. He was housed by various relatives, but never truly taken care of. As Jenny remembers, 'I think the sad thing is that Kurt just wanted to be with his mom.'

The problems between Kurt and father had begun earlier though and, as his mother saw it, Don struggled with Kurt's hyperactivity even as a young child, and responded (according to Wendy) by trying to undermine his son: 'He belittled and ridiculed Kurt and Kurt would be shamed. I mean, it really hurt him – to be embarrassed.' Having uncovered humiliation so clearly in the emotional bedrock of Kurt Cobain's character, Brett Morgen lets it lie. It surfaces later as the implied reason for Cobain's overdose on pills in Milan in 1994, which Courtney Love attributes in the film to Cobain's reaction to her *thinking* about cheating on him. In his *Talkhouse* piece, Buzz Osborne was unequivocal about this supposition: 'History becomes elastic every time Courtney Love opens her mouth.'

Osborne is no fan of the film but the younger him participates in one of its most effective sequences: muttering darkly about how shitty life is in their hometown of Aberdeen, Washington, in a taped phone conversation with Kurt (Buzz: 'What an isolated hell-hole this really is – if witch-burnings were legal we'd all be dead now'). Cobain asks Osborne if he's seen the film *Over the Edge* and Morgan overlays their back-and-forth about it with footage from the 1979 film itself: students lay siege to their own high school (Kurt: 'I wanted to hold everyone captive in the school'), kicking into a superb montage of the movie soundtracked to the frenetic Nirvana song 'School', one of the rawest and catchiest tracks from their debut, *Bleach* (1989). Cobain's rejection of the institution of high school in the Reagan era went deep into his psyche, as he says in the film: 'I was so anti-social I was almost insane.'

Though it is never made overt, there is an implication in Love's interviews and in the film itself concluding with Cobain's performance of American folk song 'Where Did You Sleep Last Night?' from the *MTV Unplugged* performance, that his suicide was somehow linked to Love's infidelity. Whether or not you agree with Buzz Osborne that the film is 'mostly misguided fiction', what it does certainly ram home is the potency of humiliation to undermine a person. It creates an agonising and chronic emotional instability, gnawing away like the stomach pain that Cobain claimed plagued him all his life.

Cobain has been mythologised for decades, but it is time to reclaim the heaviness of that emotional experience, the rawness which surfaces in the yelps and screams on his unbelievably heavy acoustic rendition of 'Where Did You Sleep Last Night?'

A band that has been doing that reclamation is Thou, from Baton Rouge, Louisiana. Their harsh, sludgy, supremely down-tuned music reeks of the fetid marshlands of their native state, but their rejection of their hometown (one of their EPs, from 2009, is called *Baton Rouge, You Have Much To Answer For*) and Louisiana more broadly ('New Orleans Is a Hole' from 2014's *The Sacrifice* EP), has much in common with Cobain and Osborne's harsh words for cold, rainy Aberdeen in the north. On the song 'Baton Rouge, Louisiana', a protracted piece of Melvins-style drone is overlaid with a sample from a relatively obscure 2007 extra-terrestrial epidemic film called *The Invasion* starring Nicole Kidman and Daniel Craig. The conversation sampled encapsulates Thou's worldview – of the underlying feral nature of man that nevertheless possesses the capacity for making important personal and social gains – rather well. Over the soundbed, it is a slow bleed of ominousness.

On the one hand, as the character of Russian ambassador Korish opens the exchange, 'Civilisation is an illusion, a game of pretend. What is real is the fact that we are still animals, driven by primal instincts.' But Kidman, as Dr Carol Bennell, is able to end the conversation conclusively: 'Five hundred years ago, post-modern feminists didn't exist yet one sits right beside you today. And while that fact may not undo all of the terrible things that have been done in this world, at least it gives me reason to believe that one day, things may be different.'

On the *Baton Rouge, You Have Much To Answer For* and *The Sacrifice* EPs, Thou make the connection with Nirvana more solid, covering two Nirvana tracks, the *Bleach*-period 'Sifting' on the first, and 'I Hate Myself and Want to Die' on the second. Thou grew up with grunge, it is in their fabric, but these cover versions filter it through the harsh, overdriven and often deathly slow barrage of hardcore punk. They are returning Nirvana back to its roots – particularly 'Sifting', which pounds and grinds the original into a slower, nastier, bulkier version of its reincarnation.

Live, Thou have opened with the disconsolate *Nevermind* song 'Something in the Way', albeit ravaged by Bryan Funck's throat-ripping vocals, his performance countered by guest singer Emily McWilliams' faithfulness to the original melody. The recording of this set closes with 'Senseless Apprentice' from Nirvana's *In Utero*.[3] At Southwest Terror Fest in 2015, Thou went all-in, and performed a whole secret set of Nirvana covers that lasted forty-five minutes. Funck performed in a blonde wig and plaid shirt – a strange echo of Cobain's own dressing-up antics at Reading Festival 1992. Back then, Cobain was wheeled onto the stage, only to pitch himself out of the wheelchair onto the stage before resurrecting himself for his performance. Thou ended their Southwest Terror Fest performance with 'Where Did You Sleep Last Night?'[4]

What Thou are doing with Nirvana is an act of reclamation that drags Kurt Cobain back into the underground, to breathe again. Thou's methods are extreme, but they are deeply considered. Funck uses their full-length albums to explore ideas of agency and destiny ('Free Will' from 2014's *Heathen*), the abuses of the working class ('The Work Ethic Myth' from 2013's *Peasant*) and the 'sacred ego' ('Inward' from 2018's *Magus*). A lot of their work concerns identity, as did Cobain's, but they have managed to steer it from being simply about 'I' and more about 'You and I' or 'I and thou'.

Thou aren't afraid of hopelessness. On 'Fucking Chained to the Bottom of the Ocean' from 2007's *Tyrant*, Funck writes, 'Why have we been abandoned? Shadows grasp at the ghosts of memories. There is no release. There is no end in sight. Tomorrow will never come. I cannot let go. I can never let go.' The last two sentences are key, since the message is that though the narrator is chained to something he cannot escape, it is his decision not to let go. Even if it is self-torture, it is the hanging-on that counts. Kurt Cobain was ultimately unable to hang on. Thou invokes Cobain to counteract the poison of humiliation that festered in him. Their unification of the grunge of the north-west and the sludge of the south-west of the US is part of their attempt to use the latter to revivify the former, to perpetuate the heavily ego-centred heaviness that defined grunge music, and in doing so save it from itself. To beat it back to life.

II. Degradation

Perhaps it's no surprise that one of the best albums written about drug addiction also contains one of the best songs written about war. *Dirt* by Alice in Chains was released in 1992 and became synonymous with the struggle of lead singer Layne Staley against his heroin addiction – a struggle he eventually lost when he died in 2002. Alongside dope-sick anthems 'Junkhead' and 'Sickman' is the song 'Rooster', written about guitarist Jerry Cantrell's father and his experience in the Vietnam War.

The eponymous Rooster, Cantrell Sr, never spoke about the Vietnam War, which lasted two decades and inflicted deep social and personal wounds on the people who served in it and on their families back home. In the context of the album, it feels like the scourge and psychological fallout from war is as great as the effects of hard drug use. Indeed, at first I thought 'Rooster' must have been about a drug dealer. At the same time, there is a challenging – almost smirking – tone of defiance to the album that seems to say, 'I'm killing myself here: what are you going to do to stop me?' And, directly in the case of 'Rooster': 'You know he ain't gonna die.'

In the same way that Kurt Cobain could not surmount the division between himself and his father, the heaviness of the Vietnam War seemed to erect a palisade between Cantrell and his dad. Like Cobain, Cantrell's parents divorced when he was under ten and he felt that his father's experience 'splintered' their family.[5] But in writing 'Rooster', which focuses on the grit and determination required simply to keep walking in that war-torn environment as 'eyes burn with stinging sweat', the Cantrells began a process of healing their relationship. This involved Cantrell Sr speaking on camera in an interview at the start of the song's video, conducted by director Mark Pellington, which brought the veteran to tears. The war was a weird experience, he said, a sad experience, and he hoped no one else had to go through it.[6] When Cantrell asked his father whether he felt the song got close to a truthful representation of what he'd been through, he answered: 'You got too close – you hit it on the head.'[7] Embodying his father as Jerry Cantrell was becoming a man himself was 'so heavy', he later reflected.[8]

Like Thou's 'Fucking Chained to the Bottom of the Ocean', 'Rooster' is stripped to muscle and bone, as its dragging, descending guitar refrain explodes like the memory of shells in the listener's cranium. 'Rooster' attempts to process the psychic turmoil of what had happened to the fathers of 'generation grunge' when they were in Vietnam at a similar age to the members of Alice in Chains in the early nineties. *Dirt* begs the question of whether the musicians' use of drugs is in some way connected to the trauma of the war their fathers fought.

The astonishing ten episodes – seventeen and a quarter hours – of Ken Burns and Lynn Novick's 2017 documentary epic *The Vietnam War*, is interspersed with the testimonials of dozens of veterans from both sides of the fighting. One of these is Karl Marlantes, who spent thirty years writing a novel based on his experiences in the war, *Matterhorn* (2009). In the episode of *The Vietnam War* entitled 'The Veneer of Civilisation (June 1968– May 1969)', he speaks about the pliability of nineteen-year-olds in going to serve and the drug-like addictiveness of warfare. His comments, like the songs of Alice in Chains on *Dirt*, see equivalence in going to war and the self-destructive high of hard drugs: 'Combat is like crack cocaine. It's an enormous high but has enormous costs. Any sane person would never do crack. Combat is like that: you're scared, you're terrified, you're miserable. But then the fighting starts. And, suddenly, everything is at stake: your life, your friends' lives. It's almost transcendence, because you're no longer a person – you lose that sense. You're just the platoon and the platoon can't be beat. And not to mention there's a savage joy in overcoming your enemy, just a savage joy. And I think we make a big mistake if we say, "Oh no, war is hell". We all know the "war is hell" story. It is – but, there's an enormously exhilarating part of it.'

In 2018, Thou released an EP titled *Rhea Sylvia*, one of three that preceded their full-length *Magus*. Each EP was intended to expose the 'underpinnings' of the band, as Bryan Funck put it to me. They present an alternative view of the band's sound, which is usually smothered in distortion and feedback and punctured by Funck's screaming. The other two EPs released that year – *Inconsolable* and *The House Primordial* – examined a dreamlike acoustic side and distended drone respectively. *Rhea Sylvia* was the most intriguing because it was guitarist Matthew Thudium's solo material refracted through the prism of Thou. And that material was heavily influenced by Alice in Chains.

Rhea Silvia was the mother of Romulus and Remus, the founders of Rome.[9] Her name might mean several things in Latin but one theory is the 'shamed woman of the woods'. Her sons were famously raised by wolves in the forest, a metaphor for the savagery of human nature: '*Homo homini lupus est*' – 'man is wolf to man'. On 'Deepest Sun', Thudium's layered vocals echo the harmonic counterpoint of the iron-fist-in-a-velvet-glove approach of Layne Staley and Jerry Cantrell, though Bryan Funck's ragged vocal makes Staley's seem smooth by comparison. On 'Non-Entity', Funck leads the vocal attack but the song still deviates into a sullen place of subdued melodicism before picking up the trail again with a strident, mid-paced drumbeat. The band find an unusual centre for themselves between the polarities of extremity that also sharpens their bite. Funck sounds even more feral, like a wolf roaming the woods, anticipating civilisation: 'Oh, cold silent horror on desolate mountain roams. In shrivelling isolation, I fashion these walls.'

Striking out for a pastoral place of isolation and self-sufficiency has a tradition in the books *Walden* (1854) by Henry David Thoreau and latterly *Into the Wild* by Jon Krakauer (1996) – made into a 2007 film soundtracked by Pearl Jam's Eddie Vedder. Jerry Cantrell made one such journey, departing for the Cascade mountains in 1998, at a time when Alice in Chains was on hiatus mostly due to Staley's continued struggles with heroin. Cantrell spent over three months wallowing and wrangling with his demons for an album that stands up with the best of Alice in Chains and which is a monument to digging into one's inner darkness: *Degradation Trip.*

The tenor of the full double-album (the length meant Cantrell had to fight to get it released his way) is wrapped in the startlingly bleak and totemic self-explanatory heaviness of 'Hellbound', 'Castaway' and 'Feel the Void'. The whole album is as great a work of indigent art as *Dirt* and at points surpasses it, also returning to the subject of Cantrell's relationship with his father. The otherwise powerful and propulsive 'Spiderbite' is dragged into the soil by the slow poison of the 'Rooster'-like doomy turnaround of its second half: 'My old man wonders where I'm at/I'm still a child, guess I keep trying to pay him back'.

The album was not released until June 2002, four years after its songs were written. Staley had passed away two months earlier and it was as if the album had had to wait for him to die before it could be born. The lyrics of opener 'Psychotic Break' took on even greater power in the wake of Staley's death, as Cantrell sang of 'Chalking up my dead friends/And loved ones long gone'.

III. Like suicide

I was twelve years old when Kurt Cobain killed himself. I didn't become aware of the fact until I became properly aware of Nirvana, about a year later. By that point, Cobain had already ascended to his own plateau of teenage iconography. His suicide was embedded in the experience of listening to his music and the two were somehow inseparable. It was sad, it was a shame, and it provided an endpoint to the angst of his songwriting which was as brutal as it was final: feeling that way led directly to him ending it this way. But packaged up as part of popular culture (not least his entry into the damnable idea of the 'Twenty-Seven Club'), his suicide felt more like an exhibit in a museum – worthy of examination, something to learn from, but not necessarily directly speaking to my personal experience.

Chris Cornell's death by hanging in 2017 felt different. It felt totally unnecessary – he had weathered the storm of drugs and depression for a long time and was fifty-two years old when he died. I came to Soundgarden late as well, but I had been able to see them perform live when they reformed in their later years. Like Alice in Chains, with 1991's *Badmotorfinger* Soundgarden embodied a harder, more metallic version of the Seattle sound that I loved. Their live cover of 'Into the Void' from the Paramount Theater in Seattle from 1992 (with Buzz Osborne, under the moniker 'Chief Sealth') spoke through the ages and drew from that same iron-rich wellspring as Tony Iommi.

The second time I saw them was also the final time, in Hyde Park, supporting Black Sabbath on 4 July 2014. This offered Soundgarden an opportunity to perform one of their heaviest and most enigmatic songs, '4th of July' on the day itself.[10] The 'riff' of '4th of July' has a descending chord sequence, moving in dissonant intervals – akin to a guitar being slowly detuned as it is being played. With its fractured acid-trip imagery of 'scared light' that 'cracks and disappears' like the titular American holiday's firework displays, the song uses patriotic celebration to examine a profound spiritual uneasiness 'where the baptised drowned' and how, 'Down in the hole/Jesus tries to crack a smile'. The latter is a beautiful couplet since it aligns the song with Alice in Chains's best examination of self-pity, 'Down in a Hole' from *Dirt*, with Cornell's own explorations of the messianic (particularly on 'Jesus Christ Pose' from *Badmotorfinger*). But it plays even more heavily since his death, now that the flare-like intensity of his life has been extinguished: 'And I thought it was the end/And I thought it was the 4th of July'.

Thou have released versions of both 'Into the Void' and '4th of July'. On their 2009 limited vinyl EP *Through Empires of Eternal Void* (itself taking its title from part of the song's lyric), 'Into the Void' sounds like a jet engine cratering out of the bowels of hell. '4th of July' appears on another EP, *Hell Comes Home, Volume 1* (2012), on which Matthew Thudium takes the first verse in a respectable enough rendition of Cornell's resigned vocal. The bleak immensity of the opening riff, already coated in tar, is pushed further into the fire, but they also remain faithful to the song's nuances: its off-hand refrains and licks, even its brighter post-chorus guitar leads. What is different, though, is Funck's vocal – his gargling scream plays the evil twin to Thudium's more reverential singing. In this case Thou don't need to reclaim the song for the underground: it is already of the cavern – they are just taking it deeper, to where the dead now live.

IV. Supremacy

In weird fiction author Thomas Ligotti's short story 'Alice's Last Adventure', the narrator's father explains how Lewis Carroll 'was a symbol of psychic supremacy, the sterling ideal of an unstrictured mind manipulating reality to its whim'.[11] On 2018's *Magus*, Thou created a thesis statement on what Bryan Funck described to me as 'repudiating the ascendancy of victimhood ideology'. On songs like 'Transcending Dualities' and 'Sovereign Self' they are advocating that listeners dig into their own personalities, accepting the ambiguities and non-binary shades of grey that define everyone, with the self-resolve and 'rugged individualism'

(Funck's phrase) necessary to play the hand dealt to them, regard-less of how bad it is.

Fuelled as Funck might be by the nihilist philosophy of Ligotti's 2010 non-fiction work *Conspiracy Against the Human Race* (sections of which will be familiar to anyone who watched Matthew McConaughey's character, Rust Cohle, spouting cosmic despair on the first series of HBO's *True Detective* from 2014), this album offers solutions to the problems so powerfully explored by Cobain, Cantrell and Cornell in their work. Thou have embed-ded themselves in their grunge influences and wallowed in their mire. It seems to be time to wrench themselves out of it. *Magus* is a long, crushing, dense work; a journey represented in micro-cosm on first track 'Inward': 'Descend into the ever-widening/ Yawning chasm of black thought/Descend into the voidpit/That spiralling hole of self-deification'.

For Funck the record is a grand act of 'self-actualisation', and it might be the saving grace for the generation he belongs to – a heavy album that offers the way out of the hell of their heroes. How far is it from the preferred Crowleyism of Jimmy Page and Philip Anselmo – 'Do what thou wilt'? In this configuration, and closing track 'Supremacy', isolation is not the source of inner collapse and the destruction of Self but rather 'primacy in soli-tude'. Instead of being haunted by religious idols, or abandoned by all including God, Thou makes the ego – the 'I' – celebrant and ascendant: 'Assume the God form. Seize the hidden shape, that sovereign self, celestial aspect.'

The reason I've included grunge artists in a book predomi-nantly about metal music is to acknowledge grunge's impact on heaviness. The grunge bands with the closest relationship to metal negotiated misery and addiction in a way that was a revela-tion. Thou have had a similar impact on metal and a similarly uneasy relationship with it. It even manifests itself in the artwork they use. Their bandcamp page is a carefully curated series of crops of Gustav Doré woodcuts. Doré's illustrations of classical history and mythology, *Paradise Lost*, the Bible and *Dante's Inferno* have made him long overused in metal circles and Funck is aware of it: 'There is just some part of me that didn't want to let go of that stuff but also wanted to make it look cool and as unique as I could.' It is also about a digital-versus-physical identity: their *Heathen* album was illustrated by a detail of the Doré woodcut of Charon crossing the River Styx – the physical version is a defaced 1867 photograph of Virginia Woolf's mother, the pre-Raphaelite model Julia Stephen.

Thou savour any bad-mouthing they receive on the internet – their sardonic stance and hipster credentials draw some derision – and they dole out their fair share in return. Based in Baton Rouge, their ambivalence about New Orleans and its crop of sludge bands is a complicated push–pull with the bigger city that Funck grew up in. Why else cover Crowbar's 'The Lasting Dose' on *Rhea Sylvia*, or extract Eyehategod's 'Blank' onstage (both songs written by New Orleans sludge royalty)? Their capacity for mischief is an act of self-defence. They want to show they are as important as their Louisiana forebears, and to display their musical confidence and conviction in their out-of-fashion grunge re-enactments.

The biggest lesson from the grunge era, and Thou's principle message on *Magus*, is that you can only have control over yourself and your actions and, if that control is lacking, then it may end badly for you. This might be harsh. It might also be the privilege of those who are not dogged by mental illness and the physical addictions of narcotics. But psychic supremacy feels like an important alternative way of viewing the concept of struggle itself.

From the centre of the maelstrom of Thou, it is Funck's optimistic message: 'My more hopeful take on it has always been more about not just suffering through the hardships but coming out of those stronger or through willpower, or through your own actions reshaping the world around you and the people around you.'

11
REMEMBER TOMORROW

'Bringing the best of Britain to the world' –
GREAT Britain campaign slogan, 2019[1]

'They dared to go where no one would try'
– Iron Maiden, 'Where Eagles Dare'

O ur journey ends with the legacy of Iron Maiden – a legacy they are still busy creating. As progenitors of a theatrical vision of Great Britain fronted by their mascot Eddie, and adored the world over, they have successfully created a global phenomenon. But how has this been affected by a shifting sense of (trans) national identity? And what do their songs of derring-do promise for how we could and should live our lives? What does their vision of heaviness promise for the future?

I. Maiden England

When Bruce Dickinson paused during the breathless first forty minutes of Iron Maiden's set at the O2 arena in London's Docklands on 10 August 2018, he pinned his colours to the mast: 'This is not just, let's face it, an English show. This is an Iron

Maiden-fucking-show, all right?' The flags flown during the gig – from Sweden, Brazil, and of course, Great Britain, among many others – made it emphatically clear that any nationalism was being subsumed to an allegiance to Iron Maiden. Iron Maiden's form of patriotism is far from jingoism. It is a means of reaffirming the global scale and identity of the band.

The opening songs of the 2018 *Legacy of the Beast* set ran the gamut of their do-or-die military stripe of songwriting: the show began with a playback of Winston Churchill's 'We will fight them on the beaches' speech, followed in quick succession by 'Aces High', 'Where Eagles Dare', '2 Minutes to Midnight', paean to William Wallace 'The Clansman', and 'The Trooper'. The image of their mascot Eddie as the trooper is the enduring Maiden icon. He is dressed in nineteenth-century redcoat cavalry colours as he steps forward, brandishing a sword in one hand and a shredded Union Jack in the other. The song's reconfiguring of the Charge of the Light Brigade, like Tennyson's 1854 poem, is for the ages.

That night I bought a T-shirt with a spectacular image of Eddie depicted as a pilot in the bullet-shattered cockpit of a Spitfire. Best not to pick holes in the design, since the four inches of glass of a Spitfire cockpit would actually repel bullets (as artist Derek Riggs was informed by a World War II enthusiast friend after he had completed the piece in the eighties).[2] The image was used for the cover of single 'Aces High', a song about the Battle of Britain of World War II (with a titular nod to a 1976 film about the Royal Flying Corps during World War I), released in October 1984. As printed on the picture disc version, it was supposed to mimic the spiralling attack of the aircraft mid-battle.

At the O2 arena, Dickinson mentioned it was recently his sixtieth birthday before noting that many of the young men who fought in the Battle of Britain, dogfighting over the south coast of

England, had been a third of his age. That year's hundredth anniversary of the RAF clearly meant something to small-plane enthusiast and commercial airline pilot Dickinson, and it meant something to Iron Maiden. The historic defeat of fascism enabled by brave young men and women is something to be celebrated, after all. There was another undercurrent to the first third of the gig, and that was to remind a divided United Kingdom what it once stood for in the dark, disordered days of the Brexit period. What troubled many on the side of remaining in the EU had been how that image of a defiant and triumphant past had been co-opted by Brexiteer factions. It was used as part of a vision of a recoverable British glory, that leavers argued could only be accessed after the country had been extricated from the European Union.

Dickinson – a whip-smart renaissance man with numerous interests outside fronting the world's biggest metal band, including fencing, writing novels and, of course, flying – has given talks on how to succeed as an entrepreneur. Iron Maiden could be poster boys for the 'Britain is Great' campaign banner run by the UK Department of Trade and Industry.[3] But, of course, they are bigger than Great Britain and, more than any other heavy metal act, they have established a culture defiantly their own, drawing on a web of touchpoints from history, literature and film. They have moulded these into grand conceptual albums that are uniquely Iron Maiden. Iron Maiden is undoubtedly one of Britain's greatest cultural exports, but more so, Great Britain itself is Iron Maiden's greatest cultural export.

It took me a long time to feel enthusiastic about Iron Maiden. In the mid-nineties the band was in the doldrums, much like the post-albatross-slaying stricken ship of their epic version of Coleridge's 'The Rime of the Ancient Mariner' from the 1984 album *Powerslave*. Bruce Dickinson had left the band in 1993 and the less charismatic Blaze Bayley fronted the band, though bassist Steve Harris remained at the helm, as he had been since the late seventies. As we've seen, the nineties saw heaviness being redefined, sharpened up and injected with a level of raw emotion and sonic intensity that Iron Maiden had rarely touched. Instead, they had sought to create what Dickinson describes in his 2018 autobiography *What Does This Button Do?* as 'theatre of the mind':[4] storytelling on a grand scale with sweeping themes, imparted in complicated, multi-part musical compositions. They have a more direct mode of writing that speaks to their origins as a metal band forged in the punk era, but the indelible impression is of the big stuff – from war and the nature of evil onwards – writ large. As Dickinson puts it in his book, 'Maiden was hard work and tangible, substantive and complex, but also visceral and aggressive.'[5] It took Dickinson to return to the band on the eve of the new millennium to make that tangibility really count again.

Iron Maiden has reached more people than almost any other heavy metal band on a global scale. What really sets it apart is how their listeners step into their story world, fronted by their grotesque mascot Eddie. In his book, pointing to the familiar themes of bassist Steve Harris's lyrics as the band's principal songwriter, Dickinson describes 'fear, powerlessness, betrayal and inescapable prophecies'.[6] Compare these to what K. K. Downing of Judas Priest described as the core themes of heavy metal in his eyes – 'darkness, religious doubt, betrayal' – and the crossover is clear. Both bands invite their audience to stare into a glass, darkly. But both foster community at the same time – Iron Maiden to spectacular effect.

What strikes you about an Iron Maiden concert is the sheer number of Iron Maiden T-shirts. This is unusual: in some quarters it's considered naff to wear the shirt of the band you're seeing, when you could be signalling your more diverse and/or underground musical taste. At the O2 arena for the *Legacy of the Beast* tour there were multiple designs on offer, with a huge number of punters queuing at all the merchandise stalls, many having come to the gig resplendent in the T-shirt for *The Book of Souls* tour (which ran through the same venue only the year before). As I queued to get in, the white-haired fan in front of me had a Maiden T-shirt from Reading Festival 1982: a garment as old as I was. Iron Maiden's fanbase is completist and avowedly loyal.

Under the management of Rod Smallwood and Andy Taylor, Iron Maiden is a behemoth of a business operation. A dive into the Companies House filings of Iron Maiden LLP, the limited liability partnership of which the members and their various holding companies are officers, reveals it is well-structured and undoubtedly very tax efficient.[7]

Dickinson has undertaken corporate speaking gigs in recent years, in a dark suit and open-collar shirt, with themes such as how to turn a brand's customers into fans, saying fans are better because 'customers are bad things. Customers have a choice and customers will go somewhere else'. Fans show fierce allegiance to Iron Maiden because the band has successfully 'ring-fenced our creativity and kept it precious'.[8] Iron Maiden insist on moving forward, alternating new album tours with greatest hits tours. Their continued growth of 20 per cent year on year in certain markets, Dickinson explains to his corporate audience, is a result of teenagers and new fans still entering the fray – they are the contingent that help fill arenas.

The band's business-smarts innovated the idea of chartering a plane in the winter months, when the aviation business is traditionally slow in the northern hemisphere, and taking it on a tour largely south of the equator and destinations such as

Mumbai, Costa Rica and Colombia.[9] In 2008–2009 Iron Maiden travelled fifty thousand miles in forty-five days, performing twenty-three shows in thirteen countries to half a million fans. They rebranded a Boeing 757 'Ed Force One', with the band and crew in the front half and their equipment in the back, and Dickinson doing some of the flying. This prodigious continent-hopping was captured in their concert film from 2009, *Iron Maiden: Flight 666*. The jetlag was ferocious but the fans afforded a first-time live experience with the band were ecstatic to see their heroes perform.

What is ironic about Dickinson appearing at forums like Entrepreneurs Wales 2012[10] and encouraging companies to turn their customers into fans is that Iron Maiden's real success has been in doing the opposite. They take fans for whom the band has, in Dickinson's words in his book, 'represented a personal affirmation of self-worth for millions of people down the years', [11] and make them highly monetisable customers. A few years ago I asked the merchandise team at Brixton Academy for their biggest night of sales. Without hesitating they said the three nights that Iron Maiden performed in 2002 in aid of a trust fund created for their former drummer Clive Burr, who was suffering from multiple sclerosis. Apparently, it was the only time that punters had crowd-surfed to the front of the merch scrum in the foyer.

Iron Maiden have a global view; they appeal to a global audience with their visions of England, but also invite fans into an incubated space that is wholly of their creation. When the integrity of that world is threatened they can mobilise their audience to form a protective shield around them. There was the bizarre time the band were egged in San Bernardino at Ozzfest 2005 by a petulant Sharon Osbourne and others, prompting an indignant Dickinson, dressed in his 'The Trooper' cavalry costume, to deliver the excellent ad-lib,

'This is an English fucking flag and these colours do not fucking run from you asswipes!'[12] The play on words was so good it inspired a song called 'These Colours Don't Run' on their following album, *A Matter of Life and Death*, released in 2006.

There is some friction around the values that Iron Maiden projects to its fans – representations of life, death, bravery and the dangers of hubris – and what is sometimes more opaque about rallying around their flag. In November 2018, speaking to French news outlet *L'Obs*, Dickinson revealed that he had voted to leave the EU in the Brexit referendum of 2016. Proud to be a contrarian, Dickinson had his own, cogent reasons for not approving of the ever-increasing union of a federalised Europe: 'What you have at the moment is effectively the European Union obviously not doing a very good job satisfying the democracies of Europe,' he said. 'A lot of people, not just Brexit, but all kinds of other people – whether it's Italians, Greeks, Hungarians or Catalans, or whoever it is – are all having big populist movements. It's because their democratic needs are not being addressed by Brussels. The right people to address the needs is the democratically elected leaders.'

In the end, he said he was 'quite relaxed' about the prospect of the United Kingdom leaving the European Union, an opinion not uncommon within the millionaire class in the country. He went on to say, in the internationalist logic of the Brexiteer – which rejects the membership of the free market with the UK's biggest trading partner in favour of a broader outlook, shunning their nearest neighbour in favour of looking beyond the garden fence – that 'Brexit actually opens our borders, Brexit opens the United Kingdom to the whole of the world.'[13]

His sentiments echoed those expressed in an open letter of 18 October 2018 sent to the *Daily Telegraph* by the 'hard Brexit' right wing of the Conservative party, including former Brexit Secretary

David Davis, former Foreign Secretary Boris Johnson and back-bencher (and prominent member of the Tory pro-Brexit European Research Group) Jacob Rees-Mogg: 'Brexit offers the prize of a better future, global free trade and political independence.'[14] Whatever the political standpoint of individual band members, or their fans' views on the issue, Brexit came to resemble one of the inescapable prophecies of Iron Maiden's songs, with an entire nation at its mercy.

II. Fly to live

Bathed in the sodium-yellow streetlights of London as the seventies turned into the eighties, Iron Maiden's mascot Eddie was a symbol of the wasted youth and wasted years of the punk era. Created by artist Derek Riggs, and originally called Electric Matthew – with his punk-ish mohican – Eddie was the mainstay of the story world of the band that Riggs visualised for the decade that constitutes their classic era. Riggs based the anatomical effect of Eddie's withered visage on a photograph he had seen in *Time* magazine of a desiccated head mounted on a tank ('because you don't get many pictures of dried up skulls').[15] That photograph – taken in 1942 by Ralph Morse – of a Japanese soldier on the Pacific island of Guadalcanal, originally appeared in *Life* magazine and is a grim historical antecedent of Iron Maiden's vicious avatar, frozen in a silent scream.[16] On the covers of Iron Maiden's self-titled 1980 debut album and 1981's *Killers*, Riggs brought horror into the everyday and onto the streets of London, akin to the H. P. Lovecraft stories he read. Eddie was an empty vessel, without personality or back story, save for the way he was rendered to portray the subject matter of the singles and album covers. He accrued injuries and body modifications which he carried from release to release as the years went on. His incarnations evolved – holding an axe dripping with blood on the cover of

Killers, the puppet master of the devil himself on 1982's *Number of the Beast*, the lobotomised lunatic lunging at the viewer in the padded cell of 1983's *Piece of Mind*: Eddie was fast transitioning into a kind of anti-hero. As a roadie once told Riggs, 'People respond to Eddie as a hero, because he's too heavy to handle as a villain.'[17]

Eddie even locked horns with the Iron Lady herself, contesting the right of the title Iron Maiden with Prime Minister Margaret Thatcher on two occasions. Eddie has just violently mugged Thatcher on the cover of the 'Sanctuary' single (1980) after she tore down an Iron Maiden poster. By way of revenge, Thatcher lies in wait with a machine gun as Eddie makes his way down the street arm-in-arm with two nurses on the cover of 'Women in Uniform' (1981). Eddie would not be as overtly anti-Conservative again, but he was deployed to express the nuclear threat of the era on the single '2 Minutes to Midnight' (1984). A mushroom cloud erupts behind him as he sits alongside a series of UN-style flags – antipathetic and dressed in GI garb, he chomps on a cigar and points accusingly at the viewer.

The cover of the single of 'The Trooper', another portrayal of war-time wasted youth, became one of the most iconic Eddies. The subject was the Crimean War, specifically the disastrous Charge of the Light Brigade on 25 October 1854. The assault led by Lord Cardigan against Russian forces at the Battle of Balaclava became shorthand for the bravery of the average soldier alongside the stupidity of his superiors. Iron Maiden's song is sabre-sharp with its lyrics of mutually assured destruction accompanied by trilling harmonised guitars. As Alfred Lord Tennyson's poem of the event put it: 'Theirs but to do and die'. The song affirmed Iron Maiden's position as patriots reporting from the battlefield and seeing events through the dying eyes of the pawns who had to lay down their lives for no good reason.

Though Riggs referenced the apocalyptic panoramas of John Martin on his lightning-scape cover of 1985's *Live after Death* and the surrealism of Salvador Dali on 1988's *Seventh Son of a Seventh Son* (he used Dali's likeness as the face of the devil on several occasions), he successfully established his own visual language and iconography for Iron Maiden that came to represent heaviness itself. Eddie in all his guises came to be the mark of quality that metal fans could depend on. It was not without its costs for Riggs, who suffered long-term chronic fatigue syndrome in many of his busiest years working for Iron Maiden in the eighties. In the early days, he would often be called on a Thursday and asked to deliver an album cover for the Monday, staying up all weekend to hit his deadline. Each album cycle required up to twenty accompanying pieces of art, including singles, T-shirts and backstage passes – and that was before the annual Iron Maiden Christmas card.

By the mid-eighties Riggs was able to focus on bigger, more complex pieces, such as 1984's magnificent *Powerslave* album cover (for which the brief was, simply, 'Egypt')[18] and the extraordinary *Blade Runner*-esque cyberpunk Eddie and vastly detailed cityscape of 1986's *Somewhere in Time*, stuffed full of in-jokes and allusions to Iron Maiden's back catalogue. The latter piece took him three months and he was so gripped by the visions it inspired that he could think of little else, all the while struggling with long-term health problems. He discovered years later that one of the causes of his illness was the mercury in his fillings. Derek Riggs had been slowly poisoned by, of all things, a heavy metal.

If tales of derring-do are one of Iron Maiden's pillars, then 'Where Eagles Dare', the opening song from *Piece of Mind*, is one of their finest. It is based on the 1968 film directed by Brian G. Hutton and starring Richard Burton and Clint Eastwood. For a band with an interest in nature of betrayals, the film's storyline is made up of a mesh of them, plot twists and double – even triple – agents. The film opens with a Junkers Ju 52 German transport plane flying over, and through, a mountainous winterscape. It is on its way to deliver its occupants, a band of seven soldiers led by Burton and Eastwood, to rescue a British general who has crashed behind enemy lines and is being held captive in *Schloss* Adler, a fortress primarily accessed by cable car.

The song begins with a triplet-infused, rolling drum introduction from Nicko McBrain that deliberately harks back to the drum intro of Rainbow's 'Stargazer'.[19] The ra-ta-ta-tat of the drums that sets up the repeated groove passages of the song – hit alternately on the snare and the tom-toms, like the echoing report of a machine gun – recalls the marching and scattershot drum patterns of the film's opening score. Written by Ron Goodwin, the film's music summons forth the airplane out of the mountains, along with the blood-red Teutonic lettering of the opening credits.

Dickinson begins the song with a quick-fire verse-chorus/verse-chorus describing the snow-covered Bavarian Alps as the plane rumbles through the air with its anxious, expectant cargo. His histrionic, compact vocal lines serve to lift the curtain on the song and then he steps back to allow the band to tell the story of the film – this time cinema of the mind, with a particularly vertiginous Dave Murray guitar solo and the ascending harmonies that simulate our heroes' gut-wrenching cable car ascent. Dickinson comes back in towards the end of the song to recap the way the intrepid crew infiltrate the castle and then make their supremely destructive escape, powered by copious sticks of dynamite, littering their route out of the nearby village with burning vehicles.

With Burton and Eastwood posing as Nazi officers throughout, and making use of German armaments such as Luger pistols and Schmeisser machine guns, the film – with its twist and turns – has a duplicitous relationship with British patriotism. As the writer Geoff Dyer puts it in his 2018 book about the film, named after Burton's famous call-sign, 'Broadsword calling Danny Boy', 'If the getaway is a spectacularly prophetic and triumphant allegory of Brexit, then the consequences and costs of that leave-taking are impossible to ignore. Everything in the film is German.'[20] At least *Where Eagles Dare* portrays a minutely plotted and executed MI6 mission, which is more than you can say of the incompetent tragedy of errors that was the Brexit process.

The song is also an encapsulation of Iron Maiden's raiding mentality: fly in, fuck shit up, and leave. The band, and particularly Bruce Dickinson, whose heart seems closer to the RAF than the film's special forces, would probably identify most strongly with a character who doesn't really feature in Alistair MacLean's script but who does make a dashing cameo in MacLean's accompanying 1967 novelisation: Wing Commander Cecil Carpenter. The insouciant pilot drops the team off at the start of the novel and picks them up at its conclusion, twiddling his handlebar moustache and reading a book as he flies under cover of night, enjoying steaming hot coffee in the sub-zero flying conditions. For Carpenter, heroism comes easy – in fact, it is something he's entitled to.

At the *Legacy of the Beast* show at the O2 arena in 2018, Iron Maiden also played a little-performed song from *Piece of Mind* composed by Dickinson and guitarist Adrian Smith about a famously disastrous mythic attempt at flight called 'Flight of Icarus', with its exhortation to 'fly like an eagle'. During the middle and latter half of the nineties, Iron Maiden's star waned with the absence of Dickinson and Smith. With the stripped-back brutality of Sepultura and Pantera storming Castle Donington in 1994 (the year after Dickinson's departure), the spry melodicism and vaunted storytelling of Iron Maiden was beaten into submission. That was until a new movement sprang up on the eve of the millennium that incorporated the twin-guitar harmonic detail of Iron Maiden into the propulsive force of metal's late twentieth-century hostility. The 'New Wave of American Heavy Metal' (NWOAHM) was named after the New Wave of British Heavy Metal (NWOBHM), to which Iron Maiden had been originally attached in the early eighties. At the forefront of NWOAHM were Killswitch Engage, whose 2002 debut *Alive or Just Breathing* is a twenty-first-century classic. As support to Iron Maiden that night at the O2 arena – an unforgiving role for any band, particularly one so much more hardcore than the headliners – they excelled as live-in-the-flesh manifestation of Iron Maiden's influence on the evolution of other branches of heaviness.

When Iron Maiden then took the stage and tore into 'Aces High', it was a reminder of just how light on its feet Iron Maiden render heavy music. Most of their songs move at a clip, then their full-on signature gallop. Theirs is unstoppable, upbeat momentum, except when they elect to put the brakes on and indulge in one of the lengthier epics that have bestrode their career. None more so than the eighteen-minute 'Empire of the Clouds' from *The Book of Souls* (2015), a song about the vast *R101* airship that crashed on its maiden voyage in 1930.

However, Iron Maiden are not about crashing out. Songs of falling and fallen-ness are a defining characteristic of heavy metal, as much as writing about the hubristic urges that lead to such downfalls. Iron Maiden pledge a different point of view. On 'Aces High' their injunction is that to fly is to live. The consequences of reaching skywards are secondary to that vivifying impulse. When they headlined Download Festival at Donington in 2013, with their Trooper ale and limited edition Trooper-branded beer cups on sale at the onsite bars, they preceded their performance by organising a Spitfire to fly over the festival site and do multiple passes of the 100,000-plus audience, of which I was one. For all the evil that men do, they have made it their business to uplift audiences around the world with a global-facing form of British storytelling. They are the keepers of a vision of heaviness that buoys their fandom. Despite the challenges of the present, they promise a future of flying higher, and higher.

ASCENDING

I cannot claim to hold the key to unlock a full understanding of the power of heavy music. I would not want to possess it – who knows who (or what) would come for me?

What I did realise in the course of writing this book is that by looking outwards, I began looking inwards. The most powerful work in the metal genre also makes this transition, because understanding how we see the world around us leads us to understand our own motivations, passions and emotions. Heaviness is a filter through which to experience the world but that experience begins with ourselves. The wanderer through this form of music has a shadow. Metal is well acquainted with darkness, but less because of its often grim subject matter and more because it demarcates a space into which we pour ourselves.

If self-doubt and disillusionment with the world around you has ever plagued your mind, and religion, family, close relationships and the emotional ties that bind have proved fragile and untrustworthy, metal certainly has something for you. If the world is frustrating, frightening and feels illusory, heavy music might be a place to find refuge as well. If you are not in that desperate place, metal offers straight-up thrills. As early nineties wrestling tag-team Legion of Doom used to say: 'Oooh, what a rush!'

Metal is a sound so absolute and without compromise that it promises solidity and fulfilment which might be absent elsewhere. But pledging too much to its power has its risks – give it too much and you might become lost in it. Human failings, inexorable fates and raw feeling feed it. The energy rush of metal can sustain us, reconnect us to a primitive self, operate on a visceral level that is felt in the gut, and a cerebral – then transcendental level – that takes us out of ourselves, into the wider universe. Metal is as physical – pummelling, heaving, cascading – as it is ethereal – gleaming, spectral, vanishing. It is Notre-Dame cathedral burning: grand, devastating, and, in a terrible way, awe-inspiring.

This book has shown how metal music fits into a broader cultural landscape. It is a highly literate genre defined at its core by its heaviness. Heaviness embraces mythic truths and rejects popular deceptions. Heaviness is a quality that is undoubtedly shared by books, art, film, theatre and other forms of music which also pledge something of themselves to contend with the darkness. They pluck at that chord deep within us with the same unflinching intensity. Metal in turn absorbs their subject matter with vigour. That feedback loop only grows stronger and stronger.

I do not walk around in a permanent state of ecstatic revelation because of heavy music. But not long ago I was at a point in my life where the path forward was not very clear. It coincided with the release of Inter Arma's 2016 album *The Paradise Gallows*. The album's cover – an illustration of a wooden ship being battered into the rocks, with a psychedelic sky and setting sun as backdrop, evokes Melmoth's arrival in Ireland when he is shipwrecked on a stormy night. '*inter arma*' is Latin for 'in times of war' – literally, 'between weapons'. At a point where I was undergoing some personal tumult and the wider world came to feel similarly vexed, they became the band of the hour.

The album is a stone-cold masterpiece and its title track – the hymn of a man awaiting his death at the gallows pole and contemplating how his 'sullied name' will be remembered down the ages after he is gone – hit me hard. Inter Arma, like most heavy artists, successfully elevate experience to the mythic plain. The music of the song evokes the imagery of its cover: it sounds like a gigantic, turbulent sea pounding the obdurate tower of experience itself. I savoured the gritted teeth of its delivery – the almost self-mocking voice of the protagonist laughing his way to his grave.

As the fog started to lift for me and the way ahead became clearer, the opportunity came up to see the band headline a small club show in Bristol. I bought a T-shirt from their singer Mike Paparo at the merchandise stand. It depicted a hooded figure, constituted of stars and astral matter, who was drawing a bow and arrow as if he was rending a hole in the fabric of the universe. This was the 'Archer in the Emptiness' of the second song on *The Paradise Gallows*. But it could just as easily be Sparrowhawk, the archmage of Earthsea, opening up a space in reality that contains nothingness.

There were no more than fifty people in the audience that evening. As I stood only a few feet away from the band, and they proceeded to play every song I could wish for in exactly the order I hoped (not a given since they have been known to cover Tom Petty and Van Halen in their more unpredictable moments), I was transfused with the rush of pure heaviness. I channelled the band that night and I poured myself into the spectacular rendition of 'The Paradise Gallows' that ensued. I walked back to the hotel in the spring evening feeling changed, like that period of my life was in some way consummated by their performance.

This book began with falling – Lucifer, the iron man, the wizard of 'Stargazer' – and ended with flying in 'Aces High'. The risk of falling is ever present, but we must dare to fly. The title track of Inter Arma's previous album, 2013's *Sky Burial*, concerns the Tibetan practice of excarnation, where a corpse is exposed to the elements to be devoured as an offering to carrion birds. In Inter Arma's song, the protagonist scales 'the spire to the sky', touching the heavens, in order to feign death, escape the vagaries and corruptions of mankind, and invites the 'scavenger's clan' to descend on him. The song makes explicit the heavy enterprise: to willingly enter the void. But this is not just about death – it is about renewal. Heavy music takes us to the farthest shore of the human experience. Once there, it invites us to look into the darkness, and to give it our name. In doing so, we make our lives our own. Knowing our own true selves, we become invincible.

EPILOGUE:
LEAVES ARE FALLING ALL AROUND

'Don't mistake lack of talent for genius' – Type O
Negative, *Bloody Kisses* album back cover

n Type O Negative's 1998 home video *After Dark*, there is a brief
but key scene in which singer and bassist Peter Steele is out in
autumnal woodland, the leaves of the trees softly blazing in a
gentle fire of red and yellow behind him. Standing by a glassy lake,
he explains in his Brooklyn baritone why autumn is 'my most
favourite' season and how, where he is standing, he will one day
build his dream house, mainly consisting of windows so that
'every morning when I wake up I have the woods to one side, the
water to the other, the sky above, and it would always seem that I
was outside and I could enjoy nature and all the seasons'. To do
this, he explains, he will need to fell a few trees, but only a few – in
order to build a home for his woman and then 'worship her the
rest of my life'.

As with everything to do with Type O Negative, the sentiment
seems to be sincere but it is underlaid by a mordant mutual understanding between band and audience. When Type O Negative
re-released *After Dark* on DVD in 2000 they took full advantage of
the recent addition of the director's commentary feature to include

a hilarious running mockery by the band of the whole video and everyone in it. Even the original scene is soundtracked by strange Gregorian chanting that moves Steele's poetic delivery of the line 'the trees aflame and water still' into mock-solemnity. Type O Negative did this throughout their career: combining a lush gothic lovesickness with harsh, controversial hardcore music, and the ornate with the crude. It's confusing, until you come to realise that their humour is the essence of their heartfelt heaviness.

Their third album, *October Rust* (1996), made a lasting impression on me. It is redolent of the season it is named for and the brooding melancholy it can bring. But *October Rust* is not about melancholy for me. I first heard Type O Negative on a 1996 cover-mount CD with *Metal Hammer* magazine that featured 'Wolf Moon (Including Zoanthropoic Paranoia)', a risqué paean to menstrual cunnilingus in the guise of lycanthropy. A small group of us, whenever we came back from a night out, had a habit of watching *After Dark* back-to-back with Pink Floyd's 1972 *Live at Pompeii* on VHS copies in a late-night haze, through which they were not so much viewed as absorbed.

The opening song of *October Rust*, 'Love You to Death', which for Type O was almost completely sincere and washed through with lush synthesiser and Steele's mellifluous croon, came to grow in stature as I got older. Aged thirty-three, when I drove home from the hospital to get some rest at 4 a.m. on a blustery late October morning after the birth of my son, its refrain 'Am I good enough/for you?' held a piercing new significance for me and my new responsibilities as a father.

In the summer of the following year, the car driven by my wife and carrying my eight-month-old son was side-swiped by a lorry. Bizarrely, disturbingly, the lorry was owned by a company that euthanised horses. Despite my wife having to be lifted out of the driver's window of the compacted side of the written-off vehicle, they both emerged relatively unscathed.

But trapped in the six-disc CD changer of the wrecked, second-hand turquoise Ford Focus was the compilation album containing the radio edit of 'Love You to Death' I had listened to returning from the hospital after the birth of my son. It was the brilliantly titled *The Least Worst of Type O Negative* (2000). I made two trips to the scrapyard on consecutive days before eventually succeeding in extricating the CD player from its automotive tomb, bloodying my hands as I pounded the dashboard with a huge wrench I had found in a rusting toolbox abandoned in the yard.

When I saw the band live in 2007, at the now-demolished London Astoria, on their *Dead Again* album tour, Peter Steele seemed pale, thin and unwell. The album that followed *October Rust*, called *World Coming Down* (1999), had made his struggles with substance abuse plain on unnerving interludes of over-indulgence called 'Sinus', 'Liver' and 'Lung'. When he died in 2010 I was sad to lose someone who had fired my teenage imagination and enriched my adult experiences. Steele's worldview seemed at times misanthropic, his motivations were hard to fathom, his provocations difficult to ignore or deflect. And he was incredibly funny. Steele was open and honest about his vices and self-abuses, and they eventually killed him.

Type O Negative represent the best of heavy music and how it can shape an outlook on life. They were a band comfortable with tonal ambiguity but retained an ironclad sense of what they were about. They were controversial and they were also light-hearted. It is perhaps more destabilising to the twenty-first century listener immune to nuance of tone, especially by online and cultural discourse stripped of any subtleties, that sarcasm and sincerity can be intertwined to the extent that one can stand in for the other. Type O's music continues to ask, 'What the fuck does it matter if we're being serious, anyway?' Though extremely successful in their time and much-missed by their fans, I don't think their cultural impact has been fully processed in a wider sense. They remain a giant from Brooklyn slumbering in the history of New York's music scene.

On a superb soundboard bootleg recording of a 1994 show in Stockholm with the inapposite title of *Blood Melting Extremity*, there is a jaw-dropping version of 'Too Late: Frozen' from *Bloody Kisses* (1993), a song that segues from a bitter recrimination over an infidelity, to an epic, glacial section about being emotionally stranded in a windswept tundra: 'In the shadow of the light from a black sun/Frigid statue standing icy blue and numb.' Its dramatic transformation summons a cold atmosphere that perennially threatened the band's preferred bucolic, autumnal mode. Winter is always coming; enjoy your time.

Peter Steele used to work as a parks and recreation officer for Brooklyn Heights Promenade: he was literally the gigantic 'Green Man' he wrote about on another *October Rust* song – a man for all seasons. He visited my life and taught me how important it is to take matters seriously, and to not take them too seriously. The band's self-deprecatory, ironic proclamations of the mediocrity of their own output printed on their record sleeves ('Functionless art is merely tolerated vandalism') taught me how to value culture and be aware of how disposable it was. They made it clear that my love of heavy music meant everything to me, but that it was not everything.

There's a reason that their music has persisted in my life long after their demise and that is because it continues to provide a necessary energy that sustains and enthrals. They stand as an emblem for heavy metal and rock music's power more generally. I hope this book, that inevitably has dwelt on death and destruction, has made the message clear. That, ultimately, heaviness is the stuff of life itself.

NOTES

SOME KIND OF MONSTER

1 The Baroness bus crash was well-documented by the BBC's local news team in Somerset: 'American band Baroness in viaduct coach crash', BBC News on 15 August 2012, https://www.bbc.co.uk/news/uk-england-somerset-19267414; 'Baroness bus crash: Band "well on way" to recovery', BBC News, 2 October 2012, https://www.bbc.co.uk/news/uk-england-somerset-19805291; 'Baroness bus crash: Two band members leave group', BBC News on 3 April 2013, https://www.bbc.co.uk/news/uk-england-somerset-22020232; 'Baroness coach crash driver Norman Markus fined', BBC News, 10 July 2013, https://www.bbc.co.uk/news/uk-england-somerset-23257302. Baizley speaks about the accident and its aftermath: 'Killswitch Engage's Jesse Leach, Baroness' John Baizley Talk Art, Bus Accident, Moving Forward', *Revolver*, YouTube, 29 January 2018, https://www.youtube.com/watch?v=LarKDX3e--E

DESCENDING

1 From the documentary *The Blues Accordin' to Lightnin' Hopkins* (dir. Les Blank, 1970).
2 'Machine Head's Robb Flynn: I never want to play Davidian again', Scott Munro, *Metal Hammer*, 5 October 2017: www.loudersound.com/news/machine-heads-robb-flynn-i-never-want-to-play-davidian-again
3 From the interview with the band discussing the album with David Fricke, published on their YouTube channel, 1 November 2018: https://youtu.be/vMc24819DXk
4 'Metallica is latest interrogation tactic', Julian Borger, *Guardian*, 19 May 2003: https://www.theguardian.com/world/2003/may/20/iraq.julianborger
5 This paper was originally published in the *Journal of Medical Humanities*, March 2014.

6 'Elif Shafak: "I am a huge fan of Gothic metal", *Prospect* magazine, 13 June 2019: https://www.prospectmagazine.co.uk/magazine/elif-shafak-interview-turkey-populism

7 'New Liverpool Manager Jurgen Klopp Says Arsenal Play Like An Orchestra But He Likes Heavy Metal!', YouTube, BeanymanSports, 7 October 2015: https://youtu.be/eb143c9kw4s

CHAPTER ONE: ORIGIN MYTHS

1 Barney Hoskyns, *Trampled Under Foot: The Power and Excess of Led Zeppelin*, Faber and Faber, 2012, p.162.

2 Sylvie Simmons, *Guardian*, 16 May 2008: https://www.theguardian.com/music/2008/may/16/popandrock.ledzeppelin

3 Hoskyns, op. cit. p.110.

4 Page had the Crowleyisms 'Do what thou wilt' and 'So mote it be' inscribed on the lacquer during the final mastering process of *Led Zeppelin III*, which he described as 'a little milestone on the way – a point of reference' in *Light & Shade: Conversations with Jimmy Page*, Brad Tolinski, Virgin Books, 2012, p. 125.

5 Mick Wall, *Black Sabbath: Symptom of the Universe*, Orion Books, 2013, p.41.

6 'Marlon James: 'Ultimately, I'm a rock kid." *Guardian*, 6 November 2015: https://www.theguardian.com/books/booksblog/2015/nov/06/marlon-james-rock-kid-6-music

7 From James's blog entry from 25 April 2008, 'I'm too old to rock and roll': http://marlon-james.blogspot.com/2008/04/im-too-old-to-rock-and-roll.html?m=1

8 Originally broadcast on BBC Four, 29 October 2010: https://www.bbc.co.uk/programmes/b00vlq0y

9 Ted Hughes, *The Iron Man: A Children's Story in Five Nights*, Faber and Faber, 1968.

10 *Heavy Duty: Days and Nights in Judas Priest*, K. K. Downing (with Mark Eglinton), Constable, 2018, p.4.

11 Ibid., p.5.

12 Ibid., pp.100–101.

13 Ibid., p.121.

14 Ibid., p.98.

15 Ursula K. Le Guin, *A Wizard of Earthsea*, Puffin Books, 2016, p.70.

16 Dio mentions this in an audio interview included in the 2005 collector's edition of *Holy Diver*.

17 Le Guin, op. cit., p.257.

18 Richard Wagner, *The Ring of the Nibelung*, translated and edited with a new introduction by John Deathridge, Penguin Classics, 2018, p.xxviii.

19 The background to the formation of Dio's solo band is from his audio interview on the 2005 reissue of *Holy Diver*.

CHAPTER TWO: NUCLEAR WINTER AND ITS MALCONTENTS

1 *1983: The World at the Brink*, Taylor Downing, Little, Brown, 2018, p.17.
2 Ibid., p.17.
3 John Joseph's comments here are from the Noisey documentary *Hardcore History: John Joseph of the Cro-Mags*, 6 May 2013: https://youtu.be/Z0E_oe43FdU
4 The motivations of the band are covered in interview material from the band's home video of their *Live at Budokan* show from 1992.
5 The war planes detail is from Rex Brown's book *Official Truth, 101 Proof: The inside story of Pantera* (with Mark Eglinton), Da Capo Press, 2013, p.89. The behaviour of the military on the day (clubbing fans with batons) is evident in the Pantera home video release, *Vulgar Video*. Pantera played further down the bill that day and almost stole the show. More of that later.
6 This comment and the one that follows are taken from the superb Los Angeles episode of the 2014 Foo Fighters *Sonic Highways* documentary mini-series, first shown on HBO in 2014 (directed by Dave Grohl).
7 This is from an interview with NBC in 1965, widely available online.
8 Cormac McCarthy, *Blood Meridian*, Picador Classic edition, 2015, p.348.
9 This was related in an interview from a radio programme on BBC Radio 1 about *Songs for the Deaf* as part of the *Masterpieces* series presented by Zane Lowe, originally broadcast on 3 December 2012: www.bbc.co.uk/programmes/b01p1vyq
10 The impact of the latter on the former can be read about here: https://www.telegraph.co.uk/news/2017/12/11/cbeebies-wont-broadcast-josh-hommes-bedtime-stories-kicked-woman/

CHAPTER THREE: ROMAN WILDERNESS OF PAIN

1 'Pre-Aztec "Flayed god" temple uncovered in Mexico', BBC, 3 January 2019: www.bbc.co.uk/news/world-latin-america-46746842
2 '*Moisir parmi les ossements*': https://fleursdumal.org/poem/126
3 'The Good Man Jesus and the Scoundrel Christ', Canongate, YouTube, 29 March 2010: https://youtu.be/HQ3VcbAfd4w
4 From the liner notes of the Relapse Records 2012 deluxe reissue of *Spiritual Healing*.
5 This excellent piece was useful here: 'Master of gore: the violent, shocking genius of Jusepe de Ribera', Charlotte Higgins, *Guardian*, 19 September 2018:

https://www.theguardian.com/artanddesign/2018/sep/19/jusepe-de-ribera-art-of-violence-master-of-gore-dulwich

6 Anthony Burgess, *The Kingdom of the Wicked*, Abacus, 1986, p.313.

7 'Michael Åkerfeldt vomited on a wall recording Bloodbath's 'Bleeding Death' EP' – video interview published by Aggressive Tendencies on YouTube on 20 December 2016: https://youtu.be/b6XU1EaHcQ0

8 This is a well-documented incident. There's a good round-up of Benton's more out-there behaviour here: 'Deicide's Glen Benton talks Mormons, battle scars, new "old school" album', *Revolver*, 11 September 2018: https://www.revolver-mag.com/music/deicides-glen-benton-talks-mormons-battle-scars-new-old-school-album

9 Burgess, op. cit., p.379.

10 Amnesty's perspective on global violence against women: https://www.amnesty.org.uk/violence-against-women

11 '*Armin Meiwes: Interview with a Cannibal* documentary sheds new light on one of Germany's most infamous murderers', Roisin O' Connor, *Independent*, 9 February 2016: https://www.independent.co.uk/news/world/europe/armin-meiwes-interview-with-a-cannibal-documentary-sheds-new-light-on-one-of-germany-s-most-infamous-a6863201.html

12 'Death metal music inspired joy not violence', Victoria Gill, BBC News, 13 March 2019: https://www.bbc.co.uk/news/science-environment-47543875

13 A facsimile of this review was included in the booklet of the Earache Records 2008 deluxe edition reissue of *Reek of Putrefaction*. An archived image of Peel's 1988 *Observer* album round-up is here: https://peel.fandom.com/wiki/1988_LPs_Of_The_Year?file=Observer_-_11_Dec_1988.PNG

14 The story of the *Heartwork* artwork is told by Al Dawson of Earache Records in this Metal Injection video interview published on 15 November 2017 on YouTube: https://www.youtube.com/watch?v=kzzEx7CW8Qk

CHAPTER FOUR: CROSSING THE THRESHOLD

1 Charles Maturin, *Melmoth the Wanderer*, Penguin Classics, 2018, p.68.

2 This excellent lawn detail is from a Dani Filth interview with *Metal Injection*: 'Cradle of Filth On The Story Behind "Jesus . . . " Shirt, *Lords Of Chaos* Film and More', YouTube, 15 April 2019: https://www.youtube.com/watch?v=V79Uv2MPtAc

3 Some of the details here sourced from the *Rolling Stone* article 'The Story of the Most Controversial Shirt in Rock History', Dan Epstein, 25 June 2015: https://www.rollingstone.com/music/music-news/the-story-of-the-most-controversial-shirt-in-rock-history-61183/

4 'Iggy Azalea wore *that* Cradle of Filth T-shirt and everyone's kicking off', Dave Everley, *Metal Hammer*, 2 January 2019: https://www.loudersound.com/

features/iggy-azalea-wore-that-cradle-of-filth-t-shirt-and-everyones-kicking
-off

5 Joseph Campbell, *The Hero with a Thousand Faces*, New World Library, 2008, p.87.

6 Sheridan Le Fanu, 'Carmilla', *In A Glass Darkly*, Wordsworth Editions, 2008, p.225.

7 Maturin, op. cit., p.544.

8 Ibid., p.280.

9 Ibid., p.298.

10 Ibid., p.299.

11 'Dark Jester: The Strange World Of . . . Ulver', Josh Gray, *The Quietus*, 25 January 2016: https://thequietus.com/articles/19586-ulver-interview-2

12 The story of working with Head Not Found is documented in the liner notes to Century Media's 2014 release of the *Trolsk Sortmetall* box set, documenting Ulver's output between 1993 and 1997.

13 The story of the making of the album and its mythology is well captured in the Invisible Oranges interview 'Of Wolf and The Past: Ulver Reflects on Twenty Years of *Nattens Madrigal*', Jon Rosenthal, 10 March 2017: http://www.invisibleoranges.com/of-wolf-and-the-past-ulver-reflects-on-20-years-of-nattens-madrigal/

CHAPTER FIVE: LEAVING THE WORLD BEHIND

1 From the King James version of the Bible.

2 *John of the Mountains: The Unpublished Journals of John Muir*, John Muir, University of Wisconsin Press, 1979, p.427.

3 One of the best recountings of the story of *Dopesmoker,* and the source of the Billy Anderson quote, is the *Such Hawks Such Hounds* documentary (2008, dir. Jessica Hundley and John Srebalus): https://imdb.com/title/tt1377796/?ref_=m_ttpl

4 There are some other nice details like this in a 2012 interview conducted with Matt Pike in Paris by Vincent Duke for Pelecanus.net, published on YouTube on 4 February 2013: https://youtu.be/L2zWrAan5ac

5 'How it feels to . . . be a legal drug baron', interview with Damian Marley by Craig McLean, the *Sunday Times Magazine*, 14 January 2018: https://www.thetimes.co.uk/article/how-it-feels-to-be-a-legal-drug-baron-rj7f0d8dj

6 Deathridge uses the bowdlerised version's name here, but his point is valid for all versions of the song.

7 Dan Simmons, *The Terror*, Bantam, 2018, p.865.

8 Ibid., p.365.

9 Ibid., p.899.

10 'GB84: No ******* end in sight', BBC, March 2004: http://www.bbc.co.uk/bradford/culture/words/david_peace_gb84.shtml
11 'The Floating World of Edo Japan', Khan Academy: https://www.khanacademy.org/humanities/art-asia/art-japan/edo-period/a/the-floating-world-of-edo-japan

CHAPTER SIX: THE AGONY AND ECSTASY OF A SUPERMAN

1 Friedrich Nietzsche, *Thus Spoke Zarathustra*, translated by R. J. Hollingdale, Penguin Classics, 1969, p.136.
2 The most referenced videos of the events on that night are from YouTube user 'Chris R'. This first one, originally posted straight after the 2016 Dimebash, on 23 January, contains most of the footage up to and including the Nazi salute: https://www.youtube.com/watch?v=5j91yKSsFaw. The second begins with the salute but also contains the outburst, and went massively viral: 'Phil Anselmo is a racist! Ruins Dimebash 2016', published 27 January 2016: https://www.youtube.com/watch?v=rVaUlXfvOHg
3 'Robb Flynn – Racism in Metal', Machine Head, 29 January 2016: https://www.youtube.com/watch?v=fCBKzWg4WYo
4 'A New Level – Phil Anselmo at Dimebash 2016', published by user 'Scoob's Dad's Adventures' on YouTube, 28 January 2016: https://www.youtube.com/watch?v=PqEvbM1gxnk
5 'How the metal world condemned Phil Anselmo's Nazi salute and White Power message', Larry Bartleet, *NME*, 1 February 2016: https://www.nme.com/blogs/nme-blogs/how-the-metal-world-condemned-phil-anselmo-s-nazi-salute-and-white-power-message-11509
6 'Philip Anselmo Apology' published by Housecore Records on YouTube on 30 January 2016: https://www.youtube.com/watch?v=gShmJV2BSr0
7 'Phil Anselmo Offers to Quit His Band Following Band Following Backlash From Nazi Salute', James Grebey, *Spin*, February 2016: https://www.spin.com/2016/02/phil-anselmo-nazi-salute-white-power-quit-down-apology/
8 'Phil Anselmo Giving a Speech on Races and Respect' published by YouTube user 'NASTYxNICKYx', 14 December 2009: https://www.youtube.com/watch?v=7eDp4wFUPMw.
9 Anselmo's explanation was printed in full in the 1 April 1995 issue of *Kerrang!*
10 'Phil Anselmo – Karaoke – The Smiths – How Soon Is Now?' published on YouTube by user 'upinthemtns', 9 February 2016: https://www.youtube.com/watch?v=K--rAhcKjYc
11 'Phil Anselmo Loves The Smiths – Radio.com Inside Out' published on YouTube by user 'Radio.com', 31 January 2014: https://www.youtube.com/watch?v=_kTsbuoTOKs

NOTES

12 'Phil Anselmo does karaoke with African-American group in first appearance since Nazi salute incident', Luke Morgan Britton, *NME*, 8 February 2016: https://www.nme.com/news/music/pantera-2-1204965

13 *Official Truth, 101 Proof: The inside story of Pantera*, Rex Brown with Mark Eglinton, Da Capo Press, 2013, p.168.

14 The full audio and visual interview with Eddie Trunk is here: 'Eddie Trunk interviews Philip Anselmo DECEMBER 15, 2016' published on YouTube by user 'Keymo Embryo' on 22 December 2016: https://www.youtube.com/watch?v=GhTVj_OfSfc

15 'Philip Anselmo Would "Take Back" Dimebash Incident, Recalls Kissing King's X Frontman and Irons Out Racial Comments Made in the '90s', Joe Divita, *Loudwire*, 18 October 2016: https://loudwire.com/philip-anselmo-take-back-dimebash-kiss-kings-x-frontman-racial-comments-90s/

16 'Superjoint's Phil Anselmo's First Longform Interview Since Dimebash', J. Bennett, *Decibel*, 17 October 2016: https://www.decibelmagazine.com/2016/10/17/superjoint-s-phil-anselmo-s-first-longform-interview-since-dimebash/

17 'Philip H. Anselmo & The Illegals – Moscow 29.06.2014' – published on Youtube by 'sstonedd', 29 June 2014: https://www.youtube.com/watch?v=Bxa8GSH6chU

18 'Philip H Anselmo & The Illegals Live at Saint Vitus 2018 (Full Show)' published on YouTube by 'Maze of Torment', 20 September 2018: https://www.youtube.com/watch?v=QyFTqbYbwQs

19 Nietzsche, op. cit., p.41.

20 Ibid., p.136.

21 Ibid., p.137.

22 *Kerrang!* magazine, 1 April 1995.

23 Nietzsche, op. cit., p.104.

24 Ibid., p.291.

25 'Philip Anselmo on Pantera – We Were Supermen (Pt. 2 of 5)', *Revolver* on YouTube, 9 November 2010: https://www.youtube.com/watch?v=8CCBcmRzxAo

26 Nietzsche, op. cit., p.300.

27 This extraordinary talk is worth watching in full: 'Philip H Anselmo Interview Loyola University March 2009 New Orleans Housecore Radio Complete', published by 'Aoife', YouTube, 26 March 2012: https://youtu.be/UkAhvGgGTg8

28 'Pantera US Tour 96 Part 1' published by 'przemooo93' , YouTube, 20 May 2009: https://youtu.be/6v0hkR1Q3js

29 This is captured on the unofficial release *Far Beyond Bootleg: Pantera Live From Donington '94*.

30 This scorching gig is also worth watching in full: 'Down-LIVE-Texas-09.21.1995.-FULL CONCERT' published by 'Pantera Live', YouTube on 25 January 2013: https://youtu.be/_uU03hYBjzY

31 This comment is taken from the liner notes of the twentieth anniversary deluxe edition of *The Great Southern Trendkill*, Rhino Atlantic, 2016.

32 'Nick Cave: One More Time With Feeling, Skeleton Tree and the power and language of grief', Mark Mordue, *Guardian*, 18 September 2016: https://www.theguardian.com/music/2016/sep/19/nick-cave-one-more-time-with-feeling-skeleton-tree-and-the-power-and-language-of-grief

33 *The Red Hand Files* Issue no. 48, June 2019: https://www.theredhandfiles.com/views-on-morrissey

34 'Guitarist's killer claimed victim stole his lyrics', Anita Chang, *Independent*, 12 December 2004: https://www.independent.co.uk/news/world/americas/guitarists-killer-claimed-victim-stole-his-lyrics-24333.html

35 'Vinnie Paul: How Pantera Fell Apart', Blabbermouth.net, 6 February 2014: http://www.blabbermouth.net/news/vinnie-paul-how-pantera-fell-apart/

36 This interview is preserved in three YouTube videos, published on 1 October 2006, by user 'andy harpole'. Part one is here: https://youtu.be/NRJg7KUb2II; part two is here: https://youtu.be/tF-XRtw89H0 and part three is here: https://www.youtube.com/watch?v=NUS6maBdesc

37 Nietzsche, op. cit., p.60.

38 'Philip Anselmo: If You Fuck With the US, You're Going to Have to Pay', *Metal Edge*, 6 August 2004: https://www.ilxor.com/ILX/ThreadSelectedControllerServlet?boardid=41&threadid=32387#msg1

39 'Damageplan – Walk (Live At Download Festival 2004)', published on YouTube by user 'kinkomaa', 3 May 2008: https://youtu.be/AnFCOsb7eSs

40 'Philip Anselmo: 'Dimebag Darrell Deserves to be Beaten Severely', Blabbermouth.net, 1 December 2004: http://www.blabbermouth.net/news/philip-anselmo-dimebag-darrell-deserves-to-be-beaten-severely/

41 Brown, op. cit., p.XV.

42 'Phil Anselmo giving statement about the murder of Dimebag' published on YouTube by user 'Tobias Wetzel', 4 April 2007: https://youtu.be/zA9roanWPSA

43 'Dimebag Darrell Killing "Not Motivated by Pantera Split"', *NME*, 21 October 2005: https://www.nme.com/news/music/pantera-13-1319466

44 'Dimebag's Ex Blames Phil Anselmo for His Murder', *Guitar World*, 7 January 2008: https://www.guitarworld.com/news/dimebag-s-ex-blames-phil-anselmo-his-murder

45 'Dimebag's Girlfriend Says She Hopes Vinnie Paul "Sees The Light" And Forgives Philip Anselmo', Blabbermouth.net, 22 August 2011: https://www.blabbermouth.net/news/dimebag-s-girlfriend-says-she-hopes-vinnie-paul-sees-the-light-and-forgives-philip-anselmo/

46 'Philip Anselmo on Pantera – They portrayed Me As a Villain (Pt 1 of 5)', *Revolver*, YouTube, 1 November 2010: https://youtu.be/6jQt-Tl0IGU

47 Brown, op. cit., p.215.

48 'Philip H. Anselmo and The Illegals – Dom/Hollow (Pantera Cover) @ Tree's in Dallas Texas (9-8-18)' published on YouTube by user 'Lance Lyon', 9 September 2018: https://youtu.be/eaQvYI6nCw8

49 J. D. Vance, *Hillbilly Elegy: A Memoir of a Family and Culture in Crisis*, William Collins, 2017, p.19.

50 'Pantera – Green Manalishi (Live 1989) Rehearsals' published on YouTube by user 'Rattmaster86', 3 December 2010: https://youtu.be/QkfW1e1OoIg

51 'Christchurch, Auckland venues pull metal gig over singer's past "white power" incident', *Stuff*, 19 March 2019: https://www.stuff.co.nz/national/christchurch-shooting/111383968/christchurch-auckland-venues-pull-metal-gig-over-singers-past-white-power-incident

CHAPTER SEVEN: THE ALL-PERVADING

1 Aldous Huxley, *The Devils of Loudon*, Grafton Books, 1988, p.72.

2 Sarah Jensen with Maynard James Keenan, *A Perfect Union of Contrary Things*, Backbeat Books, 2016, p.124.

3 Jensen with Keenan, ibid., p.154.

4 Huxley, *Devils*, op. cit., p.81.

5 Ibid., p.304.

6 Jensen with Keenan, ibid., p.201.

7 Huxley, *Devils*, op. cit., p.304.

8 Ibid., p.304.

9 Here's the full performance: 'Tool – Sober Live (Pro Shot) Remastered', published on YouTube by user 'ToolArchive', 19 June 2014: https://youtu.be/u7lweNCCwS0. This is a great analysis of the vocal technique: 'Voice Teacher Reacts to Tool Sober Live at Reading Festival 1993', published on YouTube by user 'Sam Johnson', 22 September 2018: https://youtu.be/9Z1L3Aq9YMs

10 Jensen with Keenan, op. cit., p.204.

11 This was the concluding punchline of a live set released as *Bill Hicks: Relentless* in 1992. It was recorded in 1991 at the annual *Just for Laughs* comedy festival in Montreal, Canada. Full transcript of the show: https://scrapsfromtheloft.com/2017/05/03/bill-hicks-relentless-1992-transcript/

12 The band probably extracted Timothy Leary's voice from his 1993 'public service video', *How to Operate Your Brain*, which contains this spoken section: http://www.openculture.com/2012/11/how_to_operate_your_brain_a_user_manual_by_timothy_leary_.html

13 'Never Before Published Photo of Timothy Leary with Aldous and Laura Huxley': http://www.timothylearyarchives.org/photo-of-timothy-leary-with-aldous-and-laura-huxley

14 Jensen with Keenan, op. cit., p.211.

15 Aldous Huxley, *The Doors of Perception*, Vintage Classics, 2004, p.25.

16 'Tool – Danny Carey talks about King Crimson', published on YouTube by user 'Fox Gonzo Humbert', 16 October 2013: https://www.youtube.com/watch?v=knJPCffGyE4 – on '7empest' from *Fear Inoculum* the band also have a very similar passage to the opening of King Crimson's 'Frame By Frame' from *Discipline*.

17 Huxley, *Doors*, op. cit., p.44.

18 'Tool Live Tulsa 2016 (Full Concert)' published on YouTube by user 'ToolArchive', s22 January 2016: https://www.youtube.com/watch?v=rntnfdQhY-U

19 Jensen with Keenan, op. cit., p.169.

20 Huxley, *Devils*, op. cit., p.293.

21 Ibid., p.293.

22 'Scientists Calculated a 'Point of No Return' for Dealing with Climate Change – and Time is Running Out', Kevin Loria, *Business Insider*, 30 August 2018: https://www.businessinsider.com/global-warming-point-of-no-return-temperature-2018-8?r=US&IR=T

23 Huxley, *Doors*, op. cit., p.79.

24 From Ballard's Foreword to *The Doors of Perception*, p.8.

25 'The Designer's Guide to the Golden Ratio', Creative Bloq, 24 October 2018: https://www.creativebloq.com/design/designers-guide-golden-ratio-12121546

26 'Joe Rogan Experience #986 – Maynard James Keenan', published on YouTube by user 'PowerfulJRE', 12 July 2017: https://www.youtube.com/watch?v=J68gH5PiSZg

27 'John Coltrane Draws a Picture Illustrating the Mathematics of Music', Open Culture, 12 April 2017: http://www.openculture.com/2017/04/the-tone-circle-john-coltrane-drew-to-illustrate-the-theory-behind-his-most-famous-compositions-1967.html

28 'Lines Composed a Few Miles Above Tintern Abbey, On Revisiting the Banks of the Wye During a Tour, July 13, 1798', William Wordsworth.

29 Huxley, *Doors*, op. cit., p.24.

CHAPTER EIGHT: EVERYTHING ENDS

1 Footage of this performance is widely available on YouTube but this version is relatively good quality: 'Korn Live at Donington 1996 Footage + Show HQ' published on YouTube by user 'Gabriel Miller', 8 December 2016: https://youtu.be/v7OtbFUN-Y4

2 This interview is part of the BBC archive held at the British Library in its Sound and Vision catalogue, under shelfmark H6442/2.

3 From p.220 of Pieslak's paper: https://www.scribd.com/doc/6375990/Re-casting-Metal-Rhythm-and-Meter-in-the-Music-of-Meshuggah

NOTES

4 'Meshuggah – New Millennium Cyanide Christ (OFFICIAL MUSIC VIDEO)' published on YouTube by Nuclear Blast Records, 15 May 2008: https://youtu.be/4A_tSyJBsRQ

5 *Flat Pack Pop: Sweden's Music Miracle*, BBC Four, 16 February 2019: https://www.bbc.co.uk/programmes/m0002k6k

6 Lostprophets were lumped in with Raging Speedhorn, Hundred Reasons, Defenestration and One Minute Silence. They were all British but there the similarities ended and the antipathy began.

7 'Lost in America', Ian Winwood, *Kerrang!* issue 1004, 8 May 2004.

8 The Watkins judgement makes for very disturbing reading but can be found here: https://www.judiciary.uk/wp-content/uploads/JCO/Documents/Judgments/r-v-watkins-and-others.pdf

9 Andrew McConnell Stott, *The Pantomime Life of Joseph Grimaldi: Laughter, Madness and the Story of Britain's Greatest Comedian* , Canongate Books, 2008, p.225.

10 'The most revolting band in the world', Neil McCormick, *Telegraph*, 23 August 2001: https://www.telegraph.co.uk/culture/4725230/The-most-revolting-band-in-the-world.html

11 'Slipknot – Corey Interview 2011 – Iowa Tenth Anniversary [Kerrang! Radio Special]' published on YouTube by user '666Gehenna', 1 November 2011: https://youtu.be/iQZ4MVQpjnA

12 'September 11 2001: Slipknot, Stone Sour Vox Corey Taylor', published on YouTube by user 'ArtisanNewsService', 9 September 2011: https://youtu.be/0rKQ0BEqL0U

13 'Banned songlist revealed as fake', *Guardian*, 20 September 2001: https://www.theguardian.com/world/2001/sep/20/september11.usa12

14 'Interview Slipknot – Chris Fehn #3 (part 1)' published on YouTube by user 'FaceCulture', 27 November 2008: https://youtu.be/8ZuI6Np1jHw Parts two, three and four are here https://youtu.be/eFkWqkVcgNw here https://youtu.be/v7d0pb5GPd8 and here https://youtu.be/9914LPcM0GY

15 'Slipknot gave Chris Fehn "take it or leave it" deal, says lawyer', Martin Kielty, *Ultimate Classic Rock*, 29 March 2019: https://ultimateclassicrock.com/slipknot-chris-fehn-deal/

16 'Slipknot Reading 2002', published on YouTube by user 'greenguitarman', 3 August 2011: https://youtu.be/C7sz5eS0zhU

17 'Statements on Record Relating to the Armenian Genocide', Adolf Hitler, Chancellor of Nazi Germany, 1933–45: https://www.armenian-genocide.org/hitler.html

18 'Will Self: my festival hell', *Esquire*, 17 June 2014: https://www.esquire.com/uk/culture/news/a6093/will-self-my-festival-hell/

19 This particular footage was in the 2002 film *9/11*, directed by Jules Clément Naudet and Thomas Gédeon Naudet, captured whilst the brothers were filming with the Engine 7, Ladder 1 firehouse in Manhattan that day.

20 'The Falling Man', Tom Junod, *Esquire*, 9 September 2016: https://www.esquire.com/news-politics/a48031/the-falling-man-tom-junod/

CHAPTER NINE: UNDER THE SURFACE

1 Sir Thomas Browne, *Religio Medici and Urne-Buriall*, edited by Stephen Greenblatt and Ramie Targoff, New York Review Books, 2012, p.xxix.
2 Ibid. p.97.
3 Ibid. p.135.
4 'Sunn O))) on their new Steve Albini-produced *Life Metal*', Christopher R. Weingarten, *Stereogum*, 5 February 2019: https://www.stereogum.com/2030796/sunn-o-2019-interview/
5 O'Malley's notes on this gig from the Sunn O))) bandcamp page attest to this: https://sunn-live.bandcamp.com/album/sunn-o-20041202-ran-m-r-glasgow-sco
6 Browne, op. cit., p.135.
7 'Hyundai Commission, Tania Bruguera: 10,142,926', press release 1 October 2018: https://www.tate.org.uk/press/press-releases/hyundai-commission-tania-bruguera-10142926
8 Steve Goodman, *Sonic Warfare: Sound, Affect, and the Ecology of Fear*, MIT Press, 2012, p.66.
9 Adam Thorpe, *Ulverton*, Vintage, 2012, p.32 and p.42.
10 *The Essential Jung* (Selected and Introduced by Anthony Storr), Fontana Press, 1998, p.223.
11 Browne, op. cit., p.135.
12 'Poem of the week: "The Lyke-Wake Dirge"', Carol Rumens, *Guardian*, 16 February 2009: https://www.theguardian.com/books/booksblog/2009/feb/16/lyke-wake-dirge-poem-week
13 Sarah Moss, *Ghost Wall*, Granta Books, 2018, p.3.
14 Charles Maturin, *Melmoth the Wanderer*, Penguin Classics, 2018, p.272.
15 'CONJURER – Live in The K! Pit (Tiny Dive Bar Show)', *Kerrang!*, 19 June 2018: https://youtu.be/WY0yOpBz4EA
16 Herman Melville, *Moby-Dick*, Vintage, 2007, p.224.
17 Ursula K. Le Guin, *A Wizard of Earthsea*, Puffin Books, 2016, p.278.

CHAPTER TEN: ALIVE IN THE SUPERUNKNOWN

1 Thomas Ligotti, *Songs of a Dead Dreamer* and *Grimmscribe*, Penguin Classics, 2015, p.58.
2 'Buzz Osborne (the Melvins) Talks the HBO Documentary *Kurt Cobain: Montage of Heck*', Buzz Osborne, *The Talkhouse*: http://www.talkhouse.com/buzz-osborne-the-melvins-talks/

NOTES

3 'Thou live at Saint Vitus Bar, Jan 7th, 2017 (full set)' published on YouTube by user 'Max Volume Silence', 10 January 2017: https://youtu.be/V6CgBngIlB8

4 'Thou (Secret Nirvana Set) live at Southwest Terror Fest 2015 (full set)', published on YouTube by user 'Max Volume Silence', 26 October 2015: https://youtu.be/fhC0bvZ57oY

5 'Jerry Cantrell on Writing Alice in Chains' "Rooster" For His Father' – interview with Dean Delray, Let There Be Talk podcast, 25 July 2016. Published on YouTube by user 'ShirleyCobain', 26 January 2018: https://youtu.be/thptpyQswJ0

6 'Alice in Chains – Rooster (PCM Stereo)', Alice in Chains, 25 October 2009: https://www.youtube.com/watch?v=uAE6Il6OTcs

7 'The Story Behind The Song: "Rooster" by Alice in Chains', Henry Yates, *Classic Rock*, 15 November 2006: https://www.loudersound.com/features/the-story-behind-the-song-rooster-by-alice-in-chains

8 'Jerry Cantrell on Writing Alice in Chains' "Rooster" For His Father' – Dean Delray, ibid.: https://youtu.be/thptpyQswJ0

9 'Romulus and Remus', *Encyclopedia Britannica*, 1 May 2019: https://www.britannica.com/biography/Romulus-and-Remus#ref127854

10 'Soundgarden – "4th of July" live in Hyde Park London, 4 July 2014', published on YouTube by user 'Kristymaycurrie': https://www.youtube.com/watch?v=7ZHwTQFoxtQ

11 Ligotti, op. cit., p.29.

CHAPTER ELEVEN: REMEMBER TOMORROW

1 http://www.greatbritaincampaign.com/#!/about

2 Martin Popoff, *Run for Cover: The Art of Derek Riggs*, Aardvark Publishing, 2006, p.70.

3 http://www.greatbritaincampaign.com/

4 Bruce Dickinson, *What Does This Button Do? An Autobiography*, Harper Collins, 2018, p.93.

5 Ibid., p.272.

6 Ibid., p.137.

7 Iron Maiden LLP, Companies House website: https://beta.companieshouse.gov.uk/company/OC335408

8 'Business Speaker Bruce Dickinson on "Turning Customers Into Fans"', CSA Celebrity Speakers, published on YouTube by user 'CSACelebritySpeakers', 10 December 2013: https://www.youtube.com/watch?v=fu5_dNTud0c

9 Dickinson, op. cit., p.319.

10 'Bruce Dickinson speaking at Entrepreneurs Wales 2012' published on YouTube by user 'Business Wales/Busnes Cymru', 23 November 2012: https://youtu.be/vq_jugoSV60

11 Dickinson, op. cit., p.272.

12 'Iron Maiden Vs. Ozzfest – band hit back', *NME*, 23 August 2005: https://www.nme.com/news/music/iron-maiden-102-1358150

13 'Brexit: Bruce Dickinson, Iron Maiden singer, explains why he voted "Yes"', published on YouTube by *L'Obs*, 15 November 2018: https://youtu.be/hAtxrfF0DI8

14 'Boris Johnson and David Davis tell Theresa May the British people "will not forgive us" for Brexit surrender', Steven Swinford, *Telegraph*, 18 October 2018: https://www.telegraph.co.uk/politics/2018/10/17/boris-johnson-david-davis-tell-theresa-may-british-people-will/

15 Popoff, op. cit., p.20.

16 'Portrait from the Brutal Pacific: "Skull on a Tank", Guadalcanal, 1942', Ben Cosgrove, *Time*, 19 February 2014: https://time.com/3518085/life-behind-the-picture-skull-on-a-tank-guadalcanal-1942/

17 Popoff, op. cit., p.55.

18 Ibid., p.98.

19 Dickinson, op cit., p.135.

20 Geoff Dyer, *Broadsword Calling Danny Boy: On* Where Eagles Dare, Penguin, 2018, p.108.

INDEX

INDEX

INDEX